Pioneer Ecologist

ROBERT A. CROKER

PIONEER ECOLOGIST

The Life and Work of

VICTOR ERNEST SHELFORD

1877–1968

SMITHSONIAN INSTITUTION PRESS

Washington and London

Copyright © 1991 by Smithsonian Institution.

All rights are reserved.

The quotation from *The Education of Henry Adams* that appears on page 5
is reprinted by permission of Houghton Mifflin Co. Copyright 1918
by the Massachusetts Historical Society; copyright 1946 by Charles F. Adams.

The lines from Robert Frost's poem "Into My Own" that appear on page 160
are reprinted from *The Poetry of Robert Frost,* edited by Edward Connery
Lathem, by permission of Henry Holt and Co., Inc. Copyright 1934 by
Holt, Rinehart, and Winston, Inc.; renewed by Robert Frost in 1962.

Figures 1, 2, and 3 are adapted from illustrations in Victor Shelford's
Laboratory and Field Ecology by permission of the Williams and Wilkins Co.,
Baltimore. Copyright 1929 by the Williams and Wilkins Co.

Edited by Rebecca Browning.

Designed by Alan Carter.

Library of Congress Cataloging-in-Publication Data

Croker, Robert A.
Pioneer ecologist : the life and work of Victor
Ernest Shelford, 1877–1968 / by Robert A. Croker.
p.   cm.
Includes bibliographical references (p.   ) and index.
ISBN 0-87474-315-X (cloth)
1. Shelford, Victor E. (Victor Ernest), b. 1877.   2. Ecologists-
-United States—Biography.   I. Title.
QH31.S49C76   1991
574.5'092—dc20
[B]   90-10098

British Library Cataloging-in-Publication Data is available.

On the cover is a 1937 photograph of Victor Shelford taken at Reelfoot Lake,
Tennessee. Courtesy of Eugene Odum.

For permission to reproduce individual illustrations appearing in this book
please correspond directly with the owners of the works as listed in the
captions. The Smithsonian Institution Press does not retain reproduction rights
for these illustrations individually or maintain a file of addresses for
photo sources.

Manufactured in the United States of America.
95 94 93 92 91   5 4 3 2 1

∞ The paper used in this publication meets the minimum requirements of the
American National Standard for Permanence of Paper for Printed Library
Materials Z39.48-1984.

TO

BARRY

JEAN

MARY ANN

Contents

Contents

Foreword

On a very hot day in early September 1961 I settled in a tiny cubicle in the vivarium building on the campus of the University of Illinois. The vivarium was built in 1917 for Professor Victor E. Shelford, who had accepted a position at Illinois after a few years in Chicago. Shelford was eighty-four in 1961 and had been Professor Emeritus for about fifteen years. I was at Illinois to spend a year as a graduate student of Professor S. Charles Kendeigh, who had obtained his Ph.D. under Shelford in 1930 and had been the doctoral adviser of noted ecologists Robert H. Whittaker and Eugene P. Odum. Thirty years ago ecology students had two bibles, Odum's *Fundamentals of Ecology* and the monumental *Principles of Animal Ecology* by W. C. Allee, A. E. Emerson, O. Park, T. Park, and K. P. Schmidt, an exhaustive, 837-page treatise. Its senior author, W. C. Allee, had been Shelford's first Ph.D. student in 1912 when Shelford was still at the University of Chicago. The first thing I did after claiming my cubicle was walk to the bookstore to purchase copies of these two books.

Thus I entered a world created largely by Shelford's views, a great ecological tradition of solid empirical work with a dual emphasis on physiological autecology on the one hand and holistic community ecology on the other. The geographical component of community ecology attracted me the most and had brought me to Illinois for that year of study. Even though Shelford himself came to the vivarium once in a while (to get his last book, *The Ecology of North America,* ready for publication) the major figure in ecology at Illinois then was Kendeigh. I believe Kendeigh's teaching style was similar to Shelford's: low-key lectures, intensive lab work, a rigorous reading program, and numerous field trips, rain or shine. Kendeigh's field trips were not on the geographic scale of Shelford's transcontinental journeys (for which he had become famous at Illinois and beyond), yet they introduced students to a wide range of habitats, techniques, and natural or human-altered situations. Two trips were especially memorable. The first was to a minuscule remnant of prairie, a nearly vanished habitat that had been very dear to Shelford's heart. The second was to the huge dunes along the shores of Lake Michigan, where Shelford had worked on succession in the early 1900s. I spent a wonderful year at Illinois under Shelford's looming influence and Kendeigh's fatherlike guidance.

Curiously, though, I have had to wait until now to learn fully about Victor Shelford's life and accomplishments, but this unfortunate gap is filled thanks to Robert A. Croker's wonderful book. As graduate students in 1961 my friends and I thought of Shelford primarily as the author of *Animal Communities in Temperate North America* and the co-author, with F. E. Clements, of *Bio-Ecology,* two seminal books in which nature was analyzed functionally in terms of interacting components within various levels of integration. In *Principles of Animal Ecology,* Allee and his coauthors wrote rather tersely that *Bio-Ecology* "assisted in drawing together the ecological researches of zoologists and botanists under a common denominator." Very few ecologists must be aware of how long and difficult a gestation period this book had or of the intellectual problems it posed Shelford. In 1991 I suspect that many ecologists have not even perused these two books and have only heard of Shelford briefly during the first lecture of Ecology 101, when the instructor paid lip service to the history of the field. How many ecologists know that Shelford was instrumental in founding the Ecological Society of America and that he was its first president in 1916? And how many ecologists remember that it was largely as a result of Shelford's untiring efforts that we now have The Nature Conservancy, one of the most important nature preservation organizations in North America?

Bob Croker describes these developments with great clarity and succeeds in interweaving Shelford's work and his life into a splendid tapestry. Once I started reading the book I could not put it down until I had finished the last page. And then I kept thinking about Shelford the man, Shelford the researcher, Shelford the teacher, and Shelford the conservationist. I remembered my own year in Shelford's vivarium, of course, but more important I placed concepts such as succession, community, and biome into a broader framework of time and space and of human intellectual curiosity about the living world. It is good to have such a book: it will go a long way toward documenting a fine and crucial period in the growth of ecological thought in America and toward making available to all ecologists knowledge of one of the most significant persons in American and world ecology. I will assign Croker's book as mandatory reading when I next teach ecology, and I urge others to do the same.

François Vuilleumier
Chairman and Curator
Department of Ornithology
American Museum of Natural History

Preface

This book began with my desire to learn more about the emergence and development of animal ecology as a self-conscious scientific discipline during the late nineteenth and early twentieth centuries. Study and reflection on the ecological and conservation literature made it apparent to me that Victor Shelford was, by any significant measure, one of the most influential world figures in animal ecology during the first half of the twentieth century. Shelford's pioneering work in a remarkable variety of ecological and conservation areas, begun early in this century when the word ecology was not fully understood even by many biologists, made him a compelling candidate for a full-length biography— the more so, since no biographies of early American animal ecologists had yet appeared.

The book is structured thematically rather than strictly chronologically. Part 1 traces Shelford's ancestry from England, Holland, and Wales and follows his progress from a rural upbringing in western New York to West Virginia University for premedical studies in 1899 and then in 1901 to the young University of Chicago. There, in the sand dunes, forests, streams, and ponds bordering Lake Michigan, Shelford first gave thought and form to the study of animal ecology. Part 2 examines Shelford's maturation into a world-renowned animal ecologist; his two decades of intense experimental work in applied ecology; and his descriptive work in community ecology, which he continued throughout his long career at the University of Illinois. Part 3 goes with Shelford on his legendary transcontinental explorations and accompanies him and Ecological Society of America colleagues in their persistent efforts for the preservation of natural areas. The book closes with glimpses of Shelford's busy and useful emeritus years—he hardly slowed his pace until the very end.

Shortly after finishing his graduate training at Chicago in 1907,

Shelford was advised by a prominent senior biologist to "discontinue this field of ecology which you have chosen. It is *ignis fatuus.* The true purpose of biology is to reduce the organism in terms of physics and chemistry." Shelford's answer to both was a resounding no. Here is his story, a story that I believe celebrates the ecology of the human spirit as much as it contributes to the history of ecology.

Acknowledgments

For assistance and advice and for numerous kindnesses, I am indebted to a great number of archivists and librarians, among them Maynard Brichford, James Carson, and Geoffrey Williams, of the University of Illinois; Hugh Pritchard, Lloyd Heidgerd, the late Reina Hart, David Lane, and Connie Stone, of the University of New Hampshire; Phyllis Burnham and Wayne Mann, of the University of Western Michigan; Emmett Chisum, of the American Heritage Center at the University of Wyoming; Michael T. Ryan, Daniel Meyer, and Brian Hyland, of the University of Chicago; Martha Squires, of the Chemung County, New York, Historical Society; Stephen Catlett, of the American Philosophical Society; Elena Danielson, of the Hoover Institution at Stanford University; Carolyn Bossard, of the Steele Memorial Library in Elmira, New York; Walter Eddy, of the Cortland, New York public library; Jane Fessenden, of the Marine Biological Laboratory at Woods Hole, Massachusetts; and J. Arthur Funston, of Earlham College.

For written and spoken remembrances and anecdotes, for probing questions and historical information without which this book could not have been written, special thanks go to Lois Shelford Bennett, the late Charles Kendeigh, Dorothy Shelford Parmelee, Jane Dirks-Edmunds, Stanley Auerbach, Drew Sparkman Wetzel, the late Curtis Newcombe, Hilda Tillman, and Arthur Twomey.

Other Shelford family members who opened their doors, hearts, and memories to me were Betty Bennett; Shelford Bennett; Mary Bennett; the late Paul Bennett; Mr. and Mrs. Donald Shelford; Mr. and Mrs. Harry Shelford; Paul Shelford, Jr.; Faith Hallock; and the late George Wohnuss. I thank them all.

Three dozen additional former students, friends, and colleagues of Shelford, most of whom are mentioned in the book, unselfishly supplied substance and color to the Shelford story. The book would be poorer without them.

Many other people too numerous to mention here supplied me with support and sustenance in this work.

Chapters of the manuscript were read by Lois Shelford Bennett, Robert Burgess, Frank Egerton, Jane Dirks-Edmunds, and the late Curtis Newcombe. Stanley Auerbach, Robert McIntosh, and two anonymous reviewers read the entire manuscript. Their advice, insight, and kindly criticism were freely given and genuinely appreciated. I did not incorporate all of their suggested changes or additions; consequently, any errors of commission or omission are mine.

I particularly want to thank my editors at the Smithsonian Institution Press—Peter Cannell for his unfailing interest and enthusiasm and Rebecca Browning for her keenly perceptive and skillful editing.

My wife, Mary Ann, cheerfully and efficiently carried out endless bibliographic and other library tasks so important to the enterprise of writing a book. The late Trixie McLean typed a succession of drafts that I thought would never end.

I began research for the book with travel and archival support from the Research Office of the University of New Hampshire. Support during subsequent years came from the Department of Zoology and the College of Liberal Arts at New Hampshire. I am especially grateful to John Foret, chair of the zoology department from 1978 to 1987, for his interest, encouragement, and support.

Prologue

In the spring of 1908, thirty-year-old Victor Ernest Shelford, associate in zoology at the University of Chicago, wrote daily in his office at Hull Zoological Laboratory. He made good progress on what would be the first systematic book-length treatment of animal communities. He had just returned with his wife, Mabel, from a belated wedding trip to Europe. There he visited museums to pursue his study of tiger beetles. The year before he had published a short paper on his pioneering investigations of plant succession and the accompanying changes in animal populations in the sand dunes and forests surrounding Lake Michigan. In 1907 he also received a Ph.D. degree from Chicago for a thesis sponsored by Charles Manning Child concerning the reproductive biology and larval habits of tiger beetles. Now, Shelford pondered future directions for his work, and the opportunity—gained through Child—to teach field zoology and to develop a natural history curriculum at Chicago. Some biologists called this work *ecology,* especially botanists who had taken the lead in fostering a holistic view of the environment since the 1890s.[1]

Shelford's appreciation for the ecological viewpoint had not come quickly. During his classical zoological training around the turn of the century, he seriously doubted the value of ecological work as it was then performed and enthusiastically embraced more traditional experimental studies. This was where the strongest emphasis lay at the time; where the coveted positions, support, and rewards were found; and where a young scientist naturally paid attention. But in the period between 1903 and 1907, Shelford was won over to ecology by the marvelous zoological and botanical field trips of Charles Child and Chicago professor Henry Chandler Cowles and by Cowles's infectious enthusiasm for the dynamic story of wind, water, and sand carving the ancient, plant-covered shores of Lake Michigan.

During the last quarter of the nineteenth century, as Shelford grew to manhood, American science came of age. The entire base of scientific knowledge broadened. New journals were established, natural history institutions thrived, laboratory instruction improved, and biology was institutionalized as an academic discipline. Ecology, too, emerged at the century's end as a recognizable scientific discipline forged from elements of physiology and natural history, after being named thirty-four years earlier by the German zoologist, Ernst Haeckel, a strong proponent of Darwinism.[2]

From the beginning of his ecological work, Shelford stressed the natural community, following the inspiration of European biologists Eugenius Warming, Karl Möbius, and Karl Semper, as well as the Americans Stephen Forbes, Henry Cowles, and Charles Adams. He kept up community work throughout his career, interrupted from 1914 to 1922 by an intensive period of experimental laboratory work. Early on, his self-imposed task was to organize the study of animal ecology, and in so doing, he provided leadership to the discipline in the decades up to World War II, helping to lay the foundation for modern ecological research.

Shelford was an average-sized man, slim and wiry, with brown hair and gray eyes. He was a slow, thoughtful talker, generally of serious demeanor. Few people knew Victor Shelford intimately: he was a truly private man. He graduated from high school late, in his twenty-second year, and felt the burden throughout life of the less-than-adequate grounding in writing and rhetorical skills he received from small country schools. He disliked hunting and grew impatient with the military but curiously held himself in what some described as military bearing. Predictably, he chafed at regulations of any kind but did not hesitate in expecting adherence to his own. He was his own man, knew where he was going, and never, ever gave up. The distinction of a Phi Beta Kappa key did not make Shelford forget his rural origins: he talked as easily with farmers as he did with scientists.

For thirty-two years, Shelford was an admirable, upright, and disciplined teacher of ecology and natural history to legions of University of Illinois students. In his explorations, published work, and teaching, he literally covered the map of North America and championed a unified animal-plant approach to natural communities. In the field he was superb. Energetic and tireless, he could outhike students one-third his age. He went to bat for students and received their strong loyalty in return.

Despite mounting opposition from highly placed colleagues, Shelford persisted over the years in his steadfast belief that ecologists should stand up, be counted, and get involved professionally in the preservation of the land and waters of North America. The existence of The Nature Conservancy is testimony to his and his colleagues' preservation efforts beginning in 1917 and continuing for three difficult decades. This achievement and the growing national awareness of the importance of conservation and human dependence on the environment were enduring satisfactions to Shelford at the end of his long, worthy, and useful life of ninety-one years.

PART ONE

Beginnings and Chicago Years

THE MAKING OF AN ECOLOGIST
1877–1908

Victor Ernest Shelford was born Saturday, September 22, 1877, the first child of Alexander Hamilton Shelford and Sarah Ellen Rumsey Shelford. The Shelfords lived on an upland farm in Chemung, New York, in view of the Pennsylvania hills, and some 26 kilometers from the railroad center of Elmira. Victor's mother was the oldest of five children born to Sylvanus D. Rumsey and Clarinda Shoemaker Rumsey. The Rumseys boasted English ancestors who had come from Wales in the seventeenth and eighteenth centuries, settling first on Long Island and eventually in Orange and Chemung counties in New York. Victor's grandmother, Clarinda Shoemaker, was a distant descendant of one Hendrick Schoonmaker, who emigrated from Holland to the Hudson Valley in 1653.[1]

The three generations of Shelfords before Victor's father were shoemakers and farmers in rural Keysoe, Bedfordshire, England, eighty kilometers north of London in the bend of the Great Ouse River—a region saturated with Anglo-Saxon, Viking, and Norman history. In 1837 John Shelford III, Victor's granduncle, left a turbulent England, sailed to America, and found his way to western New York. There he plied the shoemaking trade among men working on the Erie Railroad and the bridges, roads, and canals of the Chemung and Susquehanna valleys.[2]

John soon wrote his brother Eli, Victor's grandfather, and urged him to come to America with his new bride Phoebe. They sailed in 1844, reaching New York at Christmas. In the spring of 1845, Eli and a pregnant Phoebe gladly left the city, traveling to Middletown, New York, on the Erie Railroad and then taking the necessary, jolting 130-mile stage ride to Chemung. John and Eli prospered as shoemakers, and by 1847 Eli had saved enough money to buy 1,000 acres of land jointly with the families of his sisters, who had also emigrated from England. John left for California in 1855, and Eli then dropped shoemaking for farming. As his three sons, Alex, George, and Tom grew to manhood, they also worked the land and built their own houses for their families on the Snell Road—or the Henpath, as the Shelfords called it—east and north of Shoemaker's Mountain, above the Chemung River.[3]

Victor's first memories were of the farm and of those bucolic pleasures that make up the popular, glorified picture of late-nineteenth-century American country life. At first Victor was called Budget, then later, Ernie or Ernest. By the time he was seven, he carried his fair share of farm chores and rapidly developed a distaste for farming; even as a grown man he never planted vegetables that needed much tending. His favorite times were spent with his father: walks in the woods, milk deliveries to neighbors, and buggy trips to Elmira with its new electric lights. In Elmira there was also always a chance of catching sight of Mark Twain—a familiar figure there in summer, with his white linen suit and Panama hat.[4]

From 1884 to 1894, Victor trudged four miles round-trip with his cousins to Oak Hill School, northwest of the farm. As an adult, he vividly remembered reciting lessons against the cadence of a crackling wood stove; winter in his childhood simply meant school. Yet to the end of his life he wished for a better foundation in composition, grammar, and rhetoric than his school had provided. Of happier memories there were many: snowy winters and sleighing; scrumptious Christmas dinners; long, lantern-lit winter nights; lovely springs; buggy rides; swimming; Fourth of July family picnics; halloing across the fields to his cousins on their porches on lazy summer evenings; autumn harvests with family and neighbors; Chemung County fairs with bicycle races, livestock shows, and exhibits; excitement over the Elmira flood of 1889; exploring his own 20 acres of woods; and taking care of his two brothers, Harry and Wiley (too often, he thought).[5]

4

Victor entered his teens during the unrest of the 1890s. Neither farming, weather, business, markets, nor the money system was stable. Even the Erie Railroad went bankrupt along with sixteen thousand other businesses nationwide. He often heard his mother prophesy financial ruin for the family and then quickly reassure them that all would be well in the end.

By this time, Victor had developed persistence, a quick and practical mind, enthusiasm for doing rather than watching, and a firm belief in himself. He did well in school and, at his parents' urging, spent several summers during the nineties at Chautauqua Lake in western New York where he worked as a busboy and waiter. There he was exposed to the educators, politicians, ministers, and assorted lecturers on the Chautauqua circuit.[6]

The nineties was a curious time: many felt an urgent movement towards the new century and an impatience to be rid of the old century even before it was over. Still as Henry Adams wrote: "One knew no better in 1894 than in 1854 what an American education ought to be in order to count as success. . . . Society had failed to discover what sort of education suited it best." Victor, though, knew one thing about education: he needed more of it. After a short period in late 1894 when he taught school in Chemung County, he gained entrance by examination to Cortland Normal and Training School at Cortland, New York, on February 7, 1895.

During the second half of the nineteenth century, several states established normal schools to meet the demand for teachers in village and rural elementary schools. New York stipulated general entrance requirements for normal schools as good health, minimum age of sixteen to eighteen years, certification of good moral character, and examination on common subjects taught in district schools. Cortland examinations included questions on geography, arithmetic, and grammar. Students were required to teach in New York State schools for a time at least equal to the time spent at Cortland; however, many entering students, like Victor, already had some teaching experience. Normal school students paid no tuition but relied on state and local aid instead. Textbooks were free. Until 1896, New York State even reimbursed students for travel. Consequently, Victor's expenses were very reasonable, perhaps three to five dollars each week for room and board and less than a dollar for school supplies and recreation.[7]

Although normal school curricula were diverse, typically the first year covered academic work, followed by a second year of practice teaching under supervising teachers. Victor completed twenty-two courses at Cortland, with an average grade of eighty-nine. His highest grades were in mathematics, drawing, physical geography, botany, and United States history, his lowest in reading and zoology. No record exists of his having received a diploma from Cortland, but his failure to graduate was no reflection on his performance. His principal described him as an "industrious, reliable and successful student." Presumably, Victor decided it was time to get to work; so in 1897 he resumed teaching in Chemung County, putting to use the third grade teaching certificate he had received the previous year.[8]

After completing his teaching requirement for Cortland in 1898, Victor was faced with deciding what he wanted to do with his life. He talked freely with his father, whose patient listening he appreciated. His mother shared her son's concern and frequently reminded him of a good family example, her only brother, William. Six years before, William Rumsey had gone down to the West Virginia University Agricultural Experiment Station after graduating from Cornell in 1891 with a B.S. degree in agriculture. Victor's grandmother, Clarinda Rumsey, was proud of her son and spoke of him often. But William was not the only professional man the Shelfords knew. Others were Ebenezer Gere, who practiced medicine in Chemung for more than forty years, and Charles Sumner, who studied medicine with Gere. Victor decided he was interested in medicine; consequently his elders advised him to get a high school diploma and some University training. So during the 1898–99 school year, a determined Victor attended Waverly High School, 10 kilometers east of Chemung near Cayuta Creek in Tioga County. He took fifteen courses at Waverly, including English, Latin, history (ancient, medieval, English, and modern), plane geometry, and physiology (probably general biology). His grades are not recorded, but his father no doubt knew about them, having received in February of 1899 a tuition bill of six dollars for a ten-week session of the twelfth grade. Victor earned a "36 Count Certificate" from the University of the State of New York in March 1899 for his work at Waverly. He graduated from high school on June 21, 1899, three months short of his twenty-second birthday, and immediately

6

made preparations for matriculating at West Virginia University for premedical studies.[9]

West Virginia University in the fall of 1899 hummed with excitement. The school had changed drastically since the arrival of the new president, Jerome H. Raymond, two years before. President Raymond had things moving on the banks of the Monongahela; he was busy increasing the number of faculty and students, raising academic standards, and putting up new buildings. His efforts, and those of his enthusiastic faculty, presented a brand-new university face to the state. He and his wife eagerly worked to extend the benefits of higher education to the people, and the people responded. Raymond felt very much at home on the lecture platform, bringing to adult audiences the gleanings of his wide study and travel, begun when he was a young man and private secretary to both Frances E. Willard, president of the Woman's Christian Temperance Union, and George M. Pullman, of railroad car fame.[10]

In the Agricultural Experiment Station, Assistant State Entomologist William Rumsey was equally busy. During his six years at West Virginia, Rumsey had significantly improved the entomological collections. His concentration on fruit pests and forest insects was evidence of his close association with John H. Comstock, a fine teacher and eminent entomologist at Cornell. Rumsey was a remarkably versatile and persistent man and an important early influence on Shelford. Crippled from polio since childhood, he nonetheless excelled in tennis and outdoor photography and as a tireless hiker and natural historian. Although he had two small children of his own, Rumsey eagerly took in his nephew, providing him with living quarters, as well as quiet study space on the second floor of the experiment station. Shelford in turn prepared lantern slides and curated insects for his uncle. They enjoyed each other's company on hikes in the woods and ravines around Morgantown, where wild flowers carpeted the ground under immense walnuts and oaks. Through Rumsey, Shelford got his first taste of serious botanizing and insect collecting.[11]

Shelford completed six quarters as a special student at West Virginia, taking nine courses in zoology, two in botany, three in chemistry, four in French, and two in German. Zoology courses were taught by John B. Johnston, a vertebrate neurologist newly arrived at West Virginia in 1899 after completing his Ph.D. degree at Michigan. Johnston was impressed with Shelford's diligent work, both as a student and as his laboratory assistant. He stated in a letter of recommendation dated September 30, 1901:

> To whom it may concern:
> This will certify that Mr. Victor E. Shelford has been student and assistant in the Zoological Laboratory of this University for the past two years. During this time he has had experience in the care of apparatus, in the collection and preservation of animals for laboratory work, and especially in microscopic technique. He has evinced an unusual readiness and independence in his work, and I believe will prove a highly efficient worker in all laboratory technique.
>
> Mr. Shelford has also turned his attention to a very great variety of occupations for self-support and in everything he has shown enterprise and entire trustworthiness. He is wholly dependent upon his own efforts for support. He can be depended upon to give full satisfaction in any work which he undertakes.

Shelford proceeded to study a variety of invertebrates and vertebrates, learning the principles of evolution and immersing himself in the details of comparative anatomy and the embryology of vertebrates. He also made four formal reports on current literature for Johnston, whose classes were held on the third floor of the old University Hall. Shelford mentioned to Johnston that he might be interested in the study of parasites, and Johnston suggested that he should take a course with Professor Henry B. Ward, who was then at the University of Nebraska. Later when Shelford served as a zoology faculty member under Ward at the University of Illinois, he would jokingly say that he was too old to learn any parasitology—even from Dr. Ward. It was during his assistantship with Johnston that Shelford first became curious about the new field called ecology and asked his professor to define it for him. Johnston's definition goes unrecorded. [12]

Botany courses were offered by associate professor Edwin Copeland, who arrived at West Virginia in 1899 from California State University at Chico. Shelford appreciated Copeland's instruction in both laboratory and field botany and assisted Copeland by making drawings of plant structures. Copeland praised Shelford for "work excellently done." In a letter of recommendation to President Raymond dated March 3, 1901, Copeland noted that Shelford's work was "as satisfactory as that of any student I have had in this University. His laboratory work is excellent—as I expected, from his previous work with Dr. Johnston—and in recitations he is most certain, in my present class, to see the full bearing of every point."[13]

Shelford had realized by this time that his aptitudes and interests lay in the natural sciences, not necessarily in medical studies. His close association with Rumsey and his academic performance with Johnston and Copeland prompted him to think about moving to a more research-oriented university to finish his bachelor's degree and then continue with graduate work in the biological sciences. During his last year at West Virginia, he assumed duties as a zoology tutor and applied for entrance to several universities, subsequently receiving scholarship offers from Syracuse, Harvard, and the University of Chicago. Chancellor J. R. Day at Syracuse offered him a scholarship in zoology to work with Professor Charles W. Hargitt, whom he justly called "one of the best men in the country in Zoology." Hargitt had spent some time earlier at the Naples Zoological Laboratory working on Cnidaria (jellyfishes and allied animals), for which he is noted. But Hargitt's work did not interest Shelford. Harvard notified him that he had been awarded Price Greenleaf Aid—$150 for the academic year beginning in the fall of 1901—usable only if he entered as a regular student. Harvard's conditions for Shelford's entrance stated that he could be given "no credit towards satisfying the Harvard admission requirements in subjects which [he was] credited with at the time of [his] admission to West Virginia University." Harvard was willing to accept his West Virginia work in German and chemistry, as well as three courses in botany and zoology. His other option was to apply for admission as a special student, thus forfeiting his scholarship, and eventually transfer to regular status; but he would then need three years in Harvard College before receiving an A.B. degree.[14]

In the end, Shelford's future was tied to the destination of President Raymond. Raymond was offered an associate professorship of sociology, including lecture duties, in the Extension Department at the newly founded University of Chicago by President William Rainey Harper in early 1901. Harper's persuasiveness and success in recruiting faculty since Chicago's opening in 1891 had been spectacular. The faculty, fellows, and administration at Chicago included nine people who had at one time or another been seminary, college, or university presidents. In short, many scholars coveted a Chicago professorship more than a presidency elsewhere. Raymond put in a good word for Shelford with Harper, which resulted in a Chicago scholarship. After visiting at home in Chemung, he proceeded to Chicago and took lodgings north of the campus at 5490 Monroe Avenue, where he partially supported himself by reading and abstracting sociology books—a job found with the help of Raymond.[15]

Shelford arrived in Chicago late in the sultry summer of 1901 during the celebration of the university's first decade of operation. He was immediately impressed with the school and with the unbounded optimism of President Harper and his faculty. That fall he entered the junior college with 772 other students and registered for German, rhetoric and composition, and solid geometry to begin his work for the S.B. degree. In the winter quarter he took his first advanced biology course, embryology, with Frank Lillie, a member of the zoology faculty. Other Chicago zoologists were head professor Charles Whitman, Charles Child, and Charles Davenport. Lillie delivered his masterful lectures in a soft-spoken, undramatic style, and Shelford found his course a fine introduction to laboratory techniques and rigorous biological reasoning.[16]

With credit for his West Virginia work, Victor received advanced standing in the spring of 1902, and the associate in science degree that August. Meanwhile, he earned his keep at the Monroe Avenue boarding house by waiting on tables and stoking the coal furnace. At the house he met Mary Mabel Brown, a twenty-six-year-old schoolteacher. Mabel Brown was one of four daughters of Martha J. Weir and former Civil War surgeon Isaac W. Brown. She had graduated from Chicago Teachers' College. Victor's personal notes—and his mediocre grades during 1902—show that he was taken with Mabel. She was independent, sharp-minded, and industrious; and she rapidly became very special to him. She accepted his proposal of marriage in February 1902. Their engagement was to last five years and their marriage, thirty-three. Mabel spurred Victor on through his last undergraduate year filled with courses in botany, French, geology, history, mathematics, philosophy, physiology, and zoology.

The high point of his senior year lay squarely in Charles Davenport's variation and experimental zoology courses. Zoologist, natural historian, statistician, and later geneticist, Davenport had completed his doctoral degree at Harvard under Edward Mark, who had himself studied at Leipzig, probably under the eminent invertebrate zoologist, Karl Leuchart. [17]

Davenport stressed experiments, quantitative methods, and the inductive approach in examining the relationships between animal form and geographic variation. These were complex subjects for 8:30 A.M. lectures on snowy winter mornings early in 1903, but Davenport excited students by presenting specimens, photos, and field notes covering his own research in individually arranged laboratory sessions. They heard about Davenport's 1902 research trips to Europe and to the Mississippi Gulf Coast with Chicago botanist Henry Cowles and about his work on the animal ecology of the Cold Spring Harbor, New York, sand spit, which he began in 1898 before he came to Chicago. Davenport emphasized to Shelford and his classmates how disgraceful it was that animal ecology lagged so far behind plant ecology and promoted it as a fertile area for meaningful advances. [18]

Davenport suggested to Shelford that he tackle a course project on color variation in tiger beetles (Cicindelidae). After only one look at several drawers of these vividly patterned, swift-flying, predatory insects from the Cold Spring Harbor beach and the Lake Michigan dunes, Shelford agreed. These beetles would keep him well occupied for the next dozen years. Following Davenport's lead, he noted that only the elytra, or wing covers, were colored. Their hues ranged from green to red, brown, golden yellow, and purple. (Shelford was later able to report that these colors were caused by microscopically thin metallic surface films on a melanin base.) The contrast between colored and clear areas produced the patterns; the so-called markings were actually clear areas. There were bars, spots, curved and sinuous lines, winding borders, and what looked like amorphous doodlings. These markings showed up in both longitudinal and transverse arrays. Shelford wrote up his preliminary results that winter, continuing the work under Davenport's direction the following spring and subsequent fall.

Victor received his S.B. degree on June 16, 1903, as one of 150 students in the spring graduating class. Within a week he was off to Woods Hole, Massachusetts, and Cold Spring Harbor, New York, where he worked the entire summer, devoting as much time as possible to his tiger beetles. His mother wrote in early July asking, "How much pay do you get for your work?" Victor never did answer her question; apparently he did not think the money sufficient to brag about. Following a brief trip to Chemung in late summer after an absence of exactly two years, Victor returned to Chicago in late September to find a letter from President Harper saying that he'd won a scholarship of $120 for beginning graduate studies in the university's Ogden School of Science, granted for excellence in senior college work in zoology. [19]

From his arrival at Chicago in 1892, head professor of zoology Charles Whitman's goal was to build a strong research and graduate program. He did not allow undergraduate teaching to impede this primary objective. Teaching loads for faculty in zoology were typically light, and classes were small, except for premedical courses. Whitman also found administrative routine distasteful. He held no staff meetings, nor did he consult the faculty about the budget or staff appointments. Although Shelford had no formal courses with Whitman, they became acquainted through the head professor's interest in advanced student research and natural history studies. Whitman provided Shelford with sound advice for his early studies of tiger beetles and sponsored his summer work at Woods Hole. [20]

Shelford's two primary mentors at Chicago were Charles Child and Henry Cowles. Curiously, both men were born in February 1869 during Ulysses Grant's administration and both were raised in Connecticut. Child was primarily a developmental biologist whose work with the lower invertebrates sought the governing factors for regeneration of parts and served as a stimulus for his treatment of eggs and embryos as metabolic systems. Nevertheless, Child had a lifelong interest in nature, and he taught a course in field zoology that Shelford took during his first year in graduate school in the fall of 1903. Shelford's performance in this course was average: Child gave him a B− for the lectures and field work and a C for his exam. But these grades did not reflect fully what Shelford had learned. He later credited this course as his "first serious inspiration in natural history." The collaboration between

Child and Shelford continued through 1907. Child advised Shelford on his tiger beetle experimental work, and Shelford assisted Child in the field zoology course. In the interim, Shelford made up for his earlier mediocre grades with a solid B+ in Child's invertebrate zoology course. Although Child was a reserved man, and not easy to know, Shelford and he grew close. They regularly shared the long hikes in the field for which they each became legendary.[21]

To prepare him for assisting in the field zoology course, Child suggested that Shelford audit the elementary ecology course taught by Henry Cowles, of the botany department, during the summer of 1904. This class would prove epochal to Shelford's intellectual development. He knew, of course, that Cowles had won international acclaim as one of the leading plant ecologists in the world for his studies of succession, which were based on the ideas of the Danish scientist, Eugenius Warming. Shelford quickly came under Cowles's spell. Cowles believed, "The field of ecology is chaos," and felt unprepared "to define or delimit ecology." Yet in class that summer, he laid out a panoply of facts, processes, and principles about plants and their environments in a way such that Shelford understood what ecology should be. Shelford described Cowles as a "first class man" and the "teacher who influenced [him] most." Cowles, in turn, saw that Shelford had good field sense and determination.[22]

Shelford's diligence was particularly evident in his study of tiger beetles. During the 1904–5 academic year, he fit in side trips to Kansas and Indiana, in addition to a variety of Illinois locations, to continue fieldwork. He began laboratory thesis work on the reproductive habits of beetles and experimented with modifying their color patterns through radical temperature increases, areas in which Child was especially helpful. Shelford's first scientific contribution was an oral presentation entitled "Variation in Tiger Beetles," given to the Entomological Section of the Chicago Academy of Sciences on February 16, 1905, with ten members present. He argued that color patterns in tiger beetles are of little taxonomic value "owing to the great amount of variation" they display and concluded with a discussion of the interesting geographic distribution of patterns among several species, accompanying his talk with lantern slides.[23]

His first published work appeared early in 1906, in the form of a review of Horn's 1905 index of the tiger beetles. Horn had labored fifteen years on, as Shelford remarked, "practically all the large collections of the world." Shelford exulted to see his name in print, and he surged ahead with extra enthusiasm. The lights burned late in his second floor laboratory in Hull Zoology Building that year, as his doctoral research moved forward.[24]

With assisting Child, continuing his own beetle work, and taking Cowles's geographic botany and physiographic ecology courses, Shelford found himself prowling the shores, dunes, and forests of Lake Michigan more and more frequently in 1905 and 1906. There sand dunes covering a quarter of a million acres of lakeshore were fashioned over thousands of years by retreating glaciers, falling water levels, and the effects of wind on exposed sands along the lake margin. These mobile dunes could reach widths of 1 kilometer and heights of 90 meters, at times literally burying anything in their path—ponds, forests, even houses.

Cowles taught his students that changes in plant societies at any given location proceed over hundreds, or even thousands, of years; nevertheless, one could conveniently read the story of the changing vegetative mantle on a brisk walk from the open sandy beach back into the shady forest. Distinct plant societies lay at varying distances from the lake: grasses followed by brilliant wildflowers, stands of cottonwood and pine, black oak, hickory, and finally beech-maple forest as far as 25 kilometers from the present shoreline on ancient beach ridges that had been sand dunes fifteen thousand years before.[25]

The students puffed after Cowles, asking about his "dynamic ecology." To questions such as, How certain was the appearance of forest? and Were weather and climate important? Cowles took an evolutionary view, claiming that since climate and geology were always changing, vegetation could never be stable. "In other words," Cowles once wrote, "the condition of equilibrium is never reached, and when we say that there is an approach to the mesophytic [moist] forest, we speak only roughly and approximately." Like Warming, Cowles stressed plant interactions during the competitive struggle for survival as important in the development of the vegetation, downplaying Frederic Clements's belief in the dominant role of climate.

Cowles further stressed how plants are physiologically adapted to their habitats. He admitted the importance of morphology but insisted "It is far more important to know a plant's physiological adaptation; its transpiration; its water-absorbing power; its physiological plasticity." Shelford took careful notes.

To those overconfident students who felt they had a complete grasp of all this after only a few field excursions, Cowles cautioned: "The sole way to know what [vegetation] changes occur, is to make detailed studies of limited areas year by year." He repeatedly emphasized the need for further investigation of the whole subject of succession.[26]

By this time, of course, Shelford had explored the lakeshore for three years. What he had learned from Child, from his own observations, and from Cowles, churned about in his mind. Obviously, parts of the lakeshore were changing: He witnessed the building of sewers for Indiana towns like Gary, railroad and road construction, and finally the erection of the U.S. Steel plant. It was his first vivid experience of humankind's severe impact on the natural landscape. Yet, other parts of the Indiana dunes were still remote and wild. Of the place Shelford eventually chose for some of his study sites, he said, "No one lived anywhere near the shoreline. There were miles without a house."[27]

Inspired by Cowles's pioneering plant successional studies and aware that no one had yet examined the presence and role of animals in the various plant societies, Shelford homed in first on the animals he knew best—the tiger beetles. His "Preliminary Note" written in early 1907 considered the ecological distribution (defined after Haeckel) of nine species from sand beach to forest. Female beetles regularly test the soil before laying eggs, and larval beetles rarely move from the spot where they hatch. Consequently, Shelford wrote, "The larvae have been found to be more circumscribed and definite in their distribution than the adults." Adults are swift-flying when the spirit moves them.

Larvae of *Cicindela purpurea limbalis* live only on steep clay banks above the beach among scattered herbaceous vegetation. Shelford placed reproducing adults in laboratory cages with a variety of soils—both steep and level—to test the females' choice for egg laying: most females chose a steep, clay soil over four other types. Similar experiments with several other species confirmed the idea, as Shelford put it, "that the breeding place becomes the true index of [tiger beetle] habitat." Likewise, the larvae of different tiger beetle species were associated with specific types of vegetation, for example, *C. lepida* with cottonwood trees on shifting sand, *C. repanda* on pond margins with soil stained by decomposing reeds, and *C. sexguttata* with forests of white oak, red oak, and hickory. Shelford closed his article by stating confidently:

> The general principles here set forth apply to the *Cincindelas* associated with the development of rivers and the erosion of uplands. Observations now under way go to show that they apply to the fauna in general. Strikingly different faunas are to be found in the different forest stages herein mentioned. Plant succession is then a factor which we cannot afford to neglect in considering distribution and evolution.[28]

Tiger beetle and plant distribution on the sandy shores of Lake Michigan was not, as is commonly believed, the subject of Shelford's doctoral thesis. His thesis, which he wrote simultaneously with the "Preliminary Note" paper, actually concerned tiger beetle life histories and larval biology. Professor Whitman recommended his candidacy for the Ph.D. degree on March 11, 1907, and the zoology faculty formally approved it on April 27. Even before all this and unknown to Shelford, as he said later, "Dr. Child went to Professor Whitman, and proposed that I be appointed a member of the staff, and [be] given an opportunity to see what could be done with this field of natural history." He added, "But [I] never knew whether or not he thought I had made good with the opportunities which he secured for me and support which he gave me." Shelford received formal notice of his appointment to the Chicago faculty as associate in zoology beginning July 1, 1907, at an annual salary of eight hundred dollars. With this development, his financial picture brightened. Also, his recent move to housing on Woodlawn Avenue closer to campus seemed smart. It was there on June 7, 1907, that he learned of his election to Phi Beta Kappa and where four days later he robed for commencement ceremonies.[29]

His thesis for the doctoral degree amounted to only twenty-seven pages in published form. The introduction began:

> During the past quarter century, the consideration of life-histories and habits as a basis for experimental work and for the study of distribution, variation and other evolutionary topics has been far too much neglected. In the study of variation, investigators have too often collected large numbers of specimens, arranged them in classes, calculated indices, constructed curves, and drawn conclusions regarding the direction of evolution without knowing the life-history of the form and without

determining whether the characters studied are easily modified by varying conditions during development, or whether they change during the life of the individual.

Shelford presented data for twelve species of tiger beetles, taking into account life cycles (three basic types); eggs; burrows; and anatomical characteristics of first, second, and third larval stages. He then proceeded to discuss the relationship of life histories and larval characteristics to environmental factors. Data were included on hibernation, depth of burrow, and location of pupation cell in relation to temperature, behavior, soil moisture, and food. He emphasized that in three species there are overlapping generations; a phenomenon that, if not known, would confuse a study of variation. Last, he suggested that there is the potential for soil temperature and moisture to influence the variability of color patterns. Even in 1908 Shelford felt compelled— and was probably advised—to define ecology. He defined it after Haeckel as the "science of the domestic side of organic life, of the life needs of organisms and their relations to other organisms with which they live." He promised to elaborate on the ecological distribution of the beetles in a future paper.[30]

Meanwhile there were other and different matters to attend to. Shelford and Mabel were married on the evening of Wednesday, June 12, the day after his graduation. The ceremony took place at the Hyde Park Church of Disciples at 6201 Woodlawn Avenue with twenty people attending. The best man was Henry H. Parke, a zoologist friend of Shelford's from West Virginia University; the maid of honor was Florence Brown, Mabel's sister. After their marriage the couple lived a short time in Professor Lillie's house on the southeast corner of 58th and Kenwood. Shelford's mother wrote soon after the wedding that they were "sorry they couldn't come out" for the ceremony but looked forward to meeting Mabel soon.[31]

At the close of the 1907 summer quarter, Victor and Mabel left on a trip to New York. They took the Erie Railroad and arrived in Waverly on September 4. They visited around Chemung by buggy, then continued on to New York City, Philadelphia, and Washington, D.C., making a final stop at the Jamestown Exposition in Norfolk, Virginia, before returning to Chicago on October 1. The rest of their wedding trip would come in December.

Victor matriculated for a seminar in ecology given by the botany department that fall and struggled with the inevitable details of preparation for his own course in field zoology the next spring. His brother Harry wrote saying he was glad Victor and Mabel were back safely. "Since you left," he added, "we have been picking apples, have the silo filled, and the thrashing done, but have not got our potatoes dug." He went on to tell of a local robbery, which prompted him to take a gun to his room for protection. It was his last letter: as the first snow fell the young couple learned to their horror that twenty-one-year-old Harry had been killed instantly by a shotgun blast on November 26 while he sat in his room expecting an intruder. As far as is known, it was an accident. Victor's father never really got over Harry's death.

Victor and Mabel's presence in Chemung before Christmas helped the family, but it was a difficult time, as sadness and excitement are a strange mixture. The couple felt guiltily glad to leave the parents in Victor's brother Wiley's hands. They sailed from New York for England on Christmas day 1907 on the SS *Baltic* to continue their wedding trip.[32]

Two days out of Sandy Hook, Mabel remarked to her husband how much she enjoyed ordering food without worrying about the cost. To her family she wrote excitedly: "Victor says that Prof. Agassiz (Ag-a-see) the son of the great Agassiz is on board and himself a famous zoologist." And the next day: "Yesterday Victor sent one of his *Cicindela* papers with his card to Prof. Agassiz and in the afternoon he called on us. They are over in one corner of the library talking now." Mabel was in good spirits, slept soundly, and had not missed a meal. Adding a note to his wife's letter, Victor wrote: "I don't know whether to say that I am sick or not, but guess I will say not." Actually he was miserable for two days. The next day they visited the engine rooms—"like the center of the earth," Mabel remarked—and saw the boilers and the propellor shaft. Victor ended up shoveling coal at the urging of a grimy stoker. Escaping the bowels of the engine room, they went topside to a windy quarter of the ship and tried to get some exercise. They were impressed with the force of the rushing wind.[33]

Two days later they landed in Liverpool where they spent a week, and then they set off to see Victor's cousin George Shelford (Grandmother Phoebe Shelford's nephew) and more distant relatives living in Wellingborough, Northamptonshire. Afterward Victor rented a cart and horse and took his young wife on a nostalgic 20-kilometer ride to ancestral Keysoe.

Victor and Mabel were captivated by the village: thatched-roof houses on Keysoe Row; stone walls; the green fields of Shelford Farm; Staughton Moor; quaint Baptist and Anglican churches with Norman facades; the ruins of Great-grandfather John Shelford, Jr.'s, old house and shoe shop and the Checkers and White Horse inns where he drank his ale and bragged to his friends about his sons John III and Eli far away in America. Victor and Mabel diligently leafed through musty birth, marriage, and death records in Keysoe Church; exchanged pleasantries with Henry Dickens, a neighbor in his nineties, who fondly remembered both John III and Eli Shelford; and had tea with Mary Beebe, great-granddaughter of the first John Shelford. Mary surprised Victor by presenting him with her great-grandfather's favorite Windsor chair. Victor's daughter years later recalled the story of how her father "carried the chair down a country road at night to a nearby town where it could be shipped home."[34]

The couple next came down from the uplands to Bedford, where Mabel was intrigued with the pillow lace and plaited straw. They crossed the Great Ouse and continued to Cambridge, finally settling down in Little and Great Shelford on the River Cam. While Victor visited the university museum, Mabel bought colored picture cards, and "had an awful time with [British] money." Valiantly the Shelfords traveled southwest through Hertfordshire, crossed the Lea, and tarried near the ancient Danelaw line. Leaving the chalky Chiltern Hills behind, they reached Oxford where they watched a fine theatrical performance and had tea at the home of Oxford zoologist Professor Poulton.

Their European tour was structured around Victor's visits to museums to study tiger beetle collections. With letters of introduction from Frank Lillie and Charles Whitman, he was warmly greeted at Oxford, Cambridge, the British Museum of Natural History in London, the Zoologisches Museum in Berlin, and the Jardin des Plantes in Paris. He also examined the private collections of Mr. Basil Nevinson in London, Dr. Walther Horn in Berlin, and Dr. Gestio in Genoa.[35]

In London Mabel and Victor stayed at the venerable Thackeray Hotel opposite the British Museum and from there visited the sights including Sir Isaac Newton's grave and, of course, Madame Tussaud's Exhibition. Mabel helped Victor with his beetles at the British Museum but did not really enjoy it. What she did like were Basil Nevinson's Japanese bronzes, his ivory-framed miniatures, and especially his exquisite ivory dragon with individually hinged scales. Victor thought Nevinson's private collection of beetles was "finer than that at the Museum," Mabel recorded. The Shelfords finished off their London visit with a delicious Entomological Club dinner at Holborn Restaurant.[36]

In late January they set out from London for Harwich and from there sailed to Hoek van Holland—Mabel was sick this time. They had visited Amsterdam, Hannover, and Berlin by early February. In Berlin they met Frank Lillie's sister and stayed ten days in a pension at Potsdamer Strasse 40, where Victor busily made notes to himself, as he readied his thesis for publication.

"Victor gets along with the German like a native," Mabel marveled from Leipzig, "but mine is very limited." The couple thoroughly enjoyed German food and sights, but time was getting short, and they had to hurry along, traveling south to Regensburg, Munich, and Innsbruck in the Tirol. They moved wide-eyed through the Alps to Italy: Verona, Venice, Florence, and Rome. Mabel always said Florence was her favorite city. But if German was hard for her, Italian was impossible. Ignoring the foreign tongue, Victor and Mabel picked daisies from the ruins of ancient Rome and enjoyed the fine wines.[37]

Returning north in late February, they visited Genoa and Milan and arrived wearily in Geneva on their way to France. Mont Blanc "looked like a great dome of white marble," Mabel wrote. With the magnificent view of snow-draped mountains against a deep blue sky and a circlet of river in the foreground, it was too tempting, so off they went to climb the foothills. They got caught in a snowstorm with snow weighing down Mabel's long dress and sticking to their eyes, noses, and mouths as they hooted and hollered their way back to a warm fire.

They spent ten days in Paris. "Victor is busy reading the proof of his [thesis] paper," Mabel wrote to her family. "He will go to work at the Museum tomorrow. . . . Think I shall spend a good deal of my time at the Louvre." She went three times. A week later she reported, "Victor has gone to visit some military museum which I care nothing about so he brot [sic] me down to the Bon Marché. . . . It doesn't come anywhere near Marshall Field's." She was thrilled however, with the chic styles. She closed this letter saying they would visit Versailles later that week and then go on to Cherbourg, cross the English Channel, and finally leave for home.

Spring approached southern England, and the Shelfords sailed from Southampton on March 18, 1908, on the RMS *Majestic,* arriving in Sandy Hook on March 26. Victor was miserably seasick for almost five days, Mabel for three—the trip was ghastly. As they neared the New York shore, Mabel recovered her balance and wrote her mother that although Victor would have to go back to Chicago right away to meet his classes by the first of April, she would "stay in Chemung for a few days, and tell the folks about the trip—it's only fair."[38]

So Mabel went dutifully to Chemung, and Victor took the train to Chicago. A decade had passed since he finished normal school and nearly seven years, since he first came to Chicago. Victor's novice phase had ended; he had become one of only five thousand scientists in the United States and one of a mere handful studying ecology. Before him lay the challenges of developing an animal ecology program at Chicago and of tracing further the complexities of ecological distribution among tiger beetles and the relationships between plant succession and animals in general. That his "Preliminary Note" had appeared in the *Biological Bulletin* the previous year was a promising start. He had been honored to have his thesis paper read to the Linnaean Society of London by Rev. Canon W. W. Fowler in February, while he and Mabel were in Rome. Victor Shelford could justly take pride in the work that had brought him so far.[39]

CHAMPION OF ANIMAL ECOLOGY

1908–1914

After returning to Chicago in April 1908, Shelford plunged into a heavy schedule of teaching, writing, and fieldwork. The scientific work he was about to begin would firmly establish his professional reputation. His research and teaching were all of a piece.· The tiger beetle data he had gathered since 1905, concerning life histories, distribution related to plant succession, and experimental modification of taxonomic characters, served as the background against which he attempted to organize his efforts. Looking back on this time, he wrote:

> It was my hope to secure guiding principles to be used in the interpretation of the tiger beetle data, in the fields where zoology [classical taxonomic and morphological approaches] has contributed only *chaos*. In 1907, an appointment, requiring that I give instruction in natural history alone, using the field method, served to stimulate my efforts in this direction in order to find a basis for the organization of field and natural history instruction. . . .
>
> An early training in zoology which was of the strictest morphological type, caused me at the outset to share the doubts of many biologists as to the value of ecological work. However . . . I was [later] able to examine the work of plant ecologists with a large degree of sympathy, which has grown as the inquiry and accompanying investigations have progressed.[1]

Shelford wanted to gain a clearer view, a comfortable experimental framework within which his work of the past eight years could proceed amidst the ferment of current ideas about ecology, evolution, morphology, and physiology. But that was only half of his motive. After he returned from Europe, he tried to expand on his 1907 "Preliminary Note," hoping to draw a more complete picture of tiger beetle ecology as he had promised, but he found that he could not employ the typically used principles of animal distribution. More important, he believed that the field of animal ecology had to be organized independently before he could ever make much headway.

The task would not be easy, although the first step, as he conceived it, sounded simple enough—"to locate the animal in its environment." Typically, naturalists did this by studying the morphology and evolution of animal groups and the geographic barriers influencing their distribution. This method relied too heavily on speculative evolution, Shelford thought, and involved dreary discussions of adaptations. Instead, Shelford wanted to address all the animals under a given set of environmental conditions, to study animal aggregations as they actually lived in nature. Today this seems obvious, but as Shelford said, "Attempts actually to study the environment in any detail, or the reactions of animals to the conditions of environment are rare indeed." He noted that "animal activities have been usually ignored or taken for granted" and complained that zoologists fail to "discriminate between the important and unimportant periods of a life history in relation to environment." In short, he claimed, many zoologists believed that "the data of natural history [could not] be organized into a science."[2]

Not that there was any lack of data. The supply of facts with some ecological significance was enormous and bewildering; scientists had only to discover what could be done with them and what fertile questions could be asked. Shelford was keenly aware of scholarly work on the natural history of animals done long before this field was labeled ecology. He particularly liked the work of Alfred Brehm, the German zoologist whose multivolume *Tierleben* had appeared between 1863 and 1869 and whose posthumous book *From North Pole to Equator* was published in 1895. Brehm's descriptions were impressive. Karl Möbius, who suggested in 1877 the concept of a "life community" or *biocönose,* and Karl Semper, who argued in 1881 for studies of the physiology of the whole organism and its relations to the conditions of existence, were other noteworthy European biologists whom Shelford read eagerly.

On the American side, Stephen Forbes from the University of Illinois had published on an astonishing variety of natural history and applied ecology subjects involving fish, birds, and insects since the late 1870s. Forbes's eloquent case for a greater understanding of whole assemblages of animals and plants struck home with Shelford.[3]

And then there was Henry Cowles, a man of incisive ideas, wide-ranging curiosity, marvelous story-telling abilities, and great kindness. Cowles often said that the "problems of physiology and ecology are identical" and that biologists should discard the notion that "physiology is experimental and ecology is observational." This was a telling argument for Shelford, providing him with the impetus to combine his experimental interests with his desire to view and understand animals from the perspective of the natural community.[4]

He subsequently homed in on physiology and behavior with the reasonable assumption that these reflected the general environmental conditions under which animals lived, much in the same way that the growth form of plants (tree, shrub, grass, etc.) served as a convenient physiological index for Cowles in his studies of plant societies. Shelford wanted to examine complete "physiological life histories," for example, metabolic rate, time of reproduction, and viability of eggs, as well as habitat preferences and the "laws governing the relations of organisms in communities." Specifically, he proposed dealing with proximate causes of animal distribution:

> Reactions of the animal maintain it in its normal environment; reactions are dependent upon rate of metabolism which may be modified by external conditions. Behavior reactions throughout the life cycle are a good index of physiological life history characters. If we knew the physiological life histories of a majority of animals most other ecological problems would be easy of solution.

Shelford drew his confidence, no doubt, from the optimistic approach of experimental physiology—it borrowing in turn from the prestige the physical sciences enjoyed by virtue of their rigorous mechanistic explanations.[5]

Shelford's "law of toleration," for example, stated that "the distribution of species . . . is limited by the variation of a factor or factors beyond the limit of toleration of the species . . . in question." The tiger beetle data supported this general view: maximum numbers of particular beetle species were correlated with optimum ecological conditions; breeding activities and reproductive success consistently took place within the narrowest set of tolerance limits, with the same environmental factors presumably governing both local and geographic distribution. Shelford pinpointed temperature, light, appropriate soil, and moisture as critically important, but he wanted much more data.[6]

The biological principle behind Shelford's pioneering work deserves repeating. As he stated it, "Ecologically comparable animals living under similar conditions possess certain similarities of physiology, behavior, habitats and modes of life." (As a convenient brief descriptor of these, he used the Latin word *mores*.) His goal was to develop a useful ecological classification of animal communities based on this principle. But to do this, Shelford asserted, animal ecologists needed to view the environment dynamically after the example of the plant ecologists, who since the 1890s had demonstrated the participation of physiographic factors during plant succession. This perspective would enable animal ecologists to assess the roles of physiographic processes compared with biological factors in influencing animal succession.[7]

Shelford reported first on fish from both streams and ponds, with work beginning in 1907. His initial objective was to examine the distribution of stream fishes relative to geological base leveling, or erosion of the earth's surface. He examined seven streams on the southwestern shore of Lake Michigan, ranging from Dead Run near Waukegan, south to several streams tributary to the Calumet River within 50 kilometers of Chicago. The larger, older streams had worked their way back into the glacial moraine of ancient Lake Chicago, deepening their beds. The smaller, younger streams showed little bed erosion.

Shelford found the fish had definite habitat preferences. Smaller streams had fewer fish species, and among these horned dace, red-bellied dace, and johnny darter were also found near the source of the larger streams. Fish species in larger streams that were not present in smaller streams, such as little pickerel, largemouth bass, pike, and crappie, lived in the more eroded stream beds closer to Lake Michigan. Shelford proposed that the fish were responding to a graded series of environmental conditions related to changes in bottom type, current, and stream width. He considered groups of fishes appearing at a particular stream location and at a specific stage in the successional sequence over geological time to have similar physiological characteristics. Experimental work would be required to examine this latter idea.[8]

Shelford conducted pond studies concurrently with his stream research. The ponds lay at the southern end of Lake Michigan near Gary, Indiana, on the lakeshore between a parallel series of sandy ridges left behind as Lake Chicago receded in postglacial times. Consequently, the ponds were neatly arranged by their age: the youngest near the lake, and the oldest farther away. Although some were connected, others had been separated by railroad and road construction. Shelford could also deduce the ecological age of the ponds by the relative amounts of bare sand, vegetation, and sedimented organic matter on the pond bottoms. He then examined the fish composition of each pond and compared it with the fish in what was presumably the youngest pond, located next to a sandy beach at Waukegan, Illinois.

Fish composition reflected the age of a pond and the length of time since there had been construction activity near the site. Shelford believed that "ponds of different ages represent stages in the history of older ponds." The youngest beachfront pond had little vegetation, much bare sand bottom, and little bottom detritus; common fish were pike, Cayuga minnow, redhorse, and common shiner. In older ponds with bottom detritus and submerged and floating vegetation, such as water lillies and bladderwort, fish like largemouth bass, bluegill, little pickerel, and spotted bullhead were more numerous. Denser floating vegetation was found in still older ponds, along with large numbers of mud minnow and black bullhead, and much detritus. Finally, in the oldest ponds, thickly covered with cattails, bulrushes, and grass-covered hummocks, Shelford identified mud minnows and breeding dogfish (*Amia*).

Once the ponds were cut off from the receding lake, they could be considered physiographically quite stable, Shelford maintained. The changes in the ponds were primarily due to the actions of the animals and plants on their own environment. "Animal succession in ponds," he said, "is due to an unused increment of excretory and decomposition materials which causes an increase in vegetation, a decrease in O_2 on the bottom and a general change in surrounding conditions all primarily affecting *breeding*." These biological processes occurred much more rapidly than did physiographic events. The upshot was that each set of coexisting species made the environment less fit for itself and more fit for its successors, as Cowles had often suggested.[9]

As a result of his findings, Shelford advised ecologists not to employ particular species of plants as indicators of ecological conditions. Instead, he recommended using whole communities of plants and their growth forms. What was not clear was the amount of correspondence between growth form of plants and the physiological life history characteristics of fish. These data were not yet available, and their absence would eventually impede Shelford's progress with his method. He next pushed on to study the set of communities he had known earliest and best—the beach, dune, and forest communities on the sandy shores of Lake Michigan.[10]

Despite the fact that human disturbance had increased here, Shelford believed that the magnificent dune country at the head of the lake was still one of the best habitats in North America for successional studies. His research area lay between Indiana Harbor, Indiana, and Sawyer, Michigan. He studied the animals in five chief plant stages, denoted by the name of the dominant tree species: cottonwood, pine, black oak, red oak, and beech-maple. In all, he dealt with two hundred species of animals—only a portion of the total present. The species composition of the animals changed almost completely in the dramatic transition from bare lakefront sand to shady moist forest. Shelford stressed the importance of recognizing and comparing the vertical strata occupied by the animals in each habitat, although he acknowledged that some animals migrated from one stratum to another for breeding or feeding. The various strata were tree, shrub, field (herbs and low shrubs), ground, and subterranean. As the variety, average size, and architectural complexity of the vegetation increased, soil development, temperature, light, and available moisture changed, too. Consequently, plants were shown to be important in modifying environmental conditions; the distribution of animal species was more closely correlated with changes in these physical factors than with the presence of particular species of plants.[11]

Nearest the lakeshore, scattered groups of cottonwood trees balanced on shifting sand that held only traces of humus, grasses, and a few shrubs. Both white and copper tiger beetles, grasshoppers, digger wasps, and burrowing spiders were plentiful here, and many of the common animals were swift predators. Jack pine stood on more stable sand having more humus. Besides grasshoppers, digger wasps, spiders, and the bronze tiger beetle, these pine stands held the six-lined swift (a lizard), the blue racer snake, and a few skittery ground squirrels. As black oak mixed with pine and finally dominated, humus increased; and grasses, herbs, and shrubs added to the leaf litter on the shady forest floor. Accordingly, tree frogs, snails, ant lions, and secretive sow bugs first appeared. Shrubby undergrowth tangled the ground under taller trees. Finally, the moister red oak and beech-maple forests farthest from the lake boasted thick leaf litter and humus, abundant shrubs, and diverse herbaceous vegetation. A number of species of salamanders, frogs, snails, beetles, grasshoppers, spiders, centipedes, and millipedes hid under decaying wood, leaves, or bark, where they had sufficient moisture and could avoid strong light. All of this is deceptively easy to sum up, but in reality backbreakingly hard to put together in the field. "Succession of all the animals of the forest communities under consideration," Shelford said, "is comparable in principle to that in ponds. Succession is due to an increment of changes in conditions produced by the plants and animals at a given point. Animals through their effect upon the soil play an important though minor role in the process."[12]

Despite his continued need for much more data on what he termed "response phenomena," that is, physiological evidence, whether as growth form in plants or as mores in animals, Shelford had enough information to push ahead with a tentative ecological classification for the chief communities circling the southern end of Lake Michigan. "The classification which ecologists are striving to build up," he said, "will serve a purpose in behavior, physiology, and ecology, analogous in this respect to that served by the phylogenetic classification in morphological thought. It should however be flexible rather than rigid and true to fact rather than to schemes." It would, he suggested, provide a "new and different means of organization of data." To widen the factual base for a classification of animal communities, Shelford advised ecologists to determine experimentally the physiological life history characters of species in the communities they studied. These characters, he explained, "can be measured in terms of reactions to measured complexes of physical and other environmental factors. They are as clearly defined as any morphological taxonomic characters and can be measured with the accuracy of physical phenomena." By his account characters could be determined in three ways: "First, by the measurement of reaction to all or several of the chief environmental factors under rigidly controlled conditions . . . second, by testing the reaction of the animals to a graded environmental complex of known constitution, and third, by putting the animals out into a graded series of natural environments." Here was a prescription for a laboratory and field program in physiological ecology, a program that he would himself pursue for fifteen years. [13]

Shelford received his promotion to instructor in the spring of 1909 with a salary of twelve hundred dollars per year. From 1908 to 1910 he taught field zoology in the Junior College; animal ecology, a Senior College course covering animal societies, physiography, and succession; and a course in geographic zoology. He added his first graduate course offering, entitled Studies in Animal Ecology, in the spring of 1911. Occasional outside lectures and work in the University Extension rounded out his duties. He took satisfaction from the fact that Chicago now had one of the strongest zoology departments in the country, sharing high distinction with Harvard and Columbia. [14]

Although his research and writing went well, Shelford needed new stimulation. He also wanted to complete his tiger beetle collections as background for experimental work on color patterns, and he decided there was no substitute for seeing the animals' natural habitats. He made arrangements with Head Professor Whitman to spend the fall and winter terms of 1910–11 in the West. The Shelfords left during midsummer, taking a leisurely five-week trip, which included field work in Nebraska and New Mexico and ended at La Jolla, California, where they set up base for a while in a beachfront cottage, called the Seaweed. Later they traveled north along the California coast to visit with relatives of Victor's granduncle, John Shelford III. They planned to finish the trip with fieldwork in Nevada, Idaho, and Utah. [15]

That January, Victor's mother wrote with plans of her own: "Why can't you buy your tickets for Elmira or Waverly when you come back and come home for a week or two. . . . It would not cost near so much and then we could let you take a barrell [sic] of things home with you." The young people were on a tight budget in California and sorely needed some financial assistance. Alex Shelford wrote two weeks later.

"Glad you have found Uncle John's people. Yes, we can send you the $15 until then, that is Wiley and I together so you may look for a money order."[16]

Spring came late to Chemung that year: by early April none of the Shelfords or their neighbors had even plowed yet. Nor had the family heard a word from Victor and Mabel since mid-March when the couple sent a card from the Grand Canyon. "Why don't you write?" Victor's mother asked, annoyed, in her early April letter to Chicago. She knew that Victor should have been back by then for the opening of the spring quarter at the university. Wiley wrote that he, too, thought they "might be coming to Chemung for a few days this spring." He closed the letter saying: "Guess you were afraid we would make you cut wood as we did when you were home last, but don't worry about that for we have enough wood sawed to last a year." They had bought a three-horsepower gas engine the previous fall, which explained the ample woodpile.[17]

But Victor and Mabel would not have time to visit Chemung. They swung southeast after leaving the Grand Canyon, heading back through Texas and along the Gulf Coast before striking north to Nashville. They finally reached Chicago late in March. They stayed on the way at a small Texas hotel where they were surprised to find a wolf chained up behind the building. Mabel felt sorry for the beast, which seemed tame and forlorn. She petted and talked to it and actually let it put its paws on her shoulders. The hotel keeper was astounded: apparently the wolf had been caught only a few days prior to the Shelfords' arrival. It was a fitting end to their western trip.[18]

While they were away, head professor Charles Whitman had died of pneumonia on December 12. One era ended and a new one began as Frank Lillie assumed the direction of the zoology department at Chicago. Change came immediately. Under Lillie, biologist-historian Horatio Newman notes, "Two principal changes were inaugurated: the department was changed from an autocracy into a democracy, and the field of undergraduate teaching was greatly improved. 'I established the practice of regular meetings of the staff,' Lillie said, 'and no important decision, including new appointments and recommendations for Fellows and Assistants was made without their approval.' " But a democratic atmosphere brought corresponding responsibilities: all faculty members—including Lillie—were expected to share in a greatly expanded undergraduate teaching program. Shelford's share eventually included stints in introductory zoology, one of the prescribed premedical courses. The experience was in some ways disconcerting, as undergraduate students could be noisy and distracting. Charles Child soothed Shelford, telling him, "The things that happen to you are rarely personal, and should not be considered so, even when students appear to be laughing and joking in the rear of the room, it is usually something other than the lecture or the lecturer."[19]

During the academic year 1911–12, the first full year under Lillie, the zoology faculty consisted of associate professors Charles Child, William Tower, and Horatio Newman, and instructors Reuben Strong and Shelford. Under Lillie, advanced courses were added to the curriculum to improve the transition from undergraduate to graduate studies. By 1912 Shelford was teaching advanced courses in ecology and behavior and physiographic animal ecology. He averaged five courses per year from 1908 to 1914 and contributed an ecology seminar jointly with Henry Cowles from the botany department.[20]

In the summer of 1912, Shelford was chagrined not to have received a raise in salary, and he had a new baby daughter, Lois, to feed. He wrote to the university president, Harry P. Judson, asking why. Judson answered that it was not a matter of the quality of his work, but rather a departmental affair "based on particulars decided on by F. R. Lillie." Shelford took this to be the first signal of trouble brewing for him at Chicago, trouble that boiled over in 1914. Yet in 1913 he received a reasonable salary increase and was elected a fellow of the American Association for the Advancement of Science. As a university instructor he earned almost double what a factory worker made in a year. The Shelfords kept perspective and were grateful for their blessings, while all around them unemployment shot up as the country suffered through another recession.[21]

Shelford was delighted with his first doctoral student, the bright, enterprising Warder Clyde Allee. Allee had chosen aquatic isopod crustaceans for his doctoral research, using the water sow bug, *Asellus communis,* a common species in the Chicago area. "All fall and winter," Allee wrote, "I collected them from quiet mud-bottomed ponds, chopping the ice if necessary, and from beneath stones and leaves in clear small streams." He worked with groups of five to ten pond and stream isopods, putting them in rectangular or round metal containers with sanded wax bottoms and exposing them to straight or circular water currents. Stream isopods usually hurried against the current; pond isopods commonly headed down current, or behaved indifferently. The data piled up, and Allee and Shelford pondered the reasons for these distinctive responses. One obvious difference between streams and ponds was the oxygen content of the water, which was much higher in streams. So Allee experimented with different oxygen concentrations.[22]

He found he could reverse the reactions of the pond and stream isopods to currents. "Rather cockily," he said, "I reported after a time to my instructor . . . [that] I could send the indifferent pond isopods hauling themselves upstream, or I could reduce the stream isopods to going with the current," by varying the oxygen concentration. Further work showed that the strength of a positive response to current was correlated with overall metabolic activity: chemical agents known to stimulate metabolism elicited positive responses to currents, while metabolic depressants resulted in much lower responses.[23]

Allee's absorption with isopod behavior and the role of oxygen led to a joint project with Shelford during the academic year 1911–12. From earlier work on the Lake Michigan ponds, they knew that changes in water chemistry and pond vegetation accompanied fish breeding and succession. Realizing that fish were hardy experimental animals whose biology was reasonably well known, they devised a way of studying the behavior of fishes when exposed to gas gradients. No one had done this adequately before. They used narrow rectangular tanks and set up experimental gas gradients by introducing different gas concentrations into flowing water; tanks of a similar design are still used today. (See figure 1.) They then observed the fishes' behavior, measuring how much time the different fishes spent in treated compared to untreated water and recording the fishes' movements on strip charts showing time and concentration gradients. Both young and adults of all ten species tested in the principal experiments showed avoidance and gulping responses to low oxygen concentrations and no responses to excess nitrogen in bubble-free water. All of the fish were negatively reactive to carbon dioxide, turning away when they encountered an increase of as little as 5 cubic centimeters per liter. The results suggested that carbon dioxide content is probably the best index of water suitability for fish.[24]

True to his plans, Shelford stuck to an experimental approach in the years from 1912 to 1914. He picked his subjects carefully and related

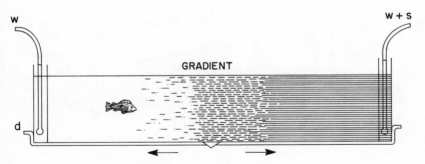

Figure 1. Shelford and Allee's gradient tank: *d*, drain; *w*, water intake; *w* + *s*, water plus substance. The introduced substance created a gradient in the water, with outflow at the bottom, and the changing positions of the fish were recorded on graph paper. Adapted from Shelford's *Laboratory and Field Ecology*, © 1930 the Williams & Wilkins Co., Baltimore.

them to principles of animal responses and animal communities— aggregates that he now practically defined as "all the animals of a given habitat." Working with animals from both terrestrial and aquatic communities, he proceeded to analyze the selection of available environments by animals and to measure the strength and frequency of abandonment of inappropriate environments.

For example, noting the lack of information on the correspondence between tolerance to water loss and geographic and ecological distribution of terrestrial animals, Shelford set up an elaborate apparatus for supplying evaporation gradients and then painstakingly tracked the reaction paths of individual animals. (See figure 2.) Animal reactions were strikingly related to comparative evaporation rates in the native environment. Survival time, too, was related to habitat, but only if animals with relatively similar integuments were compared. Species of salamander, common toad, millipede, sand spider, and ground beetle showed particularly rapid response to evaporation gradients, whether produced by air movement, temperature, or humidity.[25]

He saw behavioral agreement, as well, among stream animals from rapids compared with those from quiet pools when he tested the responses of species of fish, crayfish, snail, clam, mussel and various insect nymphs and water penny beetles to current, bottom type, and light in Allee's current apparatus. (See figure 3.) Rapids animals showed clear agreement in positive reactions to strong current and

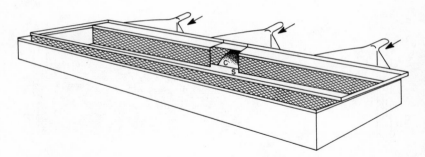

Figure 2. Shelford's gradient cage for air movement and humidity experiments: *c*, cutaway showing diffusing screens and air vent; *s*, space where animals were confined. The cover is removed in this drawing. A similar cage was used for control animals. Adapted from Shelford's *Laboratory and Field Ecology*, © 1930 the Williams & Wilkins Co., Baltimore.

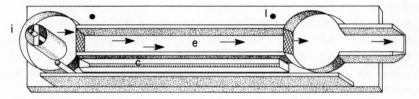

Figure 3. Allee's straight current apparatus: *c*, control animal box; *e*, experimental animal box; *i*, water inflow; *l*, light attachment. Adapted from Shelford's *Laboratory and Field Ecology*, © 1930 the Williams & Wilkins Co., Baltimore.

hard bottom; their reactions to light depended on whether they typically lived on, under, or among stones. Pool animals were alike only in their positive reaction to a sand bottom. Shelford was satisfied that he was beginning to grasp some important factors controlling animal distribution.[26]

Shelford had gained a reputation as a leader in animal ecology. Besides his written papers, he spoke on his work at the Field Museum in Chicago and the Illinois Academy of Sciences. He helped Henry Cowles guide a group of European plant ecologists through the wonders of the Indiana dunes during the International Phytogeographic Excursion in America during August 1913. There he met the eminent British botanist, Arthur Tansley. Yet none of this insulated him from the administrative decisions brewing at Chicago that would be instrumental in his leaving the university in 1914. To ecologist Charles Adams at Illinois who was on shaky tenure ground, Shelford wrote in February 1913: "You have my sympathy and good wishes. Things are going ahead here but rather roughly. I think I will get my promotion but am not certain." After learning in the fall that Adams would have to leave Illinois, Shelford offered advice and confessed the growing uncertainty of his own position: "I will do anything I can for you but don't know what it can be. I am supposedly on the slide here myself, but expect to go into entomology if worst comes to worst. . . . Forbes ought to be able to help you more than anyone. I should think a wise thing for you would be to get into Forbes' entomological service or State Lab. and remain until you get a suitable place."[27]

At this point both men were worried not only about their own careers, but about the future of animal ecology at their respective universities. The Shelfords now had a second child, John, to figure into the budget, and Victor had the curious experience of having to deal with colleagues' accolades over his first book, *Animal Communities in Temperate America,* without knowing whether it was enough to save his Chicago position. Likewise, Adams had just published his own *Guide to the Study of Animal Ecology,* a book that detailed the history of the development of ecology and demonstrated the significance of contributions by Adams, Forbes, and Shelford to American work published since 1906.[28]

Shelford's *Animal Communities* generated much interest and excitement among biologists. It represented the first book-length treatment of animal communities from a modern standpoint. The book illustrated Shelford's fine sense of the interdependence of living organisms and his insistence on natural communities as the proper focal point of ecology.[29]

Shelford used as his central theme the focus on physiological responses of whole animals, which he derived from Semper. His book was the first to consider food webs or "food relations," as he called them, for aquatic and terrestrial communities in detail. The ways in which community members ate and were eaten, he believed, were important in determining the structure of the community, including fluctuations in abundance of individual species. His argument was supported by diagrams of variously sized circles representing individual species and their interrelationships via population dynamics and available food. These anticipated the concepts of niche space and resource partitioning that would be formulated decades later. Mabel Shelford contributed a section of remarks on primeval communities near Lake Michigan. The meat of Victor's recent series of studies on succession appeared again, augmented by new data on invertebrate animals from lakeshore streams and ponds, as well as discussions on communities from swamps, marshes, forest edges, thickets, and prairies. The reviews were very favorable. Stephen Forbes wrote approvingly from Washington, D.C.:

> I put your new book on "Animal Communities" into my valise when I left home a few days ago, and so have had more time to read it than I should have had in the office.
>
> I am surprised at its comprehensive and fundamental character— quite different in that respect from the report on your "Chicago area" work which I had been expecting—and delighted with its well-balanced and thoroughly rational character. It is an admirable introduction to animal ecology, and a model of method in investigation. As such, it must do great service in opening up the field to productive work.
>
> I have a lot of things in mind to say to you on the subject, but this is hardly the time or the place. I hope that you may have every opportunity to go on as you have begun.

Shelford responded immediately: "Your remarks on my book will help me to keep at work and . . . to do a better job next time.[30]

Thoroughly encouraged, Shelford staked out his future ground with a focus on community ecology and whole organism physiology, stating, "Our first step in the task [laid] before us must accordingly be a consideration of wild nature as it really is." But there was the difficulty: nature was too wild. Although there were many animals associated with moderately narrow tolerance ranges, with particular habitats, or with other predictable coexisting animal and plant species, some animals did not fit in this mold. Instead, these species ranged across a number of habitats, changing in abundance from site to site. Shelford had anticipated this point in 1911. Obviously, his use of a physiological basis for community classification drew attention to indicator species that *were* frequently confined to relatively narrow environmental conditions. Put simply, his community concept naturally reflected the kinds of animals he dealt with in his early studies. Nevertheless, during the decades after 1913, it served many other ecologists as a working model. For example, Charles Elton, the English ecologist noted in his book, *The Pattern of Animal Communities:*

> Although my own early drive towards community ecology at the age of seventeen was a personal and internal one, it was set alight for several years by Shelford's book, which I actually carried with me in my knapsack in the course of an Oxford expedition to Spitsbergen in 1921 that I was fortunate enough to be able to accompany. It was partly to try and apply Shelford's method of treatment to the Arctic that I undertook a survey of the barrens of Bear Island and parts of West Spitsbergen . . . with the collaboration in the field of Victor Summerhayes, botanist to the expedition.[31]

During 1923, and again in 1924, the young Charles Elton returned to Spitsbergen, including the far northern islands, "where the polar ice-pack frequently pushes right against the land even in summer." This lonely, high Arctic region held fewer species than Shelford's Chicago haunts, and Elton felt he had things quite well under control. Yet he quickly realized that Shelford's community model required modifications, chiefly in regard to feeding behavior, but also concerning other species interactions. The enormous transfer of food material across a variety of habitats from sea to land impressed Elton. He identified the food chain from diatoms and phytoplankton, to zooplankton, to fish, to birds and linked the luxuriant patches of grasses and wild flowers below nesting sites on high cliffs to the recycling of nutrients from bird droppings. This interlocking of species across aquatic and terrestrial habitats stimulated Elton's later, more extensive treatment of food and feeding, providing further insight into the structure of animal communities.[32]

In the late fall of 1913 Shelford knew he had to leave Chicago. He pulled his credentials together and confidently sought another position. By winter the universities of Washington, Kansas, and Illinois had already shown interest in him, and the wide attention given his just published book was heartening. He immediately sent copies to Adams, Forbes, and Henry B. Ward, chair of zoology at Illinois. Then he made arrangements for a 1914 summer trip west and six weeks at Puget Sound Biological Station. He did not say much about it, but he knew he needed a change of scene. Nor did he fret much when the Kansas position fell through. He learned from his colleague and friend, Robert Wolcott, at Nebraska, that the position was not so desirable anyway. Wolcott would have been pleased to hire him for his own department, but all he could possibly offer was a junior subordinate position.[33]

It was beginning to look as if Illinois might offer much more. Late April 1914 not only saw Shelford going to Urbana to meet with Ward and Illinois president Edmund James but also saw K. C. Babcock, dean of the college of liberal arts and sciences, in Chicago inquiring about Shelford. J. Paul Goode, geography professor at Chicago, wrote Babcock:

> As I told you when you were here, Shelford has undertaken to develop a line which is quite new in zoology in this country, that is, the application of the geographic point of view to the study of animal life, what is called animal ecology. The old line zoologist is not at all in sympathy with this line of work. They have been interested almost wholly in morphology or taxonomy.

A few days later, Henry Cowles offered his opinion:

> I am very glad indeed to take this opportunity to say a good word for Dr. Shelford. I have known him very intimately for more than a decade, and have, perhaps, been more closely associated with him than has anybody else.
>
> I regard Dr. Shelford as one of the ablest men in the world along the line of animal ecology. In fact I know of no one who surpasses him. He has mapped out for himself in his study of physiographic ecology and animal behavior, lines that have never been so well treated by any zoologist. He has published a number of important bulletins and a book that will make an epoch in the subject. In addition [he has] stimulated investigation to a very high degree, and started a number of advanced students along ecological lines. . . . The university that enlists Dr. Shelford's services as a teacher and investigator in animal ecology is fortunate indeed.[34]

Beginning the first of May and continuing over the next six weeks, a flurry of letters, memos, notes, and meetings occupied officials at Illinois. Equally active was their correspondence with Shelford, who by early June was holed up in seaside quarters at Puget Sound Biological Station. Through it all, Forbes played a pivotal role. Shelford gave him most of the credit: "Forbes was responsible for my coming to Illinois. He liked the papers I had written." As Shelford later recounted the story, Forbes told Ward that he himself would hire Shelford for the entomology department if Ward did not put him on the zoology faculty. Forbes, the seventy-year-old patriarch of ecology and predecessor to Ward as head of the zoology department, had his way in the end: Ward hired Shelford.

In fact there were definite advantages for Ward and his department in hiring Shelford, chief among them increases in research time and equipment paid for by the State Laboratory of Natural History, which was run by Forbes. In return, Forbes would get a mature biologist interested and accomplished in experimental ecology, an area Forbes had hoped Charles Adams would develop when he hired him in 1908. Ward admired Forbes as a scientist, and respected his advice "to develop ecology." In Shelford, Ward felt he was getting the best man for the job.[35]

As worked out by Babcock with the joint approval of Forbes and Ward, Shelford's nomination was for three years as assistant professor of zoology on three-quarters time at a salary of two thousand dollars. His remaining time was devoted to serving as assistant biologist at the State Laboratory of Natural History for five hundred dollars. Periods were also arranged for Shelford's field work during the first half of the first semester and the last half of the second semester when reasonable weather could be expected. Forbes agreed to provide another five hundred dollars for research equipment and expenses during the 1914–15 academic year. Ward and the zoology department gained the services as graduate assistant of Morris Wells, Shelford's doctoral student from Chicago, and of Shelford himself for teaching responsibilities in the elementary zoology course and other advanced courses as he desired. Finally, Babcock noted that Shelford would require yet another four or five hundred dollars for an adequate teaching laboratory and that Ward had reserved "a portion of the proposed new vivarium and greenhouse building" for Shelford's research.[36]

Hearing from Babcock that his nomination had been sent to President James, Shelford wrote back in late May emphasizing his need for quality control of Urbana water and absolutely modern equipment and sufficient space. Similar requests that spring to the University of Washington during negotiations for a position there came to naught. Besides, Shelford felt the salary of fifteen hundred dollars offered at Washington was much too low. On the same day that Babcock wrote Shelford, a relieved Charles Adams wrote his botanical colleague, Arthur Vestal, in Montana, "The prospects are that Shelford will be here next year. . . . I am glad to see that ecology has now a place here—there is no longer doubt as to this point here." (Adams would move that year to the New York State College of Forestry and later build a distinguished career as a museum administrator and conservationist.) By early June, Shelford's morale was high; it did not matter that he was isolated in the remote, northwesternmost incorporated village in the United States. Friday Harbor had only wireless telegraph, and the mail took almost a week from Illinois. Moreover, there was only one ancient worn-out typewriter at the biological station—as his pick-and-peck letters show. June 13 brought news of his formal appointment at Illinois from President James. "I may say," James added, "that the Board of Trustees also approved . . . the immediate erection of a vivarium and service building which will provide better opportunities than we have at present for your special work."[37]

Shelford replied on the ancient typewriter: "I accept the appointment and shall be in Urbana Sept. 1. I am pleased that we are to have the new facilities which you mention. It will put the University of Illinois in advance of many of the large Universities in facilities for Zoological research."

The new Illinois vivarium would consist of a concrete structure of two main floors and a basement, with four doors opening into a central hall on each floor. The building would also have lateral greenhouse wings and a third attached greenhouse in the rear. "You will see," Ward wrote Shelford, "this plans to provide for your entire work in the new building, a situation which is very fortunate for you." His facilities were to include a lecture room, an office, and beyond the office, two laboratories—all on the second floor. He was assigned yet another laboratory on the first floor and a commodious section of the rear greenhouse that he planned to use for holding fishes and conducting experiments on them. The first floor laboratory was reserved for an advanced course in experimental ecology that he offered to students for thirty-two years. Shelford labored the best part of four days over the blueprints so as to speed his specifications on to Ward in Woods Hole. Ward then consulted with the architect who, in turn, inspected aquariums in Detroit with fresh- and saltwater pumping systems. Shelford carefully sent his equipment requests and copies of all his cross-continental correspondence to Forbes: he was not yet completely comfortable with Ward, but he was euphoric over the proposed facilities.[38]

At Puget Sound that summer, Shelford with his assistant, Edwin Powers, continued studies of fish reactions and tolerances to chemical and temperature gradients. They worked chiefly with young herring (*Clupea pallasi*). Powers's experience was invaluable, as he had recently completed a similar study on crayfish at Chicago. Of course, they used Shelford and Allee's gradient tank. As expected the herring showed high sensitivity to hydrogen sulphide. The young fish turned and avoided concentrations estimated as low as 0.4 to 0.5 cubic centimeters per liter. Herring showed similar responses to temperature differences as small as 0.2 to 0.5 degrees Celsius, and they preferred slightly alkaline, brackish water. Shelford believed their results threw some light on the historical decline of the Baltic herring fishery. Continual dumping of sewage and fish wastes into the low-salinity Baltic may have caused a concomitant increase in free carbon dioxide, hydrogen sulphide, and acidity in herring habitats. Overfishing may then have been enough to seal the fishing industry's fate. The summer project ignited both men's interest in pursuing the connections between animal ecology and human impact on nature—the kind of study so attractive to Forbes.[39]

As July wound down, Shelford's thoughts turned to his impending move to Illinois. He wrote Lillie of the same, and Lillie answered graciously: "I am very glad to have your kind letter, and to know the action you have taken with reference to your transfer to the University of Illinois. You will certainly have superior facilities and advantages there, although you may find the work pretty strenuous for a year or two. . . . This move will probably do you more good in an academic way than any other single act." Shelford wrapped up his work and, literally, his tent and left Puget Sound for Chicago during late July. His last professional appearance before leaving the University of Chicago was a public lecture, "The Inhabitants of Freshwater," given at Kent Theater on Monday, August 3. Later that month he moved with his family from Chicago to Urbana, settled in his temporary office in the natural history building on Green Street at the northeastern corner of the university quadrangle, and looked forward expectantly to a busy academic year at his new institution.[40]

PART TWO

The Practice of Ecology

3

PROFESSOR AT ILLINOIS

1914–1929

Champaign-Urbana, with only twenty-three thousand inhabitants in 1914, was a far different world from Chicago. Urbana itself contributed nine of those thousands and was still a small town, with all the advantages and disadvantages that implied. Most citizens would have agreed that the University of Illinois provided much of the cultural stimulus to the community and that it had made great strides during the past decade in shedding its cow college image. In 1913, for example, it proudly established museums of European and classical culture. When Shelford arrived in the fall of 1914, he joined a faculty whose list of published scholarly work covered thirty impressive pages, who served a student body of over five thousand students, and who depended heavily on a library of almost four hundred thousand volumes.[1]

The zoology faculty then consisted of five men: J. Sterling Kingsley, who specialized in vertebrate anatomy and embryology; Frank Smith, who taught ornithology and field zoology; and parasitologist Henry B. Ward were full professors. Associate professor Charles Zeleny concentrated on heredity and evolution and instructor Harley Van Cleave covered invertebrate zoology. Kingsley and Smith would retire before the twenties were half over; only the towering, red-headed Van Cleave would accompany Shelford on the faculty during his entire academic career, at times to both men's consternation. Ward was head of the department. Former dean of the college of medicine and head of zoology at the University of Nebraska, he had replaced the eminent and brilliant Stephen Forbes in 1909. Nevertheless, Forbes retained his headship in entomology and his position as director of the Illinois State Laboratory of Natural History. Ward's interests in medicine and premedical education strongly influenced the direction of the department over the next quarter century. Under Ward, the university became one of the leading centers in the world for instruction and research in parasitology. His leadership can be described in one word—forceful. Consequently, when Shelford arrived in 1914 the direction and flavor of Ward's administration were clear. In Van Cleave's words, "the concepts of head and department were rarely distinguishable." Eventually faculty unity suffered. Yet no one could deny Ward's dedication to zealous research. Under his leadership between 1909 and 1933, sixty-three doctoral degrees were granted in zoology. None had been granted before 1909.[2]

Shelford was thirty-seven when he came to Illinois. During the ensuing fifteen busy years he published forty-seven papers, edited one book, and wrote another. His field and laboratory research took four directions in overlapping stages: aquatic biology, stressing animal behavior, fishes, and pollution; terrestrial animal ecology as affected by weather and climate; light penetration into seawater; and terrestrial and marine community ecology. Shelford eagerly tangled with applied ecological problems in at least half of his research efforts.

Shelford and Charles Adams called ecology the "new natural history." Adams observed that ecology "takes the laboratory problems into the field and brings the field problems into the laboratory as never before." By 1917 some three hundred Americans considered themselves working ecologists and were acutely aware of the rapid increase in American ecological work since the turn of the century. Some, like Shelford, Forbes, and Adams, embraced the spirit of the progressive conservation movement: the increasing fund of technical and ecological knowledge, they believed, held great promise and needed to be applied to the more efficient management, use, and appreciation of natural resources. By no means were their interests limited to pristine environments.[3]

Before World War I, most research and development in wastewater treatment, for example, dealt with domestic sewage even though increasing volumes of industrial wastes accumulated in the nation's waters. By 1917 American streams, rivers, and coastal waters had suffered from fifty years of neglect, and few biologists were interested in pollution work. Fewer still appreciated that everyone was part of the pollution problem and that pollution costs were inadequately accounted for. To his credit, Shelford contributed substantially to the foundation of water pollution biology.

Of the illuminating gas wastes left over from the distillation of coal that were typically dumped into rivers and streams he once said:

> The immense commercial value of these wasted products has been more generally appreciated since the outbreak of the European war, which cut off the large supply of foreign dyes and important organic compounds and increased the demand for such products as may be used in the manufacture of explosives. The value of these wasted products should be sufficient to prevent their wastage, but their injurious effect upon fishes and other life of streams generally is itself sufficient to justify the prohibition of pollution by this means.[4]

To examine the effect of these wastes, Shelford used elaborate apparatus in lengthy experiments during 1915 and 1916 and showed that essentially all coal distillation wastes produced by the Champaign gas plant were toxic to fish—from acetone to xylene, even napthalene, which was usually rated by chemists as insoluble in water. The more tarry the substances were and, in general, the smaller or younger the fish, the greater the damage. The common orangespotted sunfish, *Lepomis humilis,* was Shelford's standard test fish. It bothered him that, curiously, fish often swam right into toxic test solutions, avoiding the pure water end of the gradient tank and obviously increasing their chances of death. Likewise, it galled him that the United States Fish Commission blithely urged the public to eat fish, and "make every day a fish day."[5]

After the United States entered the First World War, Shelford felt an increased responsibility to examine the consequences of manufacturing and sewage pollution on natural resources and public health. Large volumes of acid effluents were casually dumped by munitions factories into coastal river and marsh waters. No one had measured the effect on fish of these and other wastes from the newly proposed Miles acid process of treating raw sewage. This highly touted procedure recovered valuable fertilizer, ammonia, grease, and glycerine and put out a residual effluent of 35 to 50 parts per million of either sulfurous or sulfuric acid. During the busy summer of 1918 at Puget Sound, Shelford tested these acids on marine fish; both caused mortality, particularly to herring, in concentrations less than 39 parts per million. Even though sulfurous acid was the most toxic, he recommended its use in the Miles process, since it could escape rapidly from solution before mixing with seawater, especially if aerated.[6]

Returning to campus that fall, Shelford encountered a wartime zoology graduate student population of only eleven—the smallest number during his career at Illinois. Even though America's participation lasted a short nineteen months, Shelford found the war and its aftermath an uncomfortable time. His main concerns were with what we now call the military-industrial complex and highly inflated war profits; both offended his progressive beliefs. Earlier, he had written David Starr Jordan, president of Stanford University and well-known leader in several national and international peace organizations: "Here everything is military in tendency and has been for some time. I have been doing what I can with the Socialist party petitions to Congress . . . to my mind it is going to require strong organization to . . . shake off the equivalent of conscription after the war no matter how it ends." Jordan replied, "I think that you are right in having great concern over the conditions which surround our entrance into the war. Leaving out the question of the war itself and our temporary affiliation with the worst tories of England, [there is] a strong and concentrated effort to make conscription, with industrial and military regimentation the rule in this country after the war." Despite colorful academic gossip to the contrary, Shelford never did join the Socialist party; however, he did vote for Eugene Debs. Those that knew him best considered him a staunch progressive Democrat, eager for worthy causes.[7]

Soon the war was over, and the following two years came down hard on everyone. Mabel Shelford always said that the Shelfords' depression was during and right after World War I. Like everyone else, they agonized over prices that had doubled since their arrival in Urbana. Victor's salary, although it had increased respectably since 1914, could not keep pace. It meant frugal living for a forty-three-year-old assistant professor and his family.[8]

In a real sense the twenties was a decade torn between nineteenth- and twentieth-century attitudes and behavior. It was time of unprecedented peacetime economic growth—all at once hectic, unsettling, exasperating, and exciting. The decade spanned almost exactly the middle ground of Victor's life. His children were growing, his parents dying, and his career advancing toward a senior academic position. He was not a complicated man; he said and did what he believed. Most people who knew him agree that he had firm opinions. "He had to be persuaded fully and carefully," his daughter Lois said, "before changing his mind about a matter he had decided on." Approaching him otherwise, she added, "you were just wasting your time and effort." Adjectives pinned to him during these years include reserved, hardworking, even-tempered, dependable, and optimistic. In his forties he was still slim and wiry, and his hair still brown and full. He was not fussy about clothes. His health and stamina were excellent: students still had a hard time keeping up with his rapid field pace. Nevertheless, he had a periodic nagging sinus problem and suffered from nervous indigestion when he got bogged down in his work. His naturally serious demeanor was moderated by his good sense of humor and a practical, well-balanced sense of self. As a rule Victor was not a complainer, according to his daughter, but he did make one notable exception: "His most frequent lamentation was people's shortsightedness and unconcern for the damage being done to natural resources."

Shelford regularly rose early, had breakfast with coffee "strong enough to float a Ford axle," and bicycled off to campus. Reaching the vivarium, he would stow the bike and climb the stairs to room 200. Early arriving students and staff found him already busy at work in his small office, surrounded by shelves jammed with books and tottering apparatus. He was perpetually busy. Even so, his former student, John Savage, commented, "His door was always open to us and we were privileged to interrupt him any time we wished information or wished to discuss some phase of our research or other problems. . . . Someone once asked him if we could phone him about something interesting, say at 0300. His reply was that 'It would be OK, if the subject matter warranted it, but it had better be important.' " Students meeting with Shelford in Vivarium 200 during the 1920s faced him at his desk, outlined against an east window and the elms of north campus. His scientific reputation was hard to forget, but his measured, thoughtful speech helped put students at ease. He had a curious way of bringing his upper lip against his teeth as if he were about to smile broadly. His grin and raised eyebrows framed steady grey eyes that looked out quizzically from behind his glasses and grew more intent as meeting times wore on. When he wearied of talk and concentration, he would check out the vivarium equipment for removing chlorine from water or perhaps mosey outside to contemplate the small plot of Illinois prairie on the vivarium grounds.[9]

Occasionally Victor and Mabel attended concerts—Victor like Sousa marches—and they had a subscription to the University Dramatic Series. These outings and Presbyterian church services made up a good portion of their socializing. What Victor most enjoyed were student gatherings at his house. Host and guests sat by the fire, told stories, read mysteries, and danced the latest steps. Across the fireplace mantel was carved, at Mabel's insistence, "For You the Fire Burns." During these festive evenings the mentor and his apprentices wove that marvelous web of loyalty mentioned by Victor's admirers and detractors alike. Few failed to notice his practical side either. At home he did the plumbing and electrical wiring, built bookshelves, raised winter onions, and half-soled Lois's and John's shoes, even though Mabel despaired when the nails came through and ripped the children's socks. Unfortunately, she was inhibited by the weight of her husband's ancestral shoemaking reputation and dared not criticize him very sharply. Besides, Victor earned his points by oiling, greasing, and repairing the car and driving her about, as she never learned to drive herself. Their first car was a black, four-door, touring Durant, with side curtains, a manual windshield wiper, and no heater. The roads in the early 1920s were terrible, so the bicycle got frequent use.

Shelford did much of his writing at home after dinner, closeted in his small study at his rolltop desk. Away from vivarium interruptions, he tangled with his diverse interests, pondered points of attack, and plotted his future path. Since 1912 he had devoted his energies to developing an experimental quantitative laboratory approach with an emphasis on physical environmental factors and to creating the sophisticated apparatus needed for the work. His achievements in these areas served as currency for his tenure and promotion to associate professor in 1920.

Laboratory research alone, however, was not enough to satisfy Shelford. He had announced his long-term goal to a seminar group at Puget Sound Biological Station back in the summer of 1914. He planned to produce a treatise along the lines of his 1913 book that would describe the natural communities of all of North America, not just the Chicago area. Since then, he had not given up his belief that the community was the focal point of animal ecology, but his career dictated experimental work that would not wait.

In 1917 he convinced colleagues in the newly formed Ecological Society of America of the need to inventory natural areas across the North American continent. The project lasted seven years, during which Shelford served as chair of the preservation committee and chief editor. One hundred eighteen colleagues helped in a massive examination of plant and animal communities, the extent to which they had been modified, and their suitability for ecological research. This was a basis for much more community work, including Shelford's own planned treatise. *A Naturalist's Guide to the Americas* tied together his earlier and later work with natural communities during a period when demanding experimental research had to take precedence. [10]

In 1920 the investment value of farming in the United States surpassed that of manufacturing, railroads, and utilities combined, and approximately one-third of Americans relied on farming for a living. During wartime prosperity, banks had granted liberal credit, and farmers received high prices for their products. After the war inflation zoomed, causing agricultural profits to dwindle. Despite a rebounding economy, in 1922 farmers still carried heavy mortgages and other debts incurred during prosperous times. Many either went bankrupt or hung on by the skin of their teeth. Both the intensified interest in food supply during the war and the plight of the agricultural industry afterward brought an increased demand for the study of economic zoology problems. [11]

Stephen Forbes, in his matchless way, skillfully steered Shelford to experimental studies of codling moths and chinch bugs. Outbreaks of both pest insects caused heavy crop losses in Illinois, codling moth to apples, other fruit, and walnuts, and chinch bugs to cereal crops. Forbes had begun field studies on the codling moth in the fall of 1914 following an explosion of successive generations of caterpillars in southern Illinois during an unusually hot and dry summer. Apple growers could not come up with an adequate spraying program to stay ahead of the hordes of pinkish white, brown-headed caterpillars chewing their way into hanging apples and growing into egg-laying moths, progenitors of more caterpillars. Up to three generations of moths in a single apple-growing season were possible. To control populations, farmers needed to know the time of emergence for each generation and the effect of weather on the different life stages. Shelford determined to give them both, but it took him five years to figure the beasts out and five more to publish his findings.

Later, when he looked back, he realized how difficult and tedious the work had been. He had several dedicated student assistants who checked the thousands of developing pupal moths twice each day. The climate simulation chambers Shelford used were unique in that they allowed him to test several humidities at the same temperature. Near the end of the war, coal for the vivarium greenhouse was rationed, and it took careful tending of the furnace to maintain experimental temperatures.[12]

Rationing and heavy demands for research were not Shelford's only troubles. It was not easy then to hold progressive political views, as Shelford did, in a small midwestern town. If anything, antiradical hysteria increased after the armistice and reached a peak in the Red scares of 1919 and 1920. In the summer of 1920, in the middle of his insect study, Shelford received a telegram asking if he would be interested in a professorship at the University of Pittsburgh and saying he had been recommended by Charles Davenport. It was late in the year to consider a move, but Shelford felt perhaps he would be happier in a more tolerant environment, so he wrote Forbes a note with the details and closed wishfully, "Also Pittsburgh is free from small town gossip, and other small town isms. If this should develop well is there a possibility of getting released?" Forbes replied the same day:

> It does not seem to me that you can properly accept the Pittsburgh offer at this time. The state has provided a good deal of equipment for your use and supplied you with assistance and operating funds for experimental work on which you have made no comprehensive report of results, so that most of this product would be lost if you were to leave us now. . . .
>
> Apart from this, it seems to me that with the start and standing that you have here, you may reasonably expect that the Natural History Survey and the University of Illinois will do better by you in the long run than the University of Pittsburgh is likely to do. . . .
>
> I am glad that you have had this offer, as it will serve as a measure of the value of your services which should be helpful in securing funds for your work hereafter.[13]

Thus apprised of his position, he pushed ahead with the insect work, addressing the principles of growth and development. Since 1830 biologists had accepted the idea that the temperatures during each day in the growth period of animals and plants could be added together, giving "total degree days" for development. The number of degrees above a certain threshold temperature multiplied by the number of days was believed to have a constant value. In 1914 the Danish physiologist August Krogh showed that this was true only over a limited temperature range. The rate of development fell off at higher temperatures and was greater than predicted at low temperatures. Since many other factors influenced development, such as humidity, light, rainfall, and evaporation, Shelford searched for a new, more accurate measurement of insect development. The measure needed to be sensitive to small responses of the developing species in units of time shorter than a full day. He defined his developmental unit as the amount of development experienced by a species in one hour as a result of a change of one degree in mean temperature within the limited temperature range determined by Krogh. The number of developmental units could be added to give developmental totals for a life history stage of any insect. Shelford stressed that these were not constants, but varied with generation and environmental factors. Therefore development during a life history stage had to be expressed in more than one dimension. To this end he plotted humidity against temperature and drew lines of equal developmental time for laboratory pupal stages. Shelford pointed out that experiments with realistic variable temperatures yielded insect life history stages about 7 percent shorter than those run under constant temperatures. He and his assistants also gathered extensive temperature and rainfall data from field locations. These data showed dramatically different pictures for abundant versus scarce moth populations. Abundant populations were correlated with relatively little rainfall during spring and summer hatching after heavy rainfall the previous fall. Small populations were correlated with the opposite conditions. [14]

Shelford wrote the final, massive paper in three sections. The first section included detailed instructions to apple growers for using his method of predicting time and intensity of codling moth outbreaks, but the method may have been too complicated for some farmers to use in the field. Apple growers had to measure temperature and humidity, plod through tables of developmental units, and spy on cocoon-spinning caterpillars and egg-laying moths. Forbes hoped extension agents would help with the process, but they could not get around to all farms. Shelford's developmental units have still not been fully assessed by biologists; although now with the help of high-speed sensors, recorders, and computers this could easily be accomplished.[15]

The chinch bug work progressed in similar fashion over a ten-year period. Chinch bugs are extremely sensitive and consequently frustrating for experimentation. Shelford first examined records of chinch bug abundance in Illinois back to 1840. He then used temperature-rainfall plots for the years since 1853 to derive average climatic conditions for abundant versus scarce chinch bug years, thus confirming an 1879 contention that two dry years were needed for population outbreaks. This preliminary work, he felt, needed much more refinement.[16]

Spurred on by Forbes and eager to apply his research results to economic zoology problems, Shelford accepted every opportunity to present his ideas and findings. Beginning with a report at the 1917–18 American Association for the Advancement of Science (AAAS) meetings in Pittsburgh, he went on to present papers at the 1918 American Society of Zoologists (ASZ) meetings in Baltimore and the 1919 joint meeting of the AAAS, the ASZ, and the Ecological Society of America in St. Louis. His talks covered response physiology, physiological life histories of terrestrial animals, and details from his codling moth research. During question periods and in informal floor conversations, as well as in later papers, Shelford often commented on the need for endowed laboratories set up to make continuous studies of crop-feeding insects and the physical factors affecting their biology. He could not understand why the United States Department of Agriculture had not picked up on recent ecological work—certainly the information was relevant. His colleagues agreed. Washington finally responded in November 1923, inviting Shelford to give a series of insect ecology lectures in a graduate course on economic entomology for Department of Agriculture employees. He was offered five dollars per lecture and expenses for January 1924. It was money well spent. E. W. Ball, the Department of Agriculture's director of scientific work, wrote Shelford of his lectures, "They had a very highly stimulating effect and will I think, do a great deal of good in encouraging our students to broaden their work."[17]

Trips to Puget Sound Biological Station in alternate summers beginning in 1918 gave Shelford a welcome break from midwestern routine. Typically he left Urbana for Washington State in June and returned in August. He taught a course in marine ecology at the station and recruited students to help on his summer research projects. Participating students found the studies fascinating and knew Shelford at his best. The biological station lay nestled in picturesque Friday Harbor on San Juan Island, one of twelve larger islands and many smaller ones, making up the San Juan Islands of northern Puget Sound, hard by the United States mainland. Together these islands form a scattered circle at the junction of Puget Sound, the Straits of Georgia, and the Juan de Fuca Strait, southeast of Vancouver Island, British Columbia. San Juan Island, with its two tails, or flukes, looks like a smaller, puffed-out version of Long Island, New York. It extends 23 kilometers northwest to southeast. San Juan Channel lies to the northeast, Haro Strait to the southwest, and Friday Harbor at the base of the northern fluke. As any ecologist will appreciate, the whole area became indelibly mapped in Shelford's mind. He came to know and love the islands and the bracing seascape stretching eastward to Bellingham and Samish bays on the mainland. Shelford, his colleagues, and a legion of students dredged, seined, and dug for animals and plants; dropped water bottles and photoelectric cells; and systematically surveyed marine communities and their associated physical factors during even-yeared summers until 1930. This turned out to be Shelford's whole contribution to marine ecology. "I didn't follow up my marine work," he remarked later without apology. [18]

The project started innocently enough. In 1920 Shelford grew curious about the amount and kinds of light reaching various depths in the frequently turbid seawater near the San Juan Islands. The quality of light would presumably affect the photosynthesis of seaweeds and perhaps regulate animal behavior. Shelford's underwater light measurements in summer showed light extinction as high as 21 to 35 percent per meter within the upper 5 meters of water and underwater visibility under these conditions of less than 1 meter. Early on, he ran into so many difficulties that he teamed up with Jakob Kunz, a physicist from the University of Illinois. Kunz's photoelectric cells contained sodium or potassium elements that emitted electrons in response to light, especially in a helium, hydrogen, or argon atmosphere. Kunz and

Shelford tinkered with various kinds of cells throughout the twenties. These early cells unfortunately needed an external power source. Furthermore, their construction, calibration, and operation for biological work was very difficult. (After 1933 the self-generating selenium cells still used today became available.) Shelford and another colleague, botanist Floyd Gail, also from Illinois, used a potassium-hydrogen Kunz cell, attempting for the first time to pinpoint abundance of seaweeds in relation to depth of light penetration.[19]

Biologists had noticed for years a rough zonation of red seaweeds in deeper water, browns at middle depths, and greens in shallow areas. (We now know that the overall zonation of seaweeds is not this simple.) Shelford and Gail found a brown zone from 5 to 20 meters, overlapping a red zone from 10 to 30 meters in the San Juan Channel and adjacent waters. Short wavelength light amounted to 10 percent or less of full sunlight at these depths. The two biologists presented extensive calculations of light penetration by various wavelengths, but all these needed to be corrected later. It was tricky, dirty work wrestling with tarred electric cable, a trawl frame, steel cable, and the heavy winch from a ten-ton boat. Several colleagues put in boat time on the project, including Shelford's doctoral student, Asa Weese, and invertebrate zoologist Libbie Hyman. (Shelford's former mentor, Charles Child, was there in 1920, busy with flatworm regeneration, but not too busy to join Libbie Hyman for a daily dip in chilly Puget Sound.) Shelford decided to send his final manuscript describing these studies to Chancey Juday, limnologist at the University of Wisconsin, for review.[20]

Shelford's choice was wise. Juday was the chief colleague of Edward Birge, eminent limnologist and president of the University of Wisconsin. Their partnership had produced a prodigious amount of work on Wisconsin lakes, so Juday's comments and criticisms were helpful. In response, Shelford and Kunz put their heads together and decided to radically modify their equipment. This took five years. In addition, Shelford and Gail's initial work wrongly assumed that natural staining in seawater was not important, that dissolved organic substances would not selectively screen out certain wavelengths of light. But oceanographer Martin Knudsen's work in the meantime showed that seawater was yellow stained and light-selective, so Shelford realized he would have to screen his photocells with suitable colored filters and repeat all his measurements.

In June 1925 when they were ready to test their new equipment, Shelford and Kunz went expectantly to Madison, Wisconsin, where Birge and Juday had made arrangements for them to work on Lake Mendota. The borrowed 30-foot launch, their new microammeter for current readings, their larger glass cell, and other improved equipment did the job. Judicious use of potassium, rubidium, and cesium cells with appropriate filters showed that violet and blue light was absorbed by suspended and dissolved materials in Lake Mendota. Light at 5-meter depths was largely yellow with a hint of orange. Strikingly, 2 to 3 meters of tannish colored Mendota water absorbed as much light as 10 meters of Puget Sound water. The following summer, Shelford repeated his work at Puget Sound, adding sodium cells to his repertoire. Puget Sound water was decidedly selective: with increasing depth, progressively more blue and green light was absorbed until at 25 meters yellow light dominated. "This investigation," Shelford said, "seems to have raised many questions as to the physical properties of sea water, its suspended matter and surface [characteristics]."[21]

Just after he and Gail first published on seaweeds and light penetration in 1922, Shelford began serious fieldwork on marine bottom communities in the San Juan Islands. He stayed at this until the end of the decade, after which his broad, pioneering work languished for thirty years before it was extended by oceanographer Pat Wennekens. Since 1913 when *Animal Communities* appeared, much had happened. Shelford had become more pessimistic about the possibility of obtaining adequate data for a physiological treatment of communities, but the increasing interest of other scientists in community studies gave him cause for optimism. From 1913 to 1918, C. G. J. Petersen, director of the Danish Biological Station, published his extensive study on patterns of marine bottom communities in Scandinavian waters; and plant ecologists, particularly Frederic Clements, with his views on communities and succession, continued to produce valuable and impressive work. Clements recognized dominant plant (and sometimes animal) species that exercised a large measure of control over the composition of the biotic community. Furthermore, he asserted that a biotic community displayed a special level of organization with a unique development, structure, and function. His ideas made Shelford itch to drop his Petersen dredge in Puget Sound and see what animal aggregation patterns would emerge. Thus began the association—often tested by fire—between Shelford and Clements, a relationship that brought mixed blessings to Shelford. On the one hand, he enjoyed the privilege of working closely with one of the most influential ecologists of the time. On the other hand, he entered a struggle with the semantic jungle of Clements's classification of biotic communities, from which he could not emerge unscathed. He could always take pride, however, in their joint attempt to foster a unified approach to plant and animal ecology.[22]

After two summers' preliminary work, Shelford reported in 1925 on three provisional extensive bottom communities, which he called formations, from an area of the San Juan Channel and adjacent waters measuring 75 square kilometers. His observations and the meager literature indicated that succession, if it occurred at all, was much faster in the sea than on land. Although he and his assistant, E. D. Towler, could pick out dominant species of barnacles, mollusks, crabs, worms, and sea urchins based on abundance or size, Shelford admitted that the "way in which organisms control a habitat is not yet clear except in the case of the dominant trees in our forests." In fact, marine ecologists still pursue the answer to that question today. Shelford had no doubt, though, that marine bottom communities had to be treated quantitatively and not merely entered into a species catalogue. He emphasized that ecologists needed a better understanding of mobile predators, plankton, and seasonal population changes in individual species.[23]

As the 1920s wound down, Shelford and his assistants continued collecting and quantitatively studying marine bottom communities in an expanded study area of 1,000 square kilometers during halcyon summer days at the Puget Sound Biological Station. Quite accidentally, they left their mark. Somewhere along a jumbled stretch of rocky bottom lining the periphery of Shaw Island across from Friday Harbor lie the barnacle-encrusted remains of a snagged dredge. It was replaced through the good graces of T. C. Frye, director of the station. Frye also managed to get new botany and zoology laboratories in 1926, just in time for Shelford's increasingly large summer crowd of students. Shelford expected undivided attention to ecological business from his students. Once a California lad tested his patience in laboratory, and they exchanged harsh words. The student was amazed to see Shelford roll up his sleeves and offer to "settle this outside if necessary." Fortunately, cooler heads prevailed, and the argument was dropped.[24]

Shelford opened the monograph he wrote to sum up his research on Pacific coast bottom communities by stating, "Our primary object in this monograph is to describe several new communities . . . distinguished by a *difference* in essentially *all* the species of abundance or dominance. The general plan of community classification adopted by American and British plant ecologists has been applied." Probably the most significant finding was a subtidal soft sediment community existing at depths between 3 and 75 meters and covering about 20 percent of their study area. This *Pandora-Yoldia* community was dominated by clams and polychaete worms and was later shown to be a variant of the *Yoldia hyperborea* community of subarctic Iceland, Greenland, and the White Sea. Shelford described several other communities, too, but these early sketchy details are not of general interest anymore. More important were Shelford's comments on the difficulty of identifying the factors controlling distribution and abundance of marine bottom species without using an experimental approach.[25]

Now and then over the years, Shelford would recall Frank Lillie's prediction that the work at Illinois would be "pretty strenuous for a year or two" and chuckle to himself. In fact the work never seemed to let up. At least he was well compensated. Even after he reached full professor in 1927, Shelford still had responsibility for at least five courses in addition to sponsoring advanced research for graduate students, running a special field excursion during Easter vacation, pursuing research commitments, and keeping up with committee work and consulting. During his first decade at Illinois he also helped in the introductory general zoology course. By the mid-twenties he was easily putting in sixty- to seventy-hour weeks, counting hours at home in the evenings. He never did figure out a proper way of accounting for time spent on Saturday field trips; these were part instruction, part research, and part fun.[26]

His typical academic year during most of his thirty-two years at Illinois was extremely full: Fall semester he taught animal ecology and geography, an upper-level course stressing fieldwork and covering animal behavior and distribution as they related to climate and vegetation. This course was required of all Ph.D. candidates in ecology or related fields. Shelford saw to it that graduate students got more field experience than undergraduates taking the course, and they all worked hard. Spring semester he taught an introductory course in animal ecology with lectures and much fieldwork. In alternate years, he taught graduate courses in physiological ecology and economic zoology, which included fisheries, forestry, conservation, and pollution. Students agreed wholeheartedly with Shelford when he said he assigned "much more than can be read"—sometimes as much as one thousand pages for a semester course. Both fall and spring he also offered a graduate course in experimental ecology that consisted of laboratory experiments in physiological ecology using "modern apparatus" and an individual research course that offered graduate students research opportunities in animal ecology, zoogeography, and wildlife management.[27]

By the late twenties, a quarter of a century had passed since Shelford was introduced to tiger beetles by Davenport and since he had taken his first Chicago-area field excursions with Child and Cowles. Yet ecology still lacked unity. One can discern a rough dichotomy in ecologists' efforts at the time. On one side were studies of physical-chemical factors in the environment and on the other biotic aspects of populations and communities. Food chains and community distribution, structure, and succession, favorite topics in those years, were the subjects of Shelford's and his students' work. Two university ecology textbooks graced the decade. Both were titled *Animal Ecology*. One appeared in 1926 by Arthur S. Pearce of Duke University and the other in 1927 by Charles Elton of Oxford University. Pearce dedicated his book to Shelford, saying, "I believe you are the outstanding ecologist in North America." Elton concluded his book with a caveat:

> There is no getting away from the fact that good ecological work cannot be done in an atmosphere of cloistered calm, of smooth concentrated focusing upon clean, rounded, and elegant problems. . . . In the course of field work one should have a rather uncomfortable feeling that one is not covering the whole ground. . . .[28]

A professional ecologist might agree with both statements, but Shelford's students would not accept the second after they had experienced one of his marathon field trips: they certainly felt they walked far enough to cover the whole ground. Shelford was exhaustive and superb. I have before me as I write, a quarter-inch-thick pile of his animal ecology field trip schedules covering the years between 1925 and 1946, all impressive in organization and detail. The schedules from trips before 1925 have not survived. We do know, however, that he offered his first long trip in 1916.

Generally Shelford and his classes started with any of two dozen nearby locations from the vivarium grounds to local woods, cornfields, roadsides, and ponds; then traveled to sites in central Illinois and western Indiana, in northern and southern Illinois, and on the Lake Michigan shore; and (beginning in 1929) trekked all the way to Reelfoot Lake, 530 kilometers south, in western Tennessee. In this way they studied forests, floodplains, rivers, lakes, streams, prairie, and dunes. They went by car, bus, or interurban railroad and sometimes even on foot. Trips started early, and woe betide late students; they paid a fine of a penny per minute times the class enrollment. Few students missed more than one of Shelford's field trips. Shelford took the difficulties of these trips in stride. Undergraduates could be garrulous and tiresome, and the field work itself was physically demanding. Once a student claimed indignantly that as a result of a makeup field trip she "spent several days in McKinley Hospital with sunburn and poison ivy." (Untrue countered Shelford, she was "inattentive, interested in a man and *took off her hose*. No ivy at prairie; got it sitting under trees with a man when she should have been watching fish.") Even the dean complained when long field trips arrived back at campus on Sundays.[29]

The posted field trip itinerary always stated prominently: Go Regardless of Weather. Shelford canceled only three field trips in thirty-two years, once because of snow, subzero temperatures, and a bone-chilling wind and twice because of transportation problems. Otherwise, to students who wondered if a trip was still on during bad weather, he would ask "Might it not be important to find out what the animals are doing at this time?"[30]

Students learned collecting techniques and observational methods such as lying still and observing an animal at ground level; studied succession and seasonal communities; collected amphibian eggs; trapped mammals; made quantitative population estimates for soil animals, insects, and plankton; observed the effects of strip mining; reviewed principles of terrestrial communities; questioned hibernation; studied bird and fish behavior; and practiced instrumentation. They also tried to keep up with Shelford. Students assigned certain pieces of equipment were responsible for specific collections or measurements. Field notes were to be turned in promptly on return, additional reports were sometimes required later, and the whole affair was summarized in class discussions.[31]

It did not take students long to realize that Shelford was a demanding but fair teacher and that he would go to bat for them. They learned too, that he was not a polished lecturer; although he frequently drew on personal experiences, some found his lectures hard to follow. Outdoors was where he really shone. A common observation of former students was how easily he interacted with all sorts of people, "a good trait," as former student Clarence Goodnight remarked, "when needing permission to study on some farmer's land." Graduate students were given considerable independence and as much help as they required. Shelford genuinely enjoyed working with students and they responded in kind with their best.

He advised eight zoology Ph.D. candidates during the 1920s. Vera Smith Davidson and Martha Shackleford, both Shelford's students, were among the early women to study ecology. In Vera Davidson's words, "Neither [Martha] nor I expected or received any special consideration. We did our own field work and provided our own equipment and transportation." Characteristically, Shelford rarely commented on how he felt about women in ecology. Davidson and Shackleford were enthusiastic about the subject and absorbed with their work, which was enough for him and for them. Five of Shelford's students from the twenties completed doctoral theses on animal ecology in the forest: Asa Weese, Irving Blake, Maynard Johnson, Vera Smith, and Ralph Bird. Alvin Cahn wrote a thesis on fish, Myron Townsend on hibernation of codling moths, and Martha Shackleford on prairie animal ecology.[32]

By the late twenties, Shelford was sponsoring a dozen masters and doctoral students, representing almost a third of the zoology graduate student population at Illinois. Of necessity he spent more time on teaching than on research. As a senior professor, pressures for university service naturally increased for him yearly, and soon the allocation of 25 percent of his total time to the Natural History Survey, in force since 1914, needed readjustment. At first he tried decreasing his survey time to 20 percent, but this did not work. He no longer had the inclination to pursue the demanding experimental work needed to tackle local and regional problems, so he made his break from the survey late in 1929. That summer he published *Laboratory and Field Ecology*. Representing ten years of work, it was the final product of his desire, first expressed to Charles Adams in 1913, to produce a treatise on experimental ecology. Most of the book covers technical experimental methods, information about equipment, and practical hints, including which techniques do not work. "It was the first manual of practice in [animal] ecology," Shelford said. One gets the impression that Shelford was driven by discipline to write this book. He finished and published on just about every project he ever started.[33]

Colleagues gave *Laboratory and Field Ecology* mixed reviews. Charles Elton and others showed appreciation for Shelford's efforts to make more precise studies of physical factors and animal responses. At biologist Raymond Pearl's Johns Hopkins laboratory the book was regarded a "monumental" work according to ecologist Curtis Newcombe. Allee said he would use the book in his ecology group seminar at Chicago. Others thought the book too technical. Reviewer William Cook admitted bafflement: "After defining ecology as the science of communities, and virtually excluding autecology from that science, Shelford proceeds to write an entire book on the environmental relations of single species."[34]

Shelford was in transition during the 1920s, bringing to a close his laboratory experimental work and once again cultivating his long-held interest in field observation and analysis of natural communities. His benthic community work at Puget Sound, his increasing interactions with Frederic Clements, and his teaching emphasis on animal-plant relationships were a prologue to the full collaboration between Shelford and Clements, to which we now turn.[35]

4

BIO-ECOLOGY

1916–1939

In 1916 the newly formed Ecological Society of America (ESA) was scheduled to hold its first annual meeting in New York between Christmas and New Year's Day. Shelford was president, and William Morton Wheeler of Harvard was vice-president. Shelford was not expected to give a dinner address. In fact, secretary and treasurer Forrest Shreve "promised to put [him] in the East River if he tried to deliver one." Shelford recognized the importance of a strong meeting to the future of ecology. To minimize overlapping papers, he set up ESA sessions in cooperation with other zoological and botanical societies attending the concurrent meeting of the American Association for the Advancement of Science (AAAS). His slate of papers numbered forty-two, including two by Frederic Clements and one each by Stephen Forbes and Shelford, who planned to speak on physiological ecology and seasonal succession of animals.

In addition to professional arrangements, Shelford made plans to meet with relatives, as he often did when business brought him near. His cousin Melvia Shelford was a pastor in Hoboken, New Jersey, and Melvia's daughter Faith was a medical student to whom Victor felt especially close because of their shared interest in science. He set his visit with the family for after the conference.[1]

One hundred twenty-five ESA members attended the conference

held in conjunction with the sixty-ninth annual meeting of the AAAS, hosted by Columbia University, Barnard College, and the American Museum of Natural History. Altogether, sixty scientific and engineering societies were represented. Attendance was variously estimated from five thousand to eight thousand people. The *New York Times* grandly called it the "greatest gathering of scientific men in history."[2]

The meetings convened amidst talk of peace and war, as stock market prices dropped precipitously. Several sessions were devoted to the role of scientists in war preparations. President Wilson had recently demanded from Germany a statement on its war objectives and the terms on which it would be willing to negotiate peace with Britain. An evasive reply came just as the AAAS meetings began. Before they had closed, Shelford read reports in the *Times* of the sinking of the American steamship *Chemung* (named for his hometown and the nearby river) by an Austrian U-boat off the Spanish coast. "The *Chemung* went down with her flag flying," boasted Captain John Duffy, who refused an order to strike his colors. Thus ended any hopes for peace.[3]

The opening paper at the ESA meeting was given by Clements and titled "The Development and Structure of Biotic Communities." Clements's abstract from the program stated:

> The biotic community is regarded as an organic unit comprising all the species of plants and animals at home in a particular habitat. While plants are regarded as exerting the dominant influence in the community, it is recognized that this role may sometimes be taken by the animals. The biotic community, or *biome,* is fundamentally controlled by the habitat, and exhibits corresponding development and structure. . . .[4]

This paper marked Clements's first use of the term *biome,* which he coined. His work and writing up to this point had related almost exclusively to plants. Shelford, in contrast, had underlined the similarity of the responses of animals and plants to the environment, urging biologists to learn how organisms actually live in nature and to use this knowledge as an organizing principle of ecology. In all fairness it must be noted that, as Shelford later pointed out, the botanist Arthur Vestal first proposed a unified biotic concept two years before Clements. The owlish looking Vestal, who was a doctoral student of Henry Cowles at Chicago, acknowledged his debt to Shelford's influence. Later he worked with Shelford at Illinois, but according to ecologist Charles

Kendeigh, "It just didn't work out." They wished to cooperate because of their common interests, but apparently as Kendeigh describes it, the "two men just tolerated each other."[5]

Much of Vestal's early work dealt with Illinois sand prairie plants and animals. Since 1913, Vestal had asserted that terrestrial animals and plants were intimately and regularly related and that together they made up a biotic association. His theory differed only subtly from the views of Shelford and Clements, but the small differences provoked a long controversy. Vestal in a 1911 letter to Charles Adams said that he did not think Shelford had "much faith in the association point of view" or would go farther than saying that animals and plants "share a common environment." In retrospect, Clements and Shelford assessed the situation best claiming that both of them and Vestal had "realized the significance of the biotic community" more fully than other workers and "more or less independently." Twenty years after the New York meeting, when Shelford and Clements were sorting out the history of the biotic community concept, Shelford wrote Clements, "Vestal goes howling about to the effect that he expressed the [biotic community] idea in 1066, 1492, 1776 or thereabouts but did not use 'biome'. Let's push ourselves in the background; we will get on better. I have tried to accomplish this."[6]

Frederic Clements was born in 1874 in Lincoln, Nebraska. His father was a photographer and Civil War veteran and his paternal grandfather, like Shelford's, a refugee from England's hungry 1840s. From Somersetshire, he fled in 1842 to the small town of Marcellus in Onondaga County, New York, located about 110 kilometers north of Chemung near Syracuse. The family later moved to Nebraska. Clements revealed his Great Plains upbringing in his education, outlook, and professional interests. By the time he was nineteen and a junior at the University of Nebraska, he had already collected hundreds of plants, named many new species of fungi, and floored his classmates and teachers by identifying plants on sight wherever he traveled. He sailed easily through undergraduate work at Nebraska, including courses and independent study in languages and literature, both classical and modern. He also played scrub football and served as an officer in the Cadet Battalion. In the field he dressed nattily, often with tie, jacket, military-style campaign hat, breeches, and leather puttees. Physically he changed very little over the years: he was average in height and weight and had a long face with a prominent chin. Clements stayed on at Nebraska for graduate work under Charles Bessey. He received his Ph.D. in botany, with an emphasis on phytogeography, in 1898 when he was twenty-four. One year later he married Edith Schwartz, a teaching assistant in German at Nebraska. In 1904 Edith completed her Ph.D. in botany, studying under her husband. She described her role in their famous field expeditions as "chauffeur, typist, photographer, mechanic, commissary-general, and second field assistant." Later when Frederic developed diabetes, she artfully nursed him, making possible their punishing yearly cross-country botanical excursions. Arthur Vestal once said, "Mrs. Clements was a very stimulating person, and yet one always felt very much relieved when no longer in her presence." There were colleagues who felt the same way about her husband. Clements was idealistic and intensely philosophical. Some—including Shelford and his family—noted his haughty and, at times, prissy manner. Yet others who knew him well were impressed with his sparkling conversation, his companionable nature, his sense of humor, his kindliness and consideration for others, and his reasonable temperament. Like Shelford, he was a prodigious worker.[7]

Eight years after receipt of his doctoral degree, Clements had become professor of plant physiology at Nebraska and had established an international reputation with his 1904 book *The Development and Structure of Vegetation,* which set forth his concept of the vegetational formation as a complex organism, and his 1905 book *Research Methods in Ecology.* During this time, the Clementses founded the Alpine Laboratory, which perched at an altitude of 2,743 meters in Engelmann Canyon on Pikes Peak, about 2.5 kilometers above Manitou, Colorado.

They had honeymooned in the canyon in 1899 and were later able to buy Spruce Ridge, the cabin where they stayed. Before they could afford Spruce Ridge, they bought a two-room shack, paying for it with cash earned from the sale of Colorado plant specimens to museums. They named the shack Pinecroft and set to work. The site was perfect for the young botanical couple: below they had a clear view of the Colorado plains and within reasonable distance lay aspen woodlands, lakes and bogs, gravel slopes, meadows, and alpine summits. Visitors could either hike up on foot or take the cog railway from Manitou. Over time the Clementses built cabins, greenhouses, and experimental gardens on their property. However visitors arrived, they fell at once into the practical routine of the high-altitude research station. In the early years until 1913, the couple pinched pennies to operate the Alpine Laboratory; from 1913 to 1916 Clements received a total of seven thousand dollars in research support from the Carnegie Institution in Washington. Substantial long-term support from the Carnegie finally came in 1917 when Clements became a full-time research associate, a position he gained after the institution published his 1916 book *Plant Succession,* which is widely regarded as his best. Guaranteed a source of income, Clements resigned his position at the University of Minnesota, where he had been since 1907.[8]

Secure support put the laboratory on a productive path for the next twenty-seven years. The Clementses added Fir Lodge, a dormitory for staff, and hired nine research assistants. New faces appeared every summer, as agricultural scientists, foresters, soil scientists, botanists, and zoologists from all over the world gathered for conversation and fieldwork. The program was so successful that by 1925 Clements had coaxed Carnegie support for a second laboratory in Santa Barbara, California, where the Clementses made their winter home.[9]

From the beginning of his Colorado work in 1896, Clements's approach to plant ecology was characteristically systematic and exhaustive. His first project was a thorough reconnaissance of the vegetation of 100,000 square miles of land near Alpine Laboratory. From 1899 to 1904, he and Edith Clements made a detailed study of a 20-square-mile portion of that tract with quadrats and instruments. Beginning in 1905, they applied detailed studies to the original, larger area. At that time Clements considered animals only one component of a habitat, along with water content, light, temperature, and soils. "The animal ecology of a particular region," he wrote, "can only be properly investigated after the habitats and plant formations have been carefully studied." Although animal distribution sometimes coincided with that of particular plants, he noted that animal mobility often blurred the overall pattern. After a decade of work on plant succession and the use of plants as an index of soil and climate, Clements began to see more clearly the important role of animals in affecting plant distribution and abundance, particularly the grazing of rodents, buffalo, and cattle.

Soon after Clements came to this realization, he presented his biome concept at the 1916 ESA meetings in New York. Obviously, the idea had yet to be tested fully. To begin, Clements made plans to set up a system of quadrats in the Western states, which would be either grazed, cut, burned, or denuded and then compared with undisturbed quadrats. In this way succession of plants and animals could be monitored against the background of soil and climate. Clements wrote:

> It has been recognized for the first time that animals are a factor of profound importance in all plant associations and a number of quadrat inclosures and exclosures have been installed to measure their effects. [10]

At Pikes Peak these included some areas fenced against rodents in the shortgrass plains at 1,829 meters, in the chaparral and pine forests at 2,134 meters, and in the montane, Douglas fir forest at 2,743 meters. By 1919, Clements had in place at Alpine Laboratory a permanent belt transect, 800 meters by 2 meters, including quadrats in six selected montane habitats from gravel slide, to pine, to Douglas fir. He and his assistants monitored temperature, light, humidity, soil water, evaporation, plant growth, plant insects, and soil fauna. Here was an unparalleled opportunity to look at yearly quantitative changes in plants and animals tied to succession. Nevertheless, Clements believed that the lower altitude shortgrass plains provided the "best illustration of essential interdependence of plants and animals in the biotic community." In fact, grasslands proved to be the one North American biome on which Clements and Shelford could fully agree. [11]

Meanwhile, Shelford pursued his studies of underwater light at Puget Sound, juggled economic entomology and book writing in Illinois, and launched serious marine benthic community work in the San Juan Islands with inspiration from Clements. He was saddened during this period by his father's death in June 1922. Alexander Shelford's battered Elgin National watch was passed on to him. As long as Victor could remember, his father had carried it. He would wind the watch carefully at breakfast and then hold it snug against young Victor's expectant ear. Throughout the day, he would cock an eye to it to check the time. Victor kept the watch with him always until it quit running, and in that time it traveled farther than Alexander Shelford had in his whole life. These were taxing years for Shelford, and he felt ready for a break from routine and bad news.

His first visit to Alpine Laboratory was set for August 1923. That summer was one of the hottest in the fifty-year records of the United States Weather Bureau: Urbana-Champaign was unbearable, and the plains literally cooked as Shelford drove westward. [12]

The visit with Clements was worth the long trip. The two colleagues hiked the slopes, visited the transects and altitudinal stations, and talked late into the night before a welcome fire in Pinecroft. Clements was eager to learn of Shelford's progress with his marine community work in Puget Sound, while Shelford was curious about recent terrestrial work by Clements and his zoological associates, Charles Vorhies and Walter Taylor, in the western badlands and the California Sierra Nevadas. Their study tested, for the first time, the application of typical plant ecology field methods to quantitative work with insects, birds, and mammals associated with particular plant formations. Clements felt the methods were appropriate for animals, although some modifications were needed because of animal mobility. Shelford discussed with him the relative importance of plants and animals in marine benthic environments, where plants are sometimes secondary. But Clements preferred to concentrate on habitats where plants play a larger role. He stressed that in the grasslands plants are important indicators of climate and soil conditions and there the "correlations and reactions between the plants and animals are most evident." In fact, considerable grassland research was under way that summer. Walter Taylor, by way of his insect, bird, and rodent studies in the grasslands and in the California desert, was gathering new biome information. Likewise, Arthur Vestal was working again on plant and grasshopper assemblages in the Rockies and on the plains—work that he had started in 1911. Before their visit was over, Shelford and Clements agreed to pursue a thorough literature survey of animal work related to the biome concept. [13]

Shelford had not yet publicly used the term *biome,* even though he embraced the spirit of the concept as early as 1911. "There is every reason," he said in his 1925 Puget Sound benthic paper, "to combine plant and animal studies and to work on the biota which is the real unit." His difficulty was that data on animals from biotic communities were rarely quantitative, and dominant animals were often difficult to single out, at least much more so than terrestrial plants. The concept of dominance was fundamental to Clements's ecological philosophy. The lack of data on animals did not seem to matter much to Clements in 1925. He was obviously impressed with Shelford, particularly with his Puget Sound work. He cited it with his own work after stating confidently, "The recognition of the unity of the biome has been a slow matter, owing to the specialized training of biologists, but it now seems assured."

And yet it was assured neither in overall scope nor in Clements's excessively detailed scheme. Shelford and Clements were motivated in attempting to "correlate the field of plant and animal ecology by the common belief that it would tend to advance the science of ecology in general." As they admitted, "It was this common interest rather than agreement in all matters which led to the initiation of [their] joint project."[14]

Thus began a period of twelve years during which they exchanged working visits. Typically Shelford went to Colorado in alternate years when he was not committed to summer work at Puget Sound. He made seven trips in all, three accompanied by his family. Clements came east to Urbana six times during late summer and early fall between 1925 and 1937, each time in conjunction with transcontinental botanizing expeditions or scientific meetings. "We enjoyed our stay at Urbana very much," Clements wrote in October 1925, "and found it enjoyable quite beyond our anticipation. I hope we shall find a way to have similar conferences much more frequently in the future, especially as we both agree that ecology should undergo consistent and logical development and not 'jest grow,' topsy-like." Following their reciprocal visits that year, Shelford wrote in an article for the *Carnegie Yearbook:*

> The initial stages of [biome] study must be limited largely to determining the predominant animals and their essential correlations with the plant [successional stages]. . . . Special investigations must be carried on to determine the action and reaction of each predominant with and upon associated plants and animals. . . . Other special studies must be conducted to show the effects of animals upon soil and the abundance and rate of growth of plants, as constituting a factor in succession and in the stability of the climax stages of the biome. . . .[15]

This article was the first in which Shelford used the term *biome.* About this time, he agreed to work with Clements in a joint project on the biome concept. Clements, in his enthusiasm, reportedly said to Arthur Vestal, "Arthur, I've converted Victor Shelford." Shelford's response when he heard of this from Vestal was, "Well if he did, I must have backslid."

The most serious trial to the partnership of Clements and Shelford was always the conflict between Clements's philosophical predilections and Shelford's practicality. At first Shelford did not let their incompatibility worry him. His main concern was to collect all the evidence he could find concerning animal-plant interrelationships. Clements's zoological associates supplied him with information: L. R. Dice and R. T. Hatt on mammals, Z. P. Metcalf on crayfish and insects, W. P. Taylor and J. V. G. Loftfield on rodent grazing, F. L. Long on bees, and G. W. Goldsmith on the spadefoot toad. Shelford also relied on his former student, Asa Weese, who labored with insects and plant ecology in the sagebrush plains of western Colorado. Weese was the first of at least fifteen of Shelford's doctoral students who would carry on community research across North America and supply their mentor with field data. [16]

In this fashion Shelford geared up for the project with Clements, setting the stage for his chief research focus over the rest of his life. His other projects in Illinois were essentially finished, and he was ready to give up experimental laboratory work. He felt there was a dire need for more biologists trained in a unified approach to plants and animals. So few workers were equipped to deal with the concept at that time. His elevation to professor in 1927 freed his time and energies for more work of his own choosing. Once again Shelford found himself anxious to prove his belief, embraced first during his Chicago days, that ecology is in large measure the study of communities. He got little argument from Clements on this point. Over half of the thirty research projects conducted under Clements's Carnegie sponsorship in 1926 and 1927 related to community ecology issues. During fiscal year 1927, Clements had a total of forty-six thousand dollars available for ecological work, a considerable amount of money in those days. [17]

Clements and Shelford wrote an article together for the *Carnegie Yearbook* for the first time in 1927. Their report explained that they employed the term *bio-ecology* "with the intention of emphasizing the essential unity of ecology and the necessity of a broader approach than the specialized training of botanists and zoologists has permitted" and that they were preparing an outline for a book. In fact, three years passed before either man actually sat down to serious writing.[18]

In the summer of 1927 a twenty-six-year-old Canadian biologist left Winnipeg for southwestern Manitoba. Ralph Bird, a native of Manitoba, had just completed a year of doctoral study at the University of Illinois and was eager to push ahead on his research. His destination was the rural town of Birtle, near the Manitoba-Saskatchewan border, about 100 kilometers north of North Dakota. The country there is aspen parkland, where forest and prairie intermingle as they do westward into Saskatchewan and Alberta. Bird's plan—approved by Shelford—was to study and describe the biotic communities of the aspen parkland of central Canada. For more than a year, he dug, swept, sifted, trapped, observed, and listened, returning to Illinois with a detailed picture of species composition, successional sequences, feeding relationships, and seasonal fluctuations of selected animal populations. Bird wasted no time in writing a thesis draft for Shelford, who wanted to get Clements's opinion on it. Clements wrote back in March 1929 with "appreciation [for] the fine work Bird has done" and with technical criticisms. For example, Bird considered aspen parkland a climax community, while Clements did not. Clements insisted, "These are questions which must be settled for the 'book'." A month later, referring to his part of the book, Clements predicted confidently, "I shall hope to write much if not all of it before midsummer." Yet by December after visiting Shelford in Illinois, he admitted, "I can hardly take up bio-ecology seriously before the latter part of next summer," but promised, "It will go forward rapidly once the actual writing begins."[19]

Clements had optimistically miscalculated. Both men had other books. Clements had exacting experimental work in Colorado, and Shelford had a dozen demanding graduate students and work still to be completed with the Illinois Natural History Survey. Although neither Shelford nor Clements progressed on the book as they had hoped, their stimulating meetings, discussions, and correspondence were an inspiration to both. Shelford finished 1929 by reading a paper at the Ecological Society of America meetings in Des Moines, the purpose of which, as he put it, was "to re-state the unity of the plant-animal community."[20]

As usual, Shelford's argument was practical and realistic. His main point was that animals were not being properly considered in community dynamics, whether in short-term phenomena like food relations and behavior or in longer-term successional events. He took plant ecologists to task for referring falsely to "our science" and for over-emphasizing the role of climate in plant climax communities while underestimating the influence of large and small animals. Once again he claimed the biome to be the "natural ecological unit," suggesting that it was "convenient to liken the biome to an amoeboid organism." His chief example of the analogy was the creeping movement of the deciduous forest edge into Illinois grasslands. Here, birds and mammals dropped seeds of wild haw, sumac, and wild plum into crevices in the prairie sod made by moles, pocket gophers, or Franklin ground squirrels. Invasion of bare ground by pioneer animals and plants also occurred in postglacial times, as tundra, coniferous forest, and finally deciduous forest appeared during climatic changes. Shelford closed by pointing out the role of both physical and biotic factors in controlling invasions and subsequent successional sequences of plants and animals, adding the caveat that in some, especially marine, communities "succession was obscure or wanting."[21]

Early the following spring, Clements dashed off a note to Shelford alerting him to a fall visit by the South African plant ecologist John Phillips. Clements hoped that Shelford would be able to stop in Colorado to meet with Phillips on his return from Puget Sound. Shelford replied that he thought he "might be able to catch him" in late August or early September. He also complained that he had only a hazy idea of their joint outline for the book. He spent time at Puget Sound that summer solidifying his own thoughts on the project. "We shall remedy all this before beginning to write," Clements promised in July. In response to criticism by colleagues of the word *bio-ecology,* Shelford suggested they use *general ecology* instead. Clements did not agree. "I have tried 'general ecology' on a number of people since your letter came and no one could guess what it meant," he argued. Clements believed the qualifier *bio* should stand—despite the obvious redundancy—to counteract the historical tendency of plant and animal ecologists to go their separate ways.[22]

On August 19, 1930, John Phillips spoke at the International Botanical Congress in Cambridge, England. In his paper, "The Biotic Community," Phillips reviewed the development of the concept, including the work of Clements and Shelford and their associates and students. He then related his own experiments and observations made in the evergreen forests of South Africa and while conducting tsetse fly research in the savanna region of eastern Africa. In both areas, humans played a prominent biological role, and Phillips accounted for them in his analysis. "My inclusion of man," Phillips said, "doubtless will call for much criticism." The response, however, was not so vehement as expected. Phillips also addressed Clements's view of the biotic community itself as a complex organism. "The concept," said Phillips, "while philosophically perhaps not wholly true, has definite practical value." Shelford agreed with Phillips that the organism is a useful analogy; although in practice he rarely referred to the organismic concept and showed little recorded interest in the sophisticated, philosophical implications of Clements's ontological ideas.[23]

As the midwestern drought worsened and the depression deepened, 1930 mercifully drew to a close. Both Shelford and Clements finally began serious writing. Shelford said he was "making a little progress," but still showed ambivalence toward their proposed title. In one way he felt *ecology* was adequate. "A considerable body of animal ecologists have always maintained that ecology is bioecology," he noted, adding, "I believe [bio-ecology] would be objectionable in Europe, which perhaps, is not very important." At the same time, he felt the use of *bio-ecology* "might have some advantage from the standpoint of sales and circulation."[24]

"Too much new knowledge proves unsettling," Clements wrote in March as he struggled to fit aquatic communities into his overall scheme. He had to answer questions such as Could the vertical structure of the ocean be directly compared with the layered structure of a deciduous forest? and Could they single out dominant species and describe the nature and limits of climaxes in water? "My hope of completing much or most of the ms. by June," Clements wrote Shelford, "promises to be illusory. . . . We must arrange a meeting in Colorado if at all possible." Shelford saw as the problem a lack, rather than an excess, of knowledge available about aquatic communities. "If the arrangement of the book is dependent upon establishing these climaxes, I don't see much hope ahead," he told Clements. By 1933 Shelford had decided that it was stretching the succession-climax idea "to the limit to apply it to the sea." Nevertheless, Shelford realized that

Clements's conscientious struggle to clarify the issues brought progress on the book, so he urged his colleague to state his views fully. "I have no difficulty with letting you write the entire book. It will be the best guide I can have to the arrangement of my parts," he said facetiously. Shelford worked steadily, consulting texts from the Illinois library, and suggested that a meeting at Alpine Laboratory that summer might wait until they had "all the facts that seem essential brought together." Clements too was weighed down with "much preliminary study" and the press of other duties. He hoped they could meet on the tundra at Hudson Bay that summer, but in the end they settled on Colorado. [25]

The weather in 1931 was unusual. The amount of ice on the Great Lakes in January and February was the least ever recorded. By summer the parched Midwest needed a foot of rain, and grasshoppers plagued the West. Returning from their third trip East in late November, the Clementses got marooned by a blizzard on the New Mexico high plains. Never one to sit idle, Clements caught up on his correspondence. The ensuing exchange between him and Shelford continued for five weeks. In these letters the two spun out a complex web of descriptive terms for the classification of natural communities. Most of the detailed classification they finally erected is forgotten today, but their work does show what can happen when ecologists try—not so gently—to fit groups of plants and animals into an elaborate hierarchical scheme. And it is an example of the age-old human desire to define wholes, parts, and patterns even where parts intergrade and sharp boundaries are uncommon, where, in fact, boundaries can be set according to the kind of questions asked. [26]

The largest natural unit used by Shelford and Clements, the biome, did seem to apply fairly well to terrestrial environments. It is best seen, they wrote, "in the great landscape types of vegetation with their accompanying animals, such as grassland or steppe, tundra, desert, coniferous forest, deciduous forest, and the like. . . . which have been noted by naturalists since the early days of biology." On a large scale—in areas of several million square miles—the differences among biomes are not overly difficult to grasp. Trouble arises when intermediate-sized areas and then smaller and smaller units of landscape are delimited and considered individually. These smaller units "present unusual difficulties," Shelford admitted in a 1932 paper, although he still believed extensive travel and fieldwork could generate a logical nomenclature based on principles of successional development and climaxes that included areas of every size. He acknowledged in closing the paper that agreement on different points could not be guaranteed, but he remained hopeful for a unified system, saying, "With the same facts in mind men rarely disagree."[27]

One might speculate that Shelford's confidence was based more on wishful thinking than on evidence. As early as 1931 he had a glimmer of the disagreements to come when Clements wrote him about including a tremendous variety of biomes in their book. Shelford answered, "It will not be possible to treat all the biomes that you mentioned." He believed they should give grasslands the most detailed treatment. Shelford became discouraged about their pace and began to suffer from indigestion, which their growing conflict would only exacerbate. He felt slightly relieved when Clements wrote that he expected to "devote mornings to the book. . . . This should permit consistent progress and yet not cause you to feel that you are under too great pressure, in view of your other tasks." By early 1932, Clements had accepted Shelford's view and confessed, "Your suggestion for limiting the detailed consideration of biomes is a wise one." Yet their difficulties were only beginning.[28]

1932 was the cruelest depression year. Estimates put anywhere from twelve to fifteen million Americans out of work; many were even thrown bodily out of their homes. Factories produced goods that hardly anyone could buy, while people without money ate from garbage cans and dumps. Certainly widespread misery helped Franklin Roosevelt win the election against Hoover that year. As a staunch Democrat, Shelford was delighted with Roosevelt's liberal policies and the nation's prospects for recovery. Urbana had been spared the most extreme miseries. Shelford did not even lose money. "When his own bank closed," his daughter said, "he owed the bank as much as they had of his."[29]

The collaboration between Shelford and Clements developed uneasily during the spring of 1933. They had finally agreed definitely that they would have to limit their detailed treatment of biomes. (The idea to describe North American biomes had been Shelford's originally.) Where they could not agree on the classification of a given biome, Shelford suggested that they "state both views and let the future decide." He thought the book would be stronger that way than it would if they compromised. Shelford also believed they needed abundance data for animals in order to set distributional limits of biomes and their smaller units. He complained that without it a "chaparral mammal wandering out onto the plains is given almost as much significance as a herd of bison." The overriding issue to Shelford, which caused the most discord between the authors, was his conviction that Clements's system would have to be revised when both animals and plants were considered together. He wrote in a long letter to Clements:

> Fully twenty-five years ago I arrived at the conclusion that there is *agreement* between the plant formations and the presence of various *animals in abundance* sufficient to produce reactions and coactions of significance. For twenty-five years I have given a course in ecological animal geography which is based very largely upon this concept but which especially emphasizes the relations of animals to the various seral stages. There is a lot more to be done than the simple finding of correlation which you have stated. Modern [quantitative] ecological studies must be used wherever available. . . . I, of course, am not interested in merely assisting in the production of your book but I am intensely interested in the point of view of bioecology and like yourself have accepted a great many details about which I am not enthusiastic. I hope you will pardon my show of apparent annoyance at what was perhaps your unconscious shifting of what I regard as important ideas into subordinate positions. I am unwilling to see the plant ecological ideas unmodified in the face of important changes necessitated by the consideration of animals.[30]

Clements reacted predictably by defending his climax system based on indicator plants, saying, "The ranges of mammals are in fair agreement with these in the case of all climaxes. . . . This is of course the basic principle on which our collaboration was begun, and it is still the only basis on which I can proceed. . . . On details I can yield frequently and gracefully, but on principles I have all the well-known qualities of the patient man." A later statement reveals the inflexibility of his position: "While it is possible to reject the entire basis on which the formations [biomes] and associations of the continent have been outlined, I do not think it possible to accept some and reject others, since all rest on the same principles."[31]

On Shelford's desire for quantitative data, Clements commented "This matter of numbers is as difficult as it is important." In another letter he wrote, "Quantitative results are still so exceptional that it is quite impossible to place animals in the various biomes on this basis." Shelford continued to believe in the possibility and necessity of obtaining quantitative data. "The community concept," he later argued, "is fundamentally quantitative and social, in other words, based upon abundance and interdependence, or upon population and interactivity." Clements could not be swayed, perhaps because statistical and mathematical approaches to ecology were not his favorite subjects. Shelford persisted, though, and managed to squeeze into their book an appendix briefly detailing quantitative collections.[32]

In May 1933 they had reached something of an impasse. Yet their letters from the time presage consensus. Each man diplomatically pressed to preserve his investment in the book. "As the one responsible for getting you into the collaboration," Clements wrote, "I can not do less than let you decide the most satisfactory way out, among the three possible solutions." These were either to treat only a few mutually acceptable climaxes, to thrash over the questions further at Alpine Laboratory or in Urbana, or to discontinue the book. "Whatever your preference," Clements closed, "I shall accept it with entire good-nature and philosophy." Shelford answered within a day or so. "To abandon the book is hardly feasible or desirable," he said, "as I get a statement from some colleague once a month or so to the effect that he hopes to see it in print soon." He suggested they go forward and made plans to stay in Urbana that summer "checking all zoological points." He admitted, though, to still having some trouble applying the biome principle: "I think we should try to develop criteria for the biome . . . sufficiently clear to enable the reader to be sure he has one when he sees it." Clements replied, "It is a pleasure indeed to have your fine letter and to realize that our accord is much closer than seemed to be the case. I am in hearty agreement with your proposal as to criteria for the biome, since no science can hope to be objective until it has developed certain basic principles to which it adheres relentlessly as long as they are sound."[33]

A concrete example of the kind of evidence Shelford and Clements were working with in the 1930s and the type of synthesis they were seeking as it is now understood may illuminate their struggles. In a broad sweep across two continents lie the vast coniferous forests of Canada, central Alaska, Siberia, and northern Europe. This is the taiga—the word is Russian for dense, marshy forest—the Great North

Woods of adventure stories. The region was only recently uncovered by the retreat of the last Pleistocene ice sheets. As a result, plant and animal distribution ranges in the taiga have continually shifted as the climate has changed over the past ten thousand years. Widespread stands of spruce, fir, larch, and pine are predominant, but hundreds of square kilometers are covered with deciduous paper birch and aspen mixed in with both white and black spruce. In yet other areas, covering thousands of square kilometers, almost the entire tree biomass is concentrated in one species, larch. Sprinkled throughout the taiga are bogs, ponds, lakes, and bare rocks. The pattern of vegetation in this northern area mirrors the pattern of its environmental gradients—both can be bewilderingly heterogeneous. Factors like snow, freeze and thaw, fire, wind, microtopography, and soil moisture help mold the vegetative mosaic. There is only a small leap from these facts to the notion that a climax vegetation here might display a variable pattern from site to site, with variety of species corresponding to the array of factors just mentioned, plus biotic influences, regional and local climate, and chance. Shelford's teacher and colleague, Henry Cowles, put it well in 1901: "As a matter of fact we have a variable approaching a variable rather than a constant." He was commenting on the course of succession from early to more mature stages and the fact that climax type is never fully predictable.[34]

By no means do all ecologists agree with the concept just hinted at, which is known as the climax pattern hypothesis. It is, however, influential and contrasts strongly with the more rigid scheme that Clements developed. Robert Whittaker, the slender, dark-haired ecologist who proposed it based on work in the southern Appalachians, completed his doctoral studies at Illinois under Charles Kendeigh. He took Shelford's climatic ecology course in 1946 and did well. Whittaker's hypothesis, to sum it up briefly, treated the climax as a partially stabilized steady state. Climax and seral stages of vegetation he thought to be only relatively different in terms of stability and directional change. Since climate was only one factor of the environment, and since it fluctuated continually, there could be no ultimate, absolute climax divorced from site characteristics (soil, topography, animals, disturbance, and local climate) for any one area or region. The upshot of his findings is that convergence of early successional stages toward a climax is only partial; climax vegetation will differ with the site. He also asserted that natural vegetation more frequently displays an array of intergrading species distributions corresponding to the pattern of environmental gradients, providing a "shimmer of populations" rather than discrete assemblages of species sharply separated from other such assemblages. This observation rendered previous classification schemes arbitrary and unrealistic.[35]

Clements's rigid vegetation system stands in contrast to Whittaker's view. Clements believed in the eventual development of a single climax plant community or formation in each region that would be determined primarily by the regional climate; consequently, any other nonclimax plant communities encountered in the same region had to be classified as stages in a successional sequence converging toward the relatively stable climax. This climax typically consisted of two or more subunits, or associations, bound together by a number of species from dominant plant genera common to all the associations. Dominance was based on the kind of vegetation, its horizontal coverage, and its height. Other smaller units were recognized within the climax, and a variety of successional communities were defined as well. All units, large and small, were considered discrete, natural entities, although Clements acknowledged that borders, or ecotones, between units showed varying degrees of intergradation.[36]

When the idea of the biome was proposed, animals entered the system. They were considered major or minor influents depending on their effect in the community. The intensity of effect depended on their size and abundance and was observed in terms of what are now considered primary niche characteristics, that is, food, space usage, and timing of activities such as reproduction. Shelford recognized early that influent animals frequently ranged very widely over both climax and seral stages of an entire biome, a fact which raised questions about their impact on succession and prompted Shelford to propose to Clements that the biome concept be revised.[37]

The classification of the coniferous forest biome was a source of contention for the coauthors; their arguments over it are illustrative of their larger problems. Both men readily accepted two associations: the spruce–balsam fir (or larch) association ranging from Atlantic Canada westward to the spine of the Rockies, and the spruce-pine association extending northwestward from the Rockies deep into the Yukon and central Alaska. Trouble arose with what was termed the pine-hemlock forest by Shelford and the lake forest by Clements. The forest in question ranged from Minnesota across the Great Lakes region into New England and southeastern Canada. Now called the pine-hemlock-hardwood forest, or northern hardwoods, it had survived the axe, fire, and insects, and lay as an ecotone between deciduous forest to the south and coniferous forest to the north. Shelford considered it to be a third association of the transcontinental coniferous forest biome, while Clements viewed it as a completely separate biome.

Shelford detailed the evidence for his opinion in a 1935 paper co-authored with the (later) noted naturalist Sigurd Olson, following their long canoe trip through the Superior-Quetico wilderness. Dominant subclimax trees ranging through the three associations and providing unity to the biome were black spruce, paper birch, aspen, and both jack and lodgepole pine. Shelford and Olson wrote:

> A characteristic feature of the northern coniferous forest in the present age is that the areas of pure climax are relatively limited in size while the subclimax areas make up the greater part throughout its entire range. This fact tends to impart to the coniferous forest a decidedly subclimax characteristic in which the seral stages become unifying elements along with the climax stages themselves.

Concerning the putative exclusive claim to climax status of white spruce, balsam fir, and red and white pine, they continued:

> Climax as used here is relative and it is still a moot question as to whether or not jack pine, black spruce, even aspen and birch may not in limited areas be climax as well as subclimax. They often are mixed with trees of the generally accepted climax.

Shelford and Olson here addressed the relativity and irregularity of the climax concept and the variable patterning it displays, even as they remained adherents to Clements's system and its ambiguities.[38]

Shelford and Olson also cited thirty common subdominant trees, nineteen shrubs, and eighteen herbs for subclimax areas throughout the coniferous forest biome as they saw it. Their inventory of animal distribution revealed that wide-ranging major influent species in both climax and seral stages included moose, lynx, and wolverine. Minor influent species for the same areas were weasel, grouse, hawk, nuthatch, junco, and warbler. Influent species primarily restricted to the climaxes included marten, red squirrel, and several bark beetles. They concluded in general that the available data "indicate the agreement of the limits of the climax and of animal influents."

Shelford and Olson had made their case for the transcontinental coniferous forest biome. They were careful to include animal indicators along with the plant data to "maintain the integrity of some of the important natural units in a bio-ecological system of classification." Because they still believed the role of animals was not properly appreciated, they specified two steps necessary to gaining a realistic understanding of animal-plant dynamics. First, distribution maps had to be made based on adequate quantitative estimates of animal abundance. Second, wide-ranging influent animals from all successional stages needed to be studied further by observation and field exclosure-enclosure experiments to determine their specific impact on succession and community composition.[39]

Clements remembered 1933 as the last time he predicted publicly that *Bio-Ecology* would be "issued by the end of the year." The country was besieged by droughts and freakish weather throughout the decade, and related research and management activities kept Clements too busy to fret much about the delay. Occasionally he would diplomatically urge Shelford for progress. As often as he could, Clements made fall visits to Illinois, but he quickly realized that they were years away from completion. Edith Clements was privately convinced that Shelford was dragging his feet. She despaired of their getting "some action on his part." She hated Urbana, thinking it had the "most abominable climate in the country." In order to endure the regular visits she engrossed herself in activities with friends and in wildflower painting. Even so she complained constantly of the gloomy fall days in Urbana. "Very difficult to get proper lighting for my painting," she wrote in her diary, "tho Dr. Shelford rigged up a huge daylight electric bulb for me." Typically the Clementses stayed with zoology chair Henry B. Ward and his wife, Harriet, while in Urbana, occupying their "usual room" and eating out.[40]

In fairness it must be remembered that Shelford was busy, too. He wrote ten papers during the 1935–36 academic year, and he sometimes almost gave up hope of "ever having any free time from editing theses."

When he did work on the book, he was reminded of the obstacles. "Animal ecology is probably 20 years behind plant ecology," he told Clements, "and with the added difficulty of working up [animal] principles for fresh water and sea as well as land, I hope you see my difficulties. Considerable of my time and attention has been taken by projects to buy land, raise game, secure grassland, etc. somewhat as yours has been by erosion."[41]

Early in June 1935 Clements and his wife set out eastward from Santa Barbara in the car they called Billy Buick. Clements was now consultant to several federal agencies, including the newly formed Soil Conservation Service, which was working on ways to ameliorate the effects of drought. Clements's plan was to spend a month in the prairie region from the Panhandle to the Canadian line in order to check on the status of projects designed to decrease evaporation of soil water and soil erosion. Clements was also becoming concerned about overgrazing; he felt there had to be a rational way of discovering the carrying capacity of grasslands. Striking northward from Texas to Kansas and Nebraska, where little rain had fallen in the past two years, the Clementses were dismayed at what they saw. Previously lush prairie had given way to weed patches and bare soil. Heretofore dominant little and big bluestem grasses were replaced by wheat grass, sometimes even in ungrazed areas. This experience and others like it in the early thirties brought home to Clements the dramatic effect that human occupation coupled with prolonged drought had on the structure of the prairie. The human species was a legitimate member of the biome, the only member who, said Clements in 1936, could "destroy the stability of the climax during the long period of control by its climate." In point of fact, Clements had accepted the human species as "an intrinsic member of the biome" as early as 1931, and he had seen and commented on overgrazing evidence back in the twenties. What struck Clements so clearly on this trip, though—and this was a new admission for him—was that if humans could upset the biome, they could also help to set it right. So convinced, he applied his usual energy and diligence to the scientific management of the Great Plains in the spirit of the New Deal.[42]

The conservationist was a different Clements from the intensely speculative botanical philosopher, the maker of verbal schemes of nature. In his new role, he became a man comfortable with peddling practical suggestions for better land use. He now fully supported federal planning and coordination of resource conservation and management. "The time is most opportune for the greater service of ecology in public affairs," he said. He was delighted that he and colleagues had been consulted and asked to serve even though he never liked committees and societies. "In my own case," Clements reported to Shelford, "the opportunities to advise, to shape policies, to draw plans and supervise installations have been as constant as they are gratifying in terms of ecological service and recognition."[43]

Shelford was also involved in ecological service, but he served in a different fashion. There was no fundamental disagreement between them concerning the human role in bio-ecology. They called the human species an "outstanding dominant of a new order" in their book. With the help of steel and machines, they believed, humans had actually become "superdominant." Nevertheless, they deemed it was premature to include human ecology in any detail in the book. Where they differed on the ecological service question was in regard to the federal government. Shelford, Clements once said, had a " 'phobia' for the federal bureaus." Instead of working for the government, Shelford threw in his lot with committees of the Ecological Society of America and the National Research Council.[44]

Clements and Shelford were recalled to their theories and their book by a frontal attack on Clements's ideas by the founder of British plant ecology, Arthur Tansley, of Oxford, a long-time friend and supporter of Clements. The occasion was a 1935 issue of *Ecology* dedicated to Shelford's mentor, Henry Cowles, now sick and four years from death. Tansley praised Cowles, apologized for some "blunt and provocative" comments he would presently make, and then proceeded to criticize Clements and Phillips and, indirectly, Shelford. Tansley could not accept progressive Clementsian succession to a single climax or the idea of biotic communities and the organismic concept. He thought nothing more than a complete listing of human impact on nature could properly fall under the purview of ecology. It was a stinging, unexpected rebuke from a colleague just two years away from retirement.[45]

Tansley had been working on his monumental *The British Islands and Their Vegetation,* which required him to come to terms with a unified view of vegetation, a goal that had remained elusive for more than three decades. His attention had been drawn to a recently published series of review articles by John Phillips expounding on the Clementsian creed. According to Tansley, Clements was presented "as the major prophet and Phillips as the chief apostle." Despite Phillips's reasonable recounting of opposing views, Tansley noted "a remarkable lack of any sustained criticism of opponents' arguments. Only here and there . . . does the author present scientific *arguments*. . . . It invites attack at almost every point." Seemingly for him the invitation was irresistable.[46]

Tansley's long-settled, much disturbed British landscape differed sharply from North America in the time of Clements and Shelford. Tansley considered heath, fen, and moor to be legitimate "highest" units of vegetation, not merely preliminary, seral stages to the oak forest climax that Clements's scheme predicted for the fairly homogeneous British climate. He judged it wisest to study and describe the existing vegetation with all of its relationships. "I plead for empirical method and terminology in all work on vegetation and avoidance of generalized interpretations based on a theory of what *must* happen because 'vegetation is an organism,' " wrote Tansley.[47]

Tansley rejected the concept of the biotic community. "Animals and plants are not common members of anything except the organic world," he opined.

> This refusal is however far from meaning that I do not realize that various 'biomes', the whole webs of life adjusted to particular complexes of environmental factors, are real 'wholes'. . . . Only I do not think they are properly described as 'organisms'. . . . I prefer to regard them, together with the whole of the effective physical factors involved, simply as 'systems'. . . . It is the systems so formed which, from the point of view of the ecologist, are the basic units of nature on the face of the earth. . . . These *ecosystems* as we may call them, are of the most various kinds and sizes.

Tansley invoked a model whose components were the physical environment, the animals and plants, and a "constant interchange of the most various kinds" between them. The task of science, he believed, was to isolate a system—of whatever size—"mentally for purposes of study. . . . The isolation is partly artificial, but is the only possible way in which we can proceed." Focus on systems would further "investigation of *all* components of ecosystems and of the ways in which they interact to bring about approximation to dynamic equilibrium. That is the prime task of the ecology of the future."[48]

Such is the nature of human endeavor that turning points are often recognized only after the fact, and that they delight historians more than participants. Shelford and Clements's book—still four years from publication—would be a high water mark for a thoroughly descriptive, classificatory treatment of ecology; Tansley's festschrift aritcle was one prologue to the functional and mathematical studies of natural systems that would one day be commonly accepted.

Shelford left no recorded response to Tansley. Clements's rebuttal stated, "I do think that the differences are fewer and less serious than your style indicates, since some are more a matter of word preference than of actuality." Despite the truth in this, Tansley's disagreement was substantial.

Clements and Shelford pressed forward, however, finishing several chapters and putting the bibliography in order by 1936. Shelford worked in time for the book around his six courses and other duties. During the spring he was too preoccupied with planning a 9,650-kilometer, six-week field trip to give it much attention. When he returned to Illinois that summer, he went right back to work and made plans for Clements's fall visit. Early in 1937 they had all ten chapters in reasonable form. Shelford braved the beastly cold and visited the University of Chicago Press in early February. In mid-March he sent a manuscript for their perusal; the book was approved in late April with the suggestion by a reviewer, whom Shelford suspected was Allee, that the first chapter covering the historical development of the biotic community concept be rewritten.[49]

"The book is not a novel," Shelford replied, "hence the persons who do not want to know the history can skip the first chapter." Clements was uncommonly compliant on seeing the letter from Chicago Press with the referee's comments. "I shall do whatever you wish," he wrote Shelford. "However, I would prefer to omit [the chapter] than to take the time to rewrite it." Shelford was incredulous at the further contents of the letter. Clements had agreed, for the first time in twenty years, to participate in two symposia, both at the June AAAS and ESA meetings in Denver. This was puzzling behavior from Clements.[50]

Returning in early September 1937 from a summer of benthic community work at Put-in-Bay on Lake Erie and a two-week trip to Mexico City, Shelford prepared for Clements's visit to Urbana later that month. This time John Phillips, who was taking a two-month tour with the

Clementses, would come, too. Edith Clements described one theme of their time spent with Phillips in her diary:

> Dr. P. has been indulging during our conversational moments, in giving Frederic fatherly advice as to becoming more humanly interested in other human beings, especially since the value of his research work depends so largely on its being put into practice by said human beings. His reputation has been that of aloofness and disdain for this aspect. . . . Gathered in his talks with other men and detailed to us, was that Frederic is very unapproachable and 'superior'—won't mingle with other lesser scientists at their meetings, refuses to descend from his high eminence or even to stop and call on men as we pass through their towns. And a lot more of the same. F. admitted he is and always has been 'intellectually arrogant' (and why not?) P. says openly and on all occasions [Clements] is the 'greatest living ecologist.'

Perhaps Phillips's influence inspired the sudden change in Clements evidenced in the letter.[51]

Phillips agreed to read the whole manuscript for *Bio-Ecology,* beginning with the first two chapters while he was in Urbana. Warming up for his substantive review with a congratulatory toast to Shelford, who was now sixty, Phillips sharply criticized their treatment of "philosophical matters involving plants." He objected to the assertion that life histories, life forms, growth, and development of individual plants can be compared with corresponding characteristics of the community. To him the meaning was unclear. Shelford concurred, admitting that he could not readily "comprehend the ideas to be conveyed" and that zoologists, particularly, would have trouble with it. Late in October Shelford worked seriously on revisions and sent both chapters back to Clements, still en route from his eastern trip.[52]

Back came a letter from Clements in November. He was willing, at this point, to cut parts of the book that had been central to his ecological work for many years, including a discussion of the complex organism concept for the biome:

> You make out an excellent case for discarding chapter two altogether. If you do not understand me, it is unlikely anybody else will. Almost no one has any interest in the philosophical aspects of the matter. . . . [Also], no one but myself seems to value the historical background, and

the risk of unfavorable criticism is as unnecessary as it is great. I am entirely willing to omit this chapter likewise.

Whether it was the despoliation of the grasslands, his new active participation in conservation, Tansley's unexpected attack, Phillips's advice, Shelford's patient loyalty, some combination thereof, or unknown factors, Clements was humbled. The tenacity with which he had always defended his doctrine had mellowed perceptibly.[53]

And yet, Shelford did not act on Clements's offer to retract. Instead he chatted about details in his next two letters in early December 1937, remarking, "The subsequent chapter will give less trouble. . . . The end of the text is in sight." He never mentioned the proposed cuts. Shelford still thought the philosophical sections pertaining to plants in the second chapter were difficult to read, but except for a minor change in chapter sequence, the book remained intact. Neither man discussed the philosophical or historical aspects of the book further.[54]

For five days in late August and early September 1938, a number of ecologists met in Cold Spring Harbor on Long Island to consider the nature and classification of plant and animal communities. The worthy authors of *Bio-Ecology* did not attend. Allee, who was there, described the meeting:

> In many ways the conference was dominated by those who were not present. The ideas of Clements, Shelford, Braun-Blanquet, Juday, Elton and Lorenz and others gave form to the discussion. . . . The participants averaged much younger than if the great pioneers had been present and perhaps were more objective and free on that account. . . . Few of the speakers became over-involved in terminology, a morass in which the conference might have become hopelessly bogged. . . . Bio-communities received lip service only.

The participants included T. Lippma, A. E. Emerson, G. MacGinitie, T. Park, H. Gleason, and J. R. Carpenter. Carpenter, a former student of Shelford's, presented a useful summary of the biome concept. Charles Elton, in a later review of the volume of proceedings from the conference, took issue with creeping scholasticism in ecology, saying, "Far too much effort has been put into the organization of terms and concepts, and far too little into the accessible arranging of our existing body of ecological records." His argument, in short, was that naming is not necessarily the same as understanding. Elton did, however, find "much good stuff in all these papers." Shelford would not have expected this conference or his book to have a miraculous influence on the study of ecology. A heavy field schedule and a lurking viral infection taxed him heavily that year, and before the winter was out, Shelford had to be hospitalized for several weeks.[55]

As reviews of *Bio-Ecology* trickled in, Clements and Shelford traded letters and copies. Most reviewers acknowledged this valiant attempt by the leading American ecologists to unify plant and animal ecology, but opinions differed as to how successful they had been. Limnologist G. Evelyn Hutchinson felt the book's greatest defect was neglect of the biogeochemical and metabolic aspects of the community. Elton deplored the terminology and the "implication of certitude and finality that the terms convey," even though he hastened to applaud the "very rich learning and acquaintance with plants and animals under natural conditions, which the text displays." Certainly the book reached its audience. Over five thousand copies were sold before *Bio-Ecology* went out of print in 1958.[56]

As was his habit with most things, whether good or bad, Shelford quickly put the book behind him. He spent time on the Hudson Bay tundra in 1939 and planned a research trip to the Panamanian moist forest in 1940. Much of Shelford's character and reputation was formed by his connection with the outdoors and his passion for seeing the land and studying it well. His affinity for the natural world motivated the work on which the next chapters focus.

PART THREE

Wilderness, Wheels, and Wrangles

5

ITINERANT ECOLOGIST

1929–1946

Shelford always thought the best part of being an ecologist was working out in the field. "I travelled," he said, "in all of the states of the U.S., all provinces of Canada, and three-fourths of the states of Mexico."[1] Bruising but exhilarating travels with the master of the ecological field trip are still recalled by many Illinois graduates. According to Eugene Odum, "Nobody before or since has organized such extensive and well run trips—excursions might be the better term. Ecology students at Illinois in the 1930s and 40s were expected to visit all major biomes of North America and to facilitate that, [Shelford] organized trips during weekends, holidays, and during the summer which were run on a clockwork basis."[2]

"I believe," speculated Jane Dirks-Edmunds, "he fervently wished that he could experience first-hand every kind of natural habitat in North America," a feat he almost accomplished.[3] Shelford's expeditions influenced his students tremendously. "I still have my note books and reports of those trips which I enjoy looking over," noted ninety-year-old Lena Feighner, who took all of Shelford's long cross-country trips when she was a student and who went on to a career as a biology and general science teacher. Long after she studied with Shelford, she still reaped benefits from their association. On a 1965 trip to Moscow University she was delighted to find how cordially she was treated by the faculty when they learned of her student days with Shelford.[4]

To see Shelford through the eyes of his students is the fairest way to judge him as a teacher, and his long field trips were perhaps his most effective teaching method. The students who made those trips with him during the 1930s and 1940s learned to know him well. Many of them were able to contribute to this biography through letters and interviews. Shelford "understood students and they had great loyalty to him," said Ralph Wetzel and Drew Sparkman Wetzel. "He stimulated students to come up fully to their capabilities," added Daniel Rasmussen. Jane Dirks-Edmunds wrote, "He also challenged us to add to the developing, unfolding science of ecology." Arthur C. Twomey commented, "He was a taskmaster, but he was fair."[5] "He certainly knew where he was going." observed Curtis Newcombe.[6]

Reports on Shelford's temperament can be contradictory. Some former students claim never to have seen him get angry. "But when he was," chuckled Drew Sparkman Wetzel, "I remember some people saying that he was like an erupting Vesuvius." Beatrice Flori described him as an "even-tempered individual." In her fine memoir, Jane Dirks-Edmunds wrote, "He was quiet, observant and perceptive, punctual and disciplined. . . . He had a dry sense of humor and liked to kid with some of the more loquacious students."[7] "But," recalled C. Lynn Hayward, "students soon learned not to take pictures of him while he was asleep on the bus!"[8]

Shelford's personal qualities, as much as his scientific achievements, earned him his popularity with students. "I was always very fond of Shelford as a person," noted Edward Baylor, "and I think he had an unusually broad tolerance of me and my teasing him. . . . I learned a lot from him about putting up with smartassed graduate students."[9] According to Charles Kendeigh, "He was an outstanding teacher, although not a polished lecturer he was full of ideas, enthusiasm, and energy." Clarence Goodnight considered him a "terrific field person," and Stan Auerbach thought him a "remarkable man, in many ways, far in advance of his time."[10]

Even Shelford's storytelling powers were renowned. "During a span of over thirty years," recalled Curtis Newcombe, "Shelford did not change much, remaining vigorous in every way, entertaining dinner guests while reminiscing on past events and mutual acquaintances.

Victor Ernest Shelford at age five in 1882, Elmira, New York. Photo courtesy of V. E. Shelford personal papers.

A northward view of the Eli and Alexander Shelford farm in Chemung, New York, around 1895. Photo courtesy of Dorothy Parmelee.

Sarah Ellen and Alexander Hamilton Shelford, circa 1895. Photo courtesy of Dorothy Parmelee.

Victor at seventeen in 1895, while a student at Cortland Normal and Training School in Cortland, New York. Photo courtesy of V. E. Shelford personal papers.

Old University Hall at West Virginia University, where Victor took his first zoology course in 1899. Photo courtesy of V. E. Shelford personal papers.

Victor Shelford and Mabel Brown at South Haven, Michigan, in 1904.
Photo courtesy of V. E. Shelford personal papers.

Shelford (second from left) with other graduate students at the University of
Chicago in 1906. Photo courtesy of V. E. Shelford personal papers.

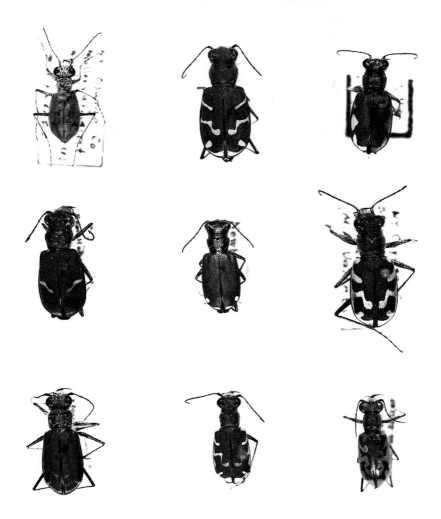

Tiger beetles (Cicindelidae): upper row, left to right, *Cicindela lepida, C. hirticollis, C. lecontei;* middle row, *C. purpurea limbalis, C. sexguttata, C. generosa;* bottom row, *C. tranquebarcia, C. repanda, C. cuprescens.* Photo courtesy of Ronald Bergeron, University of New Hampshire.

Victor Shelford at age forty in 1917, assistant professor at the University of Illinois. Photo courtesy of V. E. Shelford personal papers.

The Victor E. Shelford Vivarium at the University of Illinois. Photo courtesy of Lois Shelford Bennett.

Puget Sound Biological Station at Friday Harbor, Washington, in 1920. Tents, which served as living quarters, and dining hall are ranged along the bank; the laboratory sits at the water's edge. Photo courtesy of Vera Smith Davidson.

Shelford's animal ecology class at Puget Sound Biological Station in the summer of 1930. Photo courtesy of Vera Smith Davidson.

Shelford dressed for the field at Reelfoot Lake, Tennessee, in 1937. Photo courtesy of Eugene Odum.

Victor, Mabel, and Lois
Shelford in 1940. Photo
courtesy of Dorothy Parmelee.

A typical camp scene from Shelford's transcontinental summer field trip.
This picture, taken in the late 1930s, shows the circle of tents, the bus,
and the commissary truck. Photo courtesy of Eugene Odum.

Shelford at Indiana Dunes on Lake Michigan in 1940. Photo courtesy of Beatrice Flori.

The Easter field trip to Reelfoot Lake, Tennessee, in 1937. Shelford (wearing the hat) is with Jane Dirks and Eugene Odum. Photo courtesy of Eugene Odum.

Three ecologists at Reelfoot Lake in 1950: (left to right) Charles Kendeigh, Hurst Shoemaker, and Victor Shelford. Photo courtesy of Hurst Shoemaker.

Leaders of The Nature Conservancy at Storrs, Connecticut, in 1956: (left to right) Richard Pough, retiring president; Richard Goodwin, president-elect; and Victor Shelford, member of the first board of governors. Photo courtesy of University of Connecticut and The Nature Conservancy.

The Shelford home at 506 West Iowa in Urbana, Illinois. Photo courtesy of Lois Shelford Bennett.

Shelford instructing a class on an ecology field trip to Indiana Dunes on Lake Michigan in the mid-1920s. Photo courtesy of Vera Smith Davidson.

Victor Shelford at sixty-three in 1940, professor at the University of Illinois. Photo courtesy of V. E. Shelford personal papers.

Victor Shelford at eighty-six
in 1963, professor emeritus of
the University of Illinois.
Photo courtesy of Dorothy
Parmelee.

Frederic E. Clements in the early 1930s. Photo courtesy of Hunt Institute for Botanical Documentation, Carnegie Mellon University, Pittsburgh, Pennsylvania.

Always with a highly humorous touch, amplified at times by at least a scent of wine, his stories would unfold with characteristic ease and community spirit."[11]

Spurred on in the early thirties by his deepening association with Clements and his long-planned treatise on the natural communities of North America, Shelford became intent on gathering biome data, requiring him to take longer trips. It seemed only wise to involve the students in this enterprise. Their labor and insight were invaluable to Shelford and the trips were an excellent apprenticeship for budding ecologists, especially graduate students. The students knew that Shelford would credit their work in his books and papers, so they were very receptive to his recommendations for thesis subjects concerning biomes.

Shelford had established a long Easter field trip of three to seven days a few years earlier in the spring of 1927. The destinations were deciduous forests, caves, streams, cypress swamps, and the Mississippi River bluffs in southern Illinois. His group traveled with Parkhill Tours on special buses provided by the Illini Coach Company, Urbana. In 1929 Shelford extended this spring trip by 80 kilometers, traveling south to Reelfoot Lake in northwestern Tennessee. He made this traditional trip throughout his active years at Illinois, even after his retirement. "I went there so *many* times," Shelford said, "every year for many years. I learned a great deal about it. I was going there during the intrusion of civilization."[12] The lake was born in the cataclysm of a violent earthquake during the winter of 1811–12. "Some land was uplifted," Shelford noted, "but the oxbow ponds, cypress sloughs, and flood plain forest . . . sank 25 ft. at the south end of the present lake and 5–10 ft. near the center, and well toward the north end, thus creating the present lake."[13]

The area was dynamic, as flood plains usually are, and served as an exceptional natural laboratory for Shelford and his students. It fostered successional sequences of vegetation from cottonwood-willow to beech-maple, old Mississippi River channels, and diverse assemblages of animals. Arthur Twomey and Jane Dirks-Edmunds were two students who accompanied Shelford to Reelfoot Lake. As Twomey described it, "There were tremendous numbers of birds and mammals, and lots of reptiles including poisonous snakes like water moccasins and copperheads." Dirks-Edmunds remembers making "quantitative collections and observations at 19 different sites distributed over an area of approximately 50 square miles." The amount of work accomplished by Shelford and his students on a typical trip to Reelfoot Lake was enormous. A written report on the week's research was, according to Twomey, "practically a thesis." Part of the work at Reelfoot was devoted to birds. Alvin Cahn led the bird studies from 1929 to 1934, Arthur Twomey in 1935, Charles Kendeigh from 1936 to 1943 and again in 1946, and Hurst Shoemaker in 1944 and 1945. It wasn't all work, however. After supper the ecologists swapped stories and sang songs around the campfire.[14] Socializing with the local people also became an important and sometimes memorable feature of these trips, as Twomey proves with his favorite story:

> Shelford used to love to talk with the local fellows, and get them going. I remember one day when the locals were telling stories to students— about 300 pound snapping turtles etc. I sat down with a bag of snakes I'd just collected, and listened in. One local was telling of a large snake he'd seen. I opened a bag of non-poisonous snakes and snakes were all over the porch in no time. One big blue racer went up into a rafter and fell on top of the two locals. Both men took off, practically took the door off too, and kept going. Shelford was in hysterics.[15]

Shelford made trips to the north, as well. The Canadian tundra was one of his favorite places; he and Arthur Twomey did research there regularly for years. Shelford made his first visit in 1930 with his family, driving as far north as a car could travel to The Pas, Manitoba. At that time, Hudson Bay Railway construction extended 800 kilometers farther north to Churchill. The next year when the railroad was completed and the northern tundra finally accessible, he was anxious to get started on the "study of populations, interactions, and community development" in this fascinating region. Mabel was not pleased with Victor's suggestion that she and Lois stay in a small, lakeside cabin at The Pas while he and John traveled on to Churchill. Eventually it was decided that Victor and John would go to the tundra while Mabel and Lois stayed home in Illinois.

Arthur Twomey—at that time an undergraduate student at the University of Alberta—was collecting birds near Churchill for both the Canadian and British national museums. He had been going up to the tundra since 1928. The area, he claimed, boasted "one of the finest nesting areas for birds in the eastern Arctic." Trains arrived in Churchill about every two weeks in 1931, and Twomey noticed several new faces that summer. One of them belonged to an interesting man he frequently saw tramping about wielding an insect net. As Twomey discovered, "It turned out to be Dr. Shelford, who I hadn't met before."

Shelford began his studies of tundra animal communities that summer. He was especially in pursuit of the collared lemming (*Dicrostonyx groenlandicus*), the common herbivorous, rat-sized rodent of the tundra that changes from black to white in the fall. Victor and John searched fruitlessly; not a single lemming turned up after diligent trapping and digging. They did not know that lemming populations in the Churchill area that summer were at rock bottom. They needed advice, which they sought from Arthur Twomey:

> One night there was a knock on my lab door. It was Shelford. He admitted not being successful with collecting the lemming so far. I told him that, "yes, you can get them here." So we went out together next day. Soon I saw evidence of lemming feeding; I kicked a mound and turned up a female and eight young. Shelford was delighted. The mother and young were pickled, and are probably still in the vivarium at Illinois. After that we took a long walk and looked at Arctic birds. [16]

Shelford managed to get National Research Council support for work on the lemmings and associated tundra animal communities, and he quickly involved Twomey in his studies during 1932 and 1933. Shelford was impressed with the young man and inquired whether he planned to do graduate work. Twomey responded that he had hoped for an assistantship with the ornithologist Joseph Grinnell at Stanford but that funding had not yet been secured. Shelford seized the opportunity to offer Twomey a place at Illinois. In this way Shelford got a new doctoral student and held on to an experienced research assistant, as well. [17]

Eventually Shelford and Twomey were able to sketch a reasonable picture of tundra animal communities. They also gathered extensive data on lemming abundance as it varied with the weather. Using reports from trappers and naturalists, Twomey's data, and his own, Shelford estimated that lemming population peaks in the summers of 1929, 1933, 1936, 1940, and 1943 were followed by population minima in subsequent springs. The intervening winters were often characterized by little snow and low to subnormal temperatures. Shelford suggested that lemmings were easier prey for predatory birds during these snowless winters. Lower temperatures also dictate higher food requirements for predatory birds. Other data showed that predatory snowy owls were indeed abundant in these years and that they migrated south to the Churchill area precisely when lemming populations declined.

On the more general tundra animal community work, Shelford again got help from his son and Twomey, as well as from other eager Illinois graduate students. At the time of Victor's early tundra work, John Shelford was an engineering student at Illinois. A newspaper photo from the summer of 1932 shows John and his father in field clothes and Smokey Bear hats, posed by a railway automobile they used in their work at Little Barren, 58 kilometers south of Churchill at mile 474 on the Hudson Bay Railway. They studied the dull gray-green tundra dotted with ponds, gravel and sand ridges, rocks, bare clay, hummocks harboring mice and lemming burrows, and dwarf black spruce muskeg. Very soon the Shelfords grasped the essential features of this unique landscape; early and late successional stages were thoroughly mixed, often existing very close together. The climax stage featured low-growing reindeer lichens and heath plants in an organic, peaty surface mat resting on a frozen base. The vegetation types in all successional stages differed little in the potential shelter they offered animals. After several summers' work Shelford asserted that many insects, birds, and mammals occurred throughout the sequence of plant successional stages, although their relative abundance differed in each.[18]

Much of the work was carried out on the 9-kilometer-long peninsula between the Hudson Bay and the Churchill River. But additional habitats had to be checked. Typical of Shelford's special research trips to outlying areas was a 1932 expedition: Striking out from their quarters, painted orange and black by the local construction company, Victor and John met I. H. "Windy" Smith, the Big River trapper who was to be their guide, at his tent by Cape Merry. The three men then traveled 72 kilometers north in a freight canoe with an outboard motor along the remote western shore of the Hudson Bay to Seal River, where they conducted comparative studies. Seventeen Illinois graduate students helped Shelford make a final inventory of the Churchill area before he concluded his tundra research in the late 1930s.

So Shelford kept himself and his students busy during the years of depression, drought, dust storms, and grasshopper swarms. Four new Ph.D.'s were hooded between 1930 and 1932: Charles Kendeigh completed a thesis on temperature in the life of birds; Samuel Eddy, on freshwater plankton communities; Willard Gersbacher, on stream bottom communities; and Daniel Rasmussen, on biotic communities of the Kaibab Plateau, Arizona. Between overseeing his students and pursuing tundra ecology, Shelford felt he was too busy to accept the visiting professorship offered him by Japan's Tohoku University for the academic year 1933–34. As it turned out, he was glad he declined to go for another reason: Henry B. Ward retired from the university in June of 1933, and Shelford was curious to see how the department would fare under Ward's replacement. Charles Zeleny was "an enigma," in Shelford's opinion, and he did not have much opportunity to prove himself. Zeleny became very ill and had to resign after only two years. To Shelford's dismay, he then found himself selected, along with Harley Van Cleave and Waldo Shumway, to serve on the executive committee that would run the department from 1935 to 1938. The new responsibility did not slow Shelford down, but it did increase his efficiency, as did the continuing demands of his work with Clements and his sponsorship of the Animal Ecology Club. [19]

The Animal Ecology Club began simply as an informal seminar in the fall of 1917 at the request of Shelford's doctoral students, A. O. Weese, M. E. Jewell, and E. B. Powers. In 1925 the seminar became a formal club, with elected student officers. Its stated purpose was to provide a forum for the review of literature and the discussion of ecological research. Jane Dirks-Edmunds described the 5 P.M. Wednesday ritual in 203 Vivarium in detail:

> For these sessions, tea and cookies were a regular feature. . . . Promptly on the hour, Dr. Shelford and Dr. Kendeigh entered the seminar room with journals and other current literature to be reviewed that week and took their unvarying places—Dr. Shelford at the "near" end of the long seminar table with Dr. Kendeigh on his immediate left. We students seated ourselves around the long table—with the speaker for the day usually at the "far" end of the table. Following the literature review, the student speaker made his presentation. We graduate students . . . were required to turn in on 3 × 5 cards weekly reports of literature reviewed.

Occasionally Shelford or Kendeigh gave a presentation, or an outside speaker was featured. The club had a marvelous way of riveting student attention, especially for those students who had study cubicles along the periphery of the meeting room. Shelford had the habit of spreading out the papers to be read on the seminar table several days prior to the meetings to encourage student preparation.[20]

A perceptive professor involves students in meaningful work, provides them with the flavor of research, and practices what he or she preaches. Although Shelford could be preoccupied with his own interests and perplexities, he remained mindful of these ideals and tried his best to foster them. On balance he was successful. Students in Shelford's classes were routinely exposed to community analyses, quantitative population sampling, and bird and mammal tracking; and many graduate students contributed to long-term, quantitative studies of invertebrate and vertebrate animals on university-owned lands, which provided a valuable perspective for the population and community work performed by Shelford and his students elsewhere across North America.[21]

In 1917 the University of Illinois acquired the tract of forest called University Woods. Soon after, as noted by Kendeigh, Shelford and his students "began to measure invertebrate populations in order to see how they varied with the time of day and season, from year to year, between strata [ground, herbs, shrubs, and trees], and in successional communities." They pursued studies on mammals and birds also. In the summer of 1933 Shelford began a formal, long-term research program designed to measure seasonal and annual fluctuations of animal populations against a background of physical environmental factors and the vegetation in University Woods, which was renamed Trelease Woods in 1940. Shelford planned this as a "Century-Cycle" project, a one-hundred-year panorama of natural events. The project ran under Shelford's direction through 1946, when he retired from the university, and was continued until 1971 by Charles Kendeigh. Its thirty-eight-year lifespan yielded one of the longest continuous sets of terrestrial data of this kind.

Trelease Woods, 60 acres in size, located 6.4 kilometers northeast of Urbana, was earlier part of a large prairie grove that at one time covered 26 square kilometers along the west branch of the Salt Fork River. Before Europeans settled there, the grove was surrounded by tallgrass prairie, which is now mostly farmland. The woods had been completely protected for fifteen years when Shelford's project began and, equally important, were thereafter exposed to a minimum of human interference. Shelford and his students and colleagues identified thirty-seven species of trees in Trelease Woods. The dominant species included sugar maple, hackberry, white ash, and slippery elm. Of the five-hundred essentially resident species of invertebrate animals they identified from the woods, about fifty received Shelford's close attention. Among these were various species of spiders, harvestmen, sowbugs, millipedes, centipeded, insects (crickets, true bugs, leafhoppers, true flies, butterflies, moths, beetles, and ants), snails, and slugs. In his inimitable way, Shelford pushed the plant-animal community viewpoint both in his teaching and in his research.[22]

Eugene Odum, champion of the modern-day ecosystem concept, who completed his doctoral work under Charles Kendeigh at Illinois in the late 1930s, admits his debt to Shelford's teaching:

> Shelford essentially converted me from an animal (avian) ecologist to a holistic ecologist; his biotic community and biome concept, although but vaguely conceived in those days, has become today's ecosystem ecology. . . . We graduate students soon learned that to get the most out of a Shelford field trip one must keep within a few feet as he marched rather rapidly across the prairie or through the woods. All kinds of pearls of wisdom would drop out including appropriate sarcastic remarks about reductionist biologists, or that "Woods Hole establishment," which he viewed as anti-ecology. I think the reason he was not too well accepted by many of the more conventional biologists was that his holistic ideas were ahead of [the] time, but methods to deal with ecosystem level processes had not yet been developed. In other words, his concepts were great but field methods of the day were inadequate.

Nevertheless, Shelford's writings in the 1920s and 1930s yield an impressive list of study topics, suggested approaches, and practical methods for improving ecological work in both aquatic and terrestrial environments, all of which remain relevant today. He emphasized the need for long-term, quantitative studies; combined field and laboratory work; analysis of species interactions; identification of ecological indicators; and natural history approaches based on simple behavioral observations, life histories, and food web linkages. These several contributions testify to Shelford's leadership in the field of ecology. One might expect that Shelford would wish to slow down his pace once he reached his fifties, but he was not ready to do so by any means. He had ambitious plans for a series of field trips across the continent.[23]

An attractive, four-page, black-and-white brochure announced the first formally advertised transcontinental trip of Zoology S111, Animal Ecology, for the summer of 1936. The itinerary included the southwestern states, the Colorado Rockies, and the prairies of Iowa and Nebraska. A maximum of twenty-eight students could be accommodated, and they would make a dozen study stops, camping at twenty separate locations during the seven-week trip. The stated prerequisite was a bachelor's degree with one year of zoology courses, although outstanding senior students could also be admitted. Students could earn two units of graduate credit—one-fourth the total required for the M.S. degree at Illinois. The brochure read:

> Lodging will be provided in waterproof, insect-proof tents with sewn-in canvas floors, and electric lights. Each student is furnished a cot, mattress, two cotton and one woolen blankets. . . . Students are assigned to groups of four in tents as desired and remain together throughout the trip.
>
> A regular breakfast of fruit, hot or cold cereal, sweet rolls and butter, coffee, and eggs, ham or bacon will be provided. Lunch is carried as fruit, sandwiches, etc. with milk, iced tea or lemonade—served in the field. Dinner of meat, potatoes, two vegetables, a salad, dessert and [beverage] will be served.[24]

Shelford's first mobile summer school commenced, with bus, commissary wagon, and field gear, to study forest, grassland, desert, alpine meadow, tundra, and flood plain. Fieldwork was regularly augmented by lectures and discussions. Halfway through the trip, on July 14, they reached San Francisco Mountain near Flagstaff, Arizona, the famous peak first studied in 1889 by the intrepid naturalist, C. Hart Merriam. Merriam discovered that particular plants and animals occurred at specific altitudes, or zones, from the warmer mountain base to its colder summit. On the basis of this and later work, he presented his idea of life zones. He hypothesized that the same genera of animals would range east to west across North America, within a given temperature zone, and that the zones would change from south to north, simulating the original low- to high-altitude zones on San Francisco Mountain and correlating with cumulative temperature differences greater than 6 degrees Celsius.

Shelford could not accept this theory, nor could the ecologists John Weaver, Frederic Clements, Lee Dice, and Charles Kendeigh. Many ornithologists and mammologists were, however, quite enthusiastic. As Shelford explained and demonstrated to his students that summer on hikes up San Francisco Mountain, there was agreement between the plant and animal communities defined by modern ecologists and Merriam's life zones in the western mountains, but for large portions of North America there was little harmony. Shelford asserted that Merriam's life zones were too static and that they overemphasized the controlling rate of temperature, which could not simply be summed. He also complained that Merriam presented his ideas as a closed set of rules in too authoritative a manner.[25]

Characteristically, Shelford chafed at authoritarian rules and regulations, yet readily made his own. He ran his field trips with considerable discipline. Jake Weber, who drove a bus for Shelford on transcontinental trips from 1936 to 1946, remarked, "Some drivers thought Shelford was difficult to work for, but Dr. Shelford wanted things done properly, and he told the bus company that if they sent an undesirable driver, . . . he'd send the driver back." Weber's accounts of those summers reveal much about Victor Shelford.

> He was a quiet man. Said only what he had to. If he said be up at 6 A.M., he meant 6 A.M. In the morning he'd beat on the tent top with a heavy switch to get the students up—it was very effective. . . . Most everyone went to church on Sunday: Protestants to an available church, Catholics to theirs. Now and then Dr. Shelford would go with me to town—for mail delivery, or his half ale, half beer draught at a local tavern. Otherwise he'd often have a beer just after arrival back from the field. He really tested the students' physical stamina. He was in fine physical shape.[26]

Eugene Odum remembers that Shelford "carried two whistles; one gave off a soft warble that signalled time to get ready to move back to the bus or to the next study site; the second whistle was very loud and was the final call to everyone to collect at a designated place." The whistles topped off Shelford's field outfit, which, as Jane Dirks-Edmunds recalled, was always "basically the same—dark wool trousers, puttees above his field shoes, short dark coat, and felt hat." Shelford also wore a tie, like many naturalists of his generation.[27]

Students looked forward to informal discussions, storytelling, and singing around the campfire after supper. Invariably, ecological lessons crept in. One frequent discussion dealt with ecotones, the transitional habitats between biomes or biome elements. Edges of prairies, forests, and wetlands and forest clearings caused by fire, storms, erosion, or disease are all ecotones. Human communities, Shelford stressed, have always sought out or prepared ecotones for habitation. The cumulative effect of this behavior is destruction of a region's dominant trees and a decline in animals dependent on the original, primeval forests, such as the wild cat, gray fox, and wolf. Humans also introduced various domestic animals and plants, which carried their own pests and parasites. Shelford pointed out to his students that the animals that survived this ecological transition such as the raccoon, chipmunk, and red fox are forest-edge animals, as are humans. By means of such gentle guidance he got his students to ponder their own roles in the natural world. They learned to look at the landscape differently and see that ecology could not be isolated from human concerns and behavior, but rather that plants, humans, and other animals together are proper subjects for ecological study.[28]

Truly this concept was what Shelford considered fundamental, but the word had taken on a very different meaning to other colleagues. Shelford expressed his displeasure over modern fundamentals to his dean in 1939:

> There seems to be a strong tendency to measure all biological projects in terms of biochemistry and [to call] those features that admit of the application of physical formulae, as fundamental in character. . . . I have felt the pressure of comparison of my work with fundamental problems over a long period, during which the fundamentals have shifted more than my own projects. I find a certain satisfaction in having maintained my independence from current fads. I do not object to being told that no one on the staff is "big enough" to be head of the Department of Zoology [Shelford was acting head at this time], but this and many other things led me to the conclusion that here in Illinois we are suffering from a strong tendency to measure all values by the popular fundamentals, which tends to crowd men into a narrow field and to give

advantage to those who trim their sails to the current trends, even though they hardly sail at all.[29]

Being out of the popular current did not affect Shelford's productivity. He launched five more new Ph.D.'s between 1937 and 1938: Arthur Twomey wrote on bird populations; Harry Andrews, on animals of California kelp forests; Ralph Dexter, on Massachusetts tidal communities; Harland Roney, on the physiological ecology of *Helisoma;* and Sarah Jones, on forest invertebrates. Shelford had advised twenty-one doctoral students since Ward Allee first came to study with him at Chicago in 1911. In 1937 he logged some boat time during July and August on Lake Erie, where he was studying bottom communities, and lectured at Ohio State's Franz Theodore Stone Laboratory at Put-in-Bay. Shelford devoted some time to saltwater ecology, as well, when he visited the Chesapeake Biological Laboratory in Maryland, where his daughter, Lois, was studying paleontology in 1938. While there he fit in time for a few side field trips with Curtis Newcombe.[30]

Besides the numerous research and teaching field trips, Victor and his family made several summer visits back to Chemung during the 1930s. The drive was long, but Victor enjoyed it, and anyway, his youngest brother, Wiley, took over once they reached the farm. Wiley's daughter, Dorothy, often watched her uncle and his family pull in with their usual set of milk cans on the car's rear travel rack. The cans held wash and rinse water for clothes, and the motion of the car provided the agitation needed for washing. "I just thought Uncle Vic was a fascinating man," Dorothy says. "I probably spent more time with him than anyone else in the family when he came to Chemung; I especially liked to go along with him and my father when they visited friends and relatives." Dorothy lived in the old Eli Shelford house then with her parents and four brothers. She and Gene were the youngest children, even younger than Victor's cousin Faith Wohnus's three daughters, Faith, Hope, and Love, who spent summers in the old house that belonged to their grandfather, Tom Shelford. These kids all played together—there were nine years between the youngest and the oldest. Inevitably when one got sick, the rest did too. One summer they had an outbreak of scarlet fever.

Victor always saw to it that he visited around in Chemung. Phoebe Price, a cousin related to his paternal aunts; cousins Durward and Pearl

Shelford; his maternal aunt Ada Tillman and her daughter Hilda all lived nearby. John and Lois Shelford did not always go along on these family visits after they reached Chemung—they were in their late teens and twenties at the time—but Mabel frequently did. Dorothy remembers how Victor patiently waited for Mabel to get ready. "It seems like he was always waiting for her—but he didn't complain." Most likely he did not dare because Lois remembers her mother waiting for him just as often at home.

Victor did complain about the farm sometimes. He admitted genuine improvements, such as the new kitchen, woodshed, and workshop and the home electricity plant that was added in 1925; but other things bothered him. He criticized Wiley mildly about growing junk piles and neglected repairs. Exhibiting admirable tact, Wiley's responses were usually noncommittal. Paul Shelford, Jr., Melvia Shelford's grandson, wrote of the brother who stayed on the farm:

> Wiley was a very shrewd man; he didn't have any formal education beyond elementary school, but he evidently had a natural business sense and built the farm out far further than that which was left to him. Whenever I saw him, his face would take on a quiet smile. He was rock hard with muscle, pushed himself and family very hard. . . . Wiley was proud of Victor for his education and his accomplishments, and he respected him for it; but at the same time I'm sure that he was never so impressed that he treated him other than as the brother he grew up with.

Still, Victor and Wiley lived in two different worlds, and to some family members it was surprising that they got along as well as they did, especially to those members who spoke of "Uncle Vic and his bugs." None of the differences really mattered to the brothers; they genuinely enjoyed seeing each other and reminiscing about their boyhood. Wiley and his sons, Harry and Donald, had about 300 acres under cultivation during the thirties. They raised corn, potatoes, oats, and buckwheat; milked twenty cows; and tended maple sugar bush, too. For Victor it was a relaxing and welcome change of pace to come back to the farm.[31]

Once Shelford became fully involved in the administration of the zoology department, he did not mind the work, and he held things together rather well. His added responsibilities did reinforce his need to get away periodically, and his sights were set on southern climes. He needed biome data from the Southwest, Mexico, and Central America. Soon after he assumed the position acting chair of zoology in September 1939, students found him busily planning a summer 1940 trip to study biotic communities in Panama and Honduras. His base of operations was to be Barro Colorado Island Biological Station in the Canal Zone. The island was formed when the Chagres River was dammed in 1914 as part of canal construction. The exposed top of a high peak, the island stuck up in the middle of Gatun Lake covered with moist tropical forest, orchids, figs, monkeys, alligators, army ants, deer, coatis, tarantulas, and toucans. To get there, Victor, Mabel, and Lois faced an early July drive to New Orleans, a long sea voyage on a Standard Fruit vessel to Colón in the Canal Zone after a stop in Cuba, and finally a 30-kilometer railroad trip to Gatun Lake where a launch took them over to the island.

The biological station, with its library, mess, and living quarters, lay in a clearing on the steep shoreline. The writer John Minter describes the scene:

> From their airy cottages around the main building, the wives and children of the scientists assemble to study the butterfly collection, the jars of pickled snakes, the stuffed animals, and the file of microscope slides, or perhaps merely to chat on the veranda while they enjoy frequent concerts by the monkeys in the branches overhead. At mealtime the researchers come in from their vest-pocket jungle, and the Barro Colorado family sits down around a single long dining table.[32]

Shelford settled in to camp life and was soon exploring the spidery web of trails through black palm, mahogany, cedar, coco, breadfruit, and almendro trees festooned with lianas, orchids, and bromeliads. As usual, he had detailed work planned both on the island and in forest preserves on the adjacent mainland. Before the summer was over, he had observed, sampled, dissected, identified, and drawn plants and animals, from the sunny forest canopy down to the densely shaded forest floor. Barro Colorado was a curious place: one could emerge from a lush forest trail to see huge oceangoing vessels flying the flags of many nations, steaming for the locks in either direction. Back among the trees, one might catch howler monkeys playing or drinking nectar from blossom cups. The flavor of the place was different from anything Shelford had ever experienced.

Much too quickly the Shelfords' time was up. Early in August they started back, this time stopping in Puerto Cabezas, Nicaragua, where Mabel stretched her sea legs and bought some trinkets. On board the boat conversation centered around the German blitzkrieg and the fall of France—the war was becoming serious. The Shelfords left the boat at La Ceiba, Honduras, where Victor had planned to rent a car and drive over the mountains to Tegucigalpa to see its savanna and pine-oak forests. An acquaintance dissuaded him, warning that the malaria was bad. So instead they flew in a small plane via San Pedro Sula, arriving in Tegucigalpa none too soon for Mabel and Lois. Their spirits improved after touring around the city. In fact, it was in a public square in Tegucigalpa that Victor last saw his wife happy and healthy.

Lois recounts the story of her mother's decline:

> We [flew] on to San Salvador and stayed at the Hotel Astoria. My mother did not feel well and stayed in the hotel while my father and I visited an Agricultural Experiment Station. One of the men showed us what they were doing and then took us up a volcano to show us the different types of vegetation. My mother was feeling worse when we got back and said she did not want to be left alone. Dr. Hirleman, Swiss-trained, came the next day. He called in a heart specialist. . . . It was probably the next day that she had the chill. Dr. Hirleman came immediately and gave her something for malaria, [and soon after] told us the lab report.

Mabel lapsed into a coma and died of malaria nine hours later on Saturday, August 17. She was sixty-four. The rest of the trip was a blur for Victor and Lois, who would struggle with the conflicting emotions aroused by Mabel's funeral and Lois's wedding to Edmond H. Bennett in Chicago within the next six weeks. And so, shocked by loss but forced by circumstance to keep moving, Shelford said farewell to his partner.[33]

Victor and Lois had to make arrangements to get the body home quickly. First, Dr. Hirleman did some preliminary preservation, then "a sealed metal box within the casket was needed," Lois explained, because embalming was not the custom in El Salvador, and burial within twenty-four hours was required. Next, they had to cut through a thicket of red tape to ship the body, in its cherry casket ornamented with a black cross, via train to Puerto Barrios, Guatemala, then by sea to New Orleans, and finally by train to Champaign. That accomplished, Victor rented a car with driver, and on August 21 he and Lois motored the twisting 250 kilometers to Guatemala City. From there they flew to Veracruz stopping along the way at Tapachula and Mexico City. In Veracruz they picked up their own car, which had been shipped there from New Orleans at the beginning of the summer. The final leg of their journey was the brutal drive back home to Illinois by way of Mexico City (again), Texas, Louisiana, and the Mississippi Valley. They reached Urbana around Labor Day.

Not surprisingly, Shelford took more than a year to recover from Mabel's death: he was restless and lonely and found this new adjustment in his life very difficult. Reluctantly, he agreed to take the chair of zoology again that fall. (Finally it was offered to him as an official appointment.) The faculty numbered fourteen, and there were sixty graduate students. Shelford carried six regular courses that year, plus research supervision, a seminar, and the Reelfoot Lake trip. Mercifully Charles Kendeigh helped him out with a number of these offerings. Shelford's teaching assistant that year expended an extra measure of patience with him, too. The tragedy of the war distracted him from his grief somewhat, and he felt able to empathize with the British that fall and winter, as they staunchly withstood the all-out German air assault. His personal sorrow is marked by a contemporary photo in his album: a scene in his garden shows Mabel's favorite spot and is labeled "empty chair." He missed her dreadfully—more than anyone or anything he had ever missed.[34]

No sooner had the rains returned to the drought-ravaged farmlands in early 1942, than Americans found themselves in a far more grim fight for their survival. For World War II the country was more unified than it had been in 1917 and 1918. Even so, by mid-1942 there was not much for the Allies to cheer about as Germany and Japan pushed ahead. Beginning then, however, and continuing for the next year, the tide changed, and thanks to naval airpower at Midway, the marines at Guadalcanal, the Russian army at Stalingrad, and anti-submarine warfare in the Atlantic, the Allies were at last able to see the road home.

For years the University of Illinois had had one of the largest Army ROTC units in the country; in 1942 some four thousand students were enrolled. Including personnel involved in a myriad of training programs, more than thirty thousand uniformed men and women were stationed on University of Illinois campuses from 1942 to 1946. The Urbana-Champaign USO hummed with activity, providing old-fashioned, down-on-the-farm picnics with fried chicken and homemade pies, moonlight hayrides, and watermelon feasts. At the same time, the civilian student enrollment dropped steadily. In 1944 the university graduated its smallest class since 1903, and graduate enrollment, too, eventually dropped to a new low. Education-as-usual, was replaced by an academic fast track: the typical two-semester plan supplemented by a relatively short summer session gave way to three terms of sixteen weeks each. Freshmen could enter in any term and complete the bachelor's degree in three calendar years less one term. Zoologists and physiologists at Illinois had their own solution to a dwindling student population and departing faculty; in March 1943 they combined to form a joint department of zoology and physiology. By the end of the war, the department had twenty-seven faculty, but only thirty-six graduate students—the same number present almost twenty years before.[35]

After returning from Panama in 1940, Shelford knew he had to get back to Mexico for more biome data. He immediately engaged a tutor to help him improve his Spanish. When his work as zoology chair grew tiresome in the spring of 1941, he chucked the paperwork for a while and began planning a return trip to Mexico for that summer and a Zoology S111 trip south for the next. "Even though war had broken out," wrote Henri Siebert, Shelford's graduate assistant, "Shelford had already made plans for the [1942] trip and in typical fashion, nothing, not even a war, was going to stop him. Although gasoline was severely rationed, new tires unavailable and travel not recommended, we nevertheless set off for Mexico from Champaign via Florida in a small [1939 Ford] station wagon with extra retreads strapped to the roof." The usual bus and camp truck were not available. Shelford estimated student expenses for the six-week trip at about $195, including cabin, hotel, and restaurant accommodations. He also figured on the use of government buildings at isolated reservations. They went as far south as the base of the tropical mountains 250 kilometers from Tampico. "The wagon was cramped," Siebert remarked, "it was hot, but Shelford held

us together rather well and I don't recall any serious temper tantrums."
Nevertheless, during that year or two after Mabel's death, Siebert
found the professor "a complex of personalities—one moment as charm-
ing as a veteran foreign diplomat, the next, as fierce and stern as a
marine drill sergeant." Sometimes fledgling scientists need the strict
approach, and no one ever accused Shelford of passivity.[36]

In the academic year 1941–42, Shelford saw his last few doctoral
students finish up their thesis work: Reed Fautin researched biotic
communities of the desert shrub biome in Utah; Jane Dirks-Edmunds,
biotic community comparisons between western, Douglas fir–hemlock
and midwestern, oak-hickory stands; C. Lynn Hayward, Utah mountain biotic communities; and Tilden Roberts, the physiological ecology
of crayfish. Shelford had sponsored an even two dozen Ph.D.'s in his
twenty-eight years at Illinois.

Victor was sixty-five, but little gray showed. He had not yet lost his
energy or his ability to out-tramp students. He did lose his patience
when a much-touted operation failed to help his sinus trouble—in fact
it sharply aggravated the condition. In vain, Lois urged him to get
regular medical checkups. "No," he would answer emphatically, "the
Doctor would just tell me I was fine and send me a big bill." He still
preferred to work alone, and his chief relaxation was simply ecological
research. Now and then he would go with a colleague or older student
to Bidwell's at Wright and Green Streets near the vivarium for beer and
peanuts. He liked tequila, too. ("The three undrinkable things," he
often said, "are tea, tomato juice, and kerosene.") At home he left
vegetables and flowers needing a lot of tending to Lois; instead he
delighted in asparagus, winter onions, bulbs, and peonies. He reserved
one corner of his house lot for forest-edge plants like redbud, and
pawpaw. Out front he had a big Buick parked in the driveway; some
claim he had a bus motor put in it. Victor liked powerful cars and drove
fast, but safely. Yet his real delight in those years was something much
smaller: Betty Bennett, his first Urbana grandchild, was born in 1943.
A snapshot from the time shows him—appearing not a day over fifty-
five—gazing down on the child with an adoring Grandpa look.[37]

Inevitably, when former students reminisce about those years, they
mention Shelford's generosity and loyalty to them (as well as theirs to
him), his ability to forgive and forget, his decisiveness, his rugged
individualism and integrity, his idealism and keen perception of how

much better the environment could be treated, his tireless work habits, his dignified reserve, and his reasonable way of challenging students. The women students, in particular, comment on his fair and balanced treatment of their sex. They could "have babies and do science too," he said. A few admitted they wished they had "met him forty years before." Over time little had changed in his lecture style. He was still low-key, unpolished, and fortunate that he did not have to face a formal, written teaching evaluation. He had come a long way from Chemung and Oak Hill School, but the countrified aura stuck— despite the Phi Beta Kappa key he modestly kept concealed. "Shelford was not a good lecturer at all," recalled Stan Auerbach, who worked on centipedes for his M.S. degree with Shelford, "but his hesitancy, his not so occasional groping for words and phrases, did not bother me because what came through was an impression of tough dedication as well as an individual trying to distill out of a wide range of scientific experience, key thoughts and ideas. . . ." Shelford may never have crafted the model lecture, but former students attest that he shared attitudes longer lasting than the little-remembered utterances of more articulate professors.[38] He was not stingy with grades, at least at the end of his career. For close to one hundred students—mostly graduate, with a sprinkling of upper-level undergraduates—in seven courses from 1942 to 1946, his average assigned grade was a lofty 3.6 out of 4.0, or slightly less than A−. Fifty-seven percent of his students received an A grade.

His approach to ecology in his seventh decade was still strongly empirical; still centered on quantitative and structural descriptions of communities and observations (literally with nose to the ground) of animal activities; still based on the necessary elements of species distributions and good systematics; and still faithful to understanding what his early role model, the naturalist Alfred Brehm, called "animal life as it's lived in nature." "Evolution as a factor in understanding ecological phenomena was of little interest to Shelford," said Stan Auerbach. "More than once he declaimed to me that our challenge was to understand the workings of an ecological community as it was currently functioning—not as an attribute of the past." The evolutionary synthesis proceeding at that time had as little effect on him as it had on Clements; it passed them both by.[39]

For concentrated field work, coverage of biome types, study, and travel, the years from 1942 to 1945 unquestionably stood out. Shelford was south, southeast, east, southwest, and west getting his university-sponsored, cross-country trips in before his retirement in 1946. During most of the war years and on into 1947, Shelford worked with Drew Sparkman, whom he judged to be the "best assistant I ever had." "She took a master's degree, but she didn't care for a doctor's degree" he commented. Proper at all times, Shelford felt he could not take research trips "alone with a young woman of course," so he enlisted two female high school teachers who had been on trips with him earlier, Verna Johnston and Marie Tucker of Berwyn and Alton, Illinois, respectively. "I knew," Shelford said to Sparkman, reportedly with a sly grin, "if I took *two* women on the trip, they might vote me down on decisions, but I knew *three* women would never agree on anything."

He misjudged on at least one point with that statement: all three agreed on working like beavers for five weeks during the summer of 1943. They homed in on the animals and plants of the deciduous forest biome, traveling through Tennessee, Arkansas, and northern parts of the Gulf states; then over to the Duke Forest in North Carolina; next to Georgia; and back home in August by way of Virginia, West Virginia, and Kentucky. Shelford was getting good coverage of biomes for his last book now, and he intended to keep at it as long as the Ford wagon and his gas ration stamps held out.[40]

As if by instinct, Victor visited Chemung in September, stopping to see Wiley and his family after collecting forest insects in New York and Pennsylvania. That December, two years to the day since America entered the war, Wiley was killed instantly by a speeding train while he stubbornly tried to start his stalled truck on a local crossing. The old farm passed to Wiley's sons, Harry and Donald. Victor heard only by telegram that his brother had died and did not learn the details until later. He left late in December for a winter field trip with his son-in-law to Texas, Oklahoma, and Mexico.

The following year he set out one last time for the South and Southwest. (By this time he had made a number of friends south of the border from whom he heard for years; he had even joined the Natural History Society of Mexico.) It was June 1944, and Shelford began this final trip with the same wagon, the same party, and the same heightened expectations he had had the previous summer. They were bound first for Arkansas and Oklahoma. From there the Ford wagon held steady toward California, then swung south, then southeast into torrid southern Texas and northern Mexico. The field routine was the same this year, too: Shelford and his assistants made insect sweeps in herbs, grasses, and shrubs; cruised for birds and mammals; identified and collected plants; collected ground invertebrates; and took copious notes on biome after biome for the developing treatise on North America. Mixed prairie in Texas; piñon-juniper woodland in Colorado; cold desert in the Great Basin of Utah and Nevada; sclerophyll vegetation, sporting thick, shiny, cutinized leaves, in California where grizzly bears once reigned; desert grassland and oak-juniper woods in Arizona; grasslands in Arizona and Mexico; and hot desert in California, Texas and Mexico—Shelford covered as many biotic communities as he possibly could. Characteristically, though, he allowed the trip to be sidetracked for a visit to Drew Sparkman's relatives in western Oklahoma. She never forgot Shelford's gesture, "He simply went a little out of his way so I could see family."[41]

Hot, tired, and looking forward to getting back, they finally pulled into United States customs at Laredo, Texas, on Sunday, July 30. There they ran into old friends, who unwittingly brought them trouble. Edward Baylor tells the story:

> My wife (the former Martha Barnes, a fellow graduate student at Illinois) and I had been to Mexico to wind up some estate business for which I was on emergency leave from the Army Air Force and in uniform at the time. We were just clearing the American Customs at Laredo, when Shelford [and his crew] drove into Customs in an adjoining lane for their turn at being searched for contraband. Since we had all been students together we were delighted and surprised at the coincidence of seeing each other so far from Urbana-Champaign. Without thinking anyone would take me seriously I walked over to Shelford and said, "Hello, you old spy! What are you smuggling in your station wagon?" At this point because our car was blocking a traffic lane through the Customs House, the Customs men requested us to move along. We drove blithely away chatting of our pleasant surprise in encountering our friends. Sometime later to my chagrin, we learned that because of my teasing remarks, Shelford's field notes had been impounded as undecipherable code and sent to Washington for cryptanalysis. I understood that it took a year of correspondence to secure the release of the field notes.[42]

According to today's academic expectations, Shelford's treatment by the University of Illinois was not generous. He had received no sabbatical leave during his first thirty years on the faculty, but by 1944 he must have felt he deserved a semester off. He submitted a short, late request for leave that January. His dean forwarded the request to President Willard, enclosing a letter in support from zoology-physiology chair Carl Hartman and his own recommendation:

> Although the procedure of late application is irregular I hope you will give consideration to it. I learned a few years ago when I visited many Zoologists in the east that Dr. Shelford is regarded as probably the outstanding ecologist in the country.

Willard approved Shelford's sabbatical for the fall semester of 1944 the next day.[43]

First on Shelford's agenda that autumn was to sort out twelve years worth of collections and notes and edit manuscripts on his continuing studies of animal populations in Trelease Woods. From December through early February, he made several study visits to museums in Ann Arbor, Washington, Philadelphia, and New York, as he needed to compare against museum specimens at least a thousand animal species he and his students had collected in their study trips across North America in order to establish identities and distribution ranges. In mid-November while he labored in the vivarium on pinned and alcohol specimens of invertebrates, he got word from Chemung that the old Eli Shelford house had burned to the ground. A bucket of tar that Wiley's sons had been melting on the stove boiled over and started the fire. Very little of the house or its contents were saved. Victor decided then to visit his nephews and, no doubt, make his peace with the loss as soon as he could. The following May, he received a $200-raise bringing his salary to $6,300. The chair of his department commented to the dean in recommending the raise that it would be "a slight token to a faithful and inspiring teacher who is the peer of ecologists of America." Shelford was pleased with the money, but he got the distinct feeling that his superiors were patting him on the head before leading him out to pasture. He did not like it.[44]

In fact, Illinois state law stipulated that he had to retire no later than September 1 of the year following his sixty-eighth birthday, meaning for him September 1, 1946. That being so, Shelford had one last run of his transcontinental summer school excursion to look forward to in 1945. As he planned the trip, neither Shelford, nor anyone else, grasped fully how close they were to the brink of the modern age. Japan was struggling, but no one could know how and when the war would end. Some biology students had finished their military service and returned to college. Stan Auerbach was among them. He met Shelford for the first time in the vivarium that January and soon learned that the professor was one of the more eminent and powerful faculty members in the zoology department, although he was not quite accepted as "one of the boys." Shelford never talked much about his own research, Auerbach and his classmates noticed, except to mention that he was preparing a major treatise on natural communities of North America.

Propped up on my desk as I write this, is an aging snapshot of Auerbach's showing Shelford and a half dozen of his introductory ecology students in Brownfield Woods on a cool Saturday morning in the spring of 1945. Several students up front—Bob Chew, Don Kelly, and Jean Finger—are taking notes. Shelford stands to the right with his hands in the pockets of his twill riding breeches, in turn tucked into leather puttees. He sports a fedora, tie, vest, and short coat. And he has that peculiar half smile, almost challenging students to observe and understand the unfolding woodland around them. According to his field schedules, Shelford's classes typically repeated this trip four times between early March and mid-May each year to witness the scheme of changes in animal and plant populations related to season and weather.

Shelford appreciated physical dexterity on his field trips, as Stan Auerbach recalls:

> Don Kelly, who was my lab and field partner while I was at Illinois, swore that I earned my "A" in field ecology on our first Saturday field trip to Brownfield Woods by swinging hand over hand from a steel cable which spanned a short deep ravine within the woods near the entrance. Shelford was impressed, but then I was a somewhat atypical student for him, coming as I did from the urban milieu and a culture that did not send students into the field of ecology.[45]

That summer Shelford ran the animal ecology course for the last time as planned. The six students with him were Stan Auerbach, Bob Chew, Lena Feighner, Blanche Graff, Jean Lamon, and Helen Monroe. This time their path proceeded snakelike into Missouri, Kansas, and Colorado; across the Great Basin and up into the Pacific Northwest; then back through Idaho, Montana, Wyoming, and Nebraska. They covered almost 12,000 kilometers over six weeks, with a steady diet of prairies, cool desert, and forests, not to mention frequent restaurant meals and tourist cabins. Shelford drove the entire trip. "Not the slightest hint was ever given that somebody should relieve him at driving," Auerbach noted. "Damned night owl" is what Shelford grumblingly called Auerbach, the Army veteran, when he slipped off to the bars at night in Jackson Hole, Wyoming. Shelford took his watering at breakfast—a standard fare of beer and peanuts for the peerless leader, who otherwise ran a tight trip. But not so tight as to deny the group a chance to visit a gambling house in Reno or the sight of their zoology professor washing dishes in their quarters at a ranger experiment station in Utah. By early July they had reached coastal Oregon, which seemed to them kaleidoscopic: they explored coastal dunes and beaches, the mighty Pacific, and primeval forest. At night they feasted on broiled salmon steaks. Shelford made time for a visit with Jane Dirks-Edmunds and her husband.[46]

Most of their trip was behind them when they reached Olympic and Mount Ranier national parks. From there they turned eastward into the Columbia Basin, where Vera Smith Davidson, who took her Ph.D. with Shelford in 1927, picks up the story:

> Shelford called me . . . saying he would like to see us. I invited them out for Sunday morning breakfast. They ate a hearty farm meal, Fred [Davidson] and V.E.S. visited, the men picked cherries and lounged on the lawn, the girls and I did deviled eggs, sandwiches, etc. and about 11 A.M. Dr. Shelford said, "time to go."

A few days later, one of the group picked up a newspaper with the headlines: "Atomic Bomb Exploded in New Mexico," "Like a Thousand Suns, Say Army Observers," and "No Trace of Supporting Tower Found." The news upset and angered Shelford. "Shelford really didn't have much use for the military," noted Auerbach. "One of his wartime problems was preventing Reelfoot Lake from being used as a practice bombing range—the idea for which according to him, came from a general, but which was blocked." Shelford even suggested that a national grasslands park—complete with bison—be established somewhere on the vast army reservation lands of the western states.[47]

Next Shelford and his field class made a short visit to Yellowstone National Park, where Shelford met a bear. The students held their breath while he chased it off with his insect net. From there homeward the trip was mostly anticlimactic. Excitement came a week after their arrival back in Illinois. On August 7 an atom bomb was dropped on Hiroshima, and on August 10 a second bomb hit Nagasaki. By August 15, Japan had accepted Allied terms for peace.

Shelford, ever impatient with war, did not wait around for more news; he was off to Chemung to see family. As it turned out, this would be his last visit to the old farm. His nephews, Donald and Harry, had thrown up a temporary, prefabricated house near the old house foundation that spring to provide shelter while they prepared to move to their new farm at Dundee, New York, on Seneca Lake. The land was more productive there, and Harry had grown weary of making the trip up the Shelford road to where most of their arable land lay. The house burning only sealed their decision to leave.[48]

In the fall of 1945, his last year at Illinois, Shelford prepared for the thirty-second time for the opening of the academic year. His 200 Vivarium office may have seemed smaller and stuffier, and he was certainly a bit bored with the details of the academic routine, but he plowed ahead through the same basic five courses he had taught since 1924. On Memorial Day 1946, he led his last course-connected field trip outside of Urbana. On the itinerary were grassland studies at Loxa Prairie, 80 kilometers to the south near Mattoon, fish breeding observation at the Charleston Country Club Pond and the Patterson Springs Pond near Tuscola. Shelford and Kendeigh accompanied twenty-five students from their introductory ecology, economic zoology, and advanced field ecology courses on that trip.

Shelford continued to enjoy his contacts with students, whether over coffee in the vivarium (he kept a stone pot going with about a pound of coffee and an equal amount of water, yielding a potent brew), the occasional open house or all-soybean dinner at his home, or beer and peanuts at Bidwell's. Stan Auerbach remembers Shelford talking politics over beer: voicing his concern that generals MacArthur and Eisenhower might become president; delivering a dry, humorous exposition of his voting for Eugene Debs; and complaining about the "eastern establishment" of ecologists. "Gradually what emerged," said Auerbach, "was the story of the Ecologists' Union and Shelford's effort to have the Ecological Society of America take a strong, conservationist posture in its role as the professional society of ecologists. . . . Typical of Shelford, he provided few details and never discussed any of the personalities involved."[49]

The spring of Shelford's retirement marked both ends and beginnings in an endeavor that caused him acute frustration and disappointment over the years, but eventually gave him deep satisfaction—his lifelong struggle for preservation of natural habitats. We must now consider the most political aspect of Shelford's career, his tireless dedication to what he saw as the ecologist's responsibilities to the natural world.

6

PRESERVING NATURE

1914–1950

While still at Chicago in 1914 Shelford received a letter from his naturalist friend, Robert H. Wolcott, of the University of Nebraska. "What do you think," Wolcott wrote, "of such a thing as a society of ecologists to include both botanists and zoologists and to be a society for field work rather than a society for the reading of papers?" Such a society, he suggested, could bring ecologists into unfamiliar areas during the summer and keep them informed on current work of other ecologists. Preoccupied though he was with job hunting, Shelford discussed the idea with Henry Cowles and then replied to Wolcott:

> I have your plan for an Ecological Society and think it fine. Cowles does likewise and will help it along all he can. He suggests the thing be started at Philadelphia [AAAS meetings] in 1914. Why could it not be National? Most of the meetings would be in the Mississippi valley any way and the western country is of much interest though little worked.
>
> Do you have a plan for organization? Let's be sure that something is done.

Wolcott answered that he would be glad to join a national society, but would prefer a sectional one with simple organization to assure good attendance, adding, "In fact my idea for this society was gained from a perusal of your book [*Animal Communities,*] it having resulted in a strong desire to see the localities in which you have worked."[1]

On the evening of December 30, 1914, Henry Cowles gathered a group of twenty-two ecologists in the lobby of the Hotel Walton in Philadelphia. They agreed virtually unanimously to form an ecological society and appointed an organizing committee of J. W. Harshberger, Shelford, Cowles, Robert Wolcott, Charles Adams, and Forrest Shreve. A year later, fifty members formally approved the formation of the Ecological Society of America in the Hotel Hartman in Columbus, Ohio. Another fifty-odd charter members were absent at the founding. Annual dues for the society were set at one dollar. The first set of officers chosen were Shelford as president, William Morton Wheeler as vice-president, and Forrest Shreve as secretary-treasurer. By early 1916, membership had doubled, and the newly elected officers saw "every prospect for an active and influential organization." Shelford and Stephen Forbes quickly organized "the Illinois bunch as a section." Shreve elatedly wrote Shelford that they should be able to "pull in the Pacific men" and that foresters were "flocking right in." Support seemed tremendous for this new society for work and study in the American out-of-doors.[2]

Since the Civil War, American natural resources had felt the increasing blows of industrial society in its drive for progress. In fact, depredation of nature began much earlier. "From 1600 right down to the present," Shelford noted, "the belief that all exploitable areas should be settled and developed has been almost a national religion." Theodore Roosevelt unified conservation forces in the early 1900s after his chief forester, Gifford Pinchot, ignited the crusade that culminated in Roosevelt's White House Governors' Conference on Conservation in 1908. By the end of his second term that same year, Roosevelt had increased the national forest acreage by 172 million acres. Within a year, however, Roosevelt left office, and Pinchot was sacked by President Taft. Conservation efforts then dropped to a lower pitch, not reaching the intensity of the Roosevelt years again until the peak of the Hetch Hetchy Reservoir controversy in 1912, when San Franciscans debated the need for more water versus the protection of pristine beauty. By this time, Americans showed a lively interest in the outdoors, signaling their increased need for contact with the natural world as the population became more than 50 percent urban. Early in Wilson's administration, the federal government moved boldly into wildlife work. It declared all-out warfare on varmints, assigning money for predator control on both private and public lands to the Division of Biological Survey.

Very troublesome for naturalists was the general lack of interest in nature conservation shown by national scientific societies, although thoughtful scientists believed biologists should lead the way. William T. Hornaday, the noted wildlife conservationist, lecturing at the Yale School of Forestry in 1914, wasted no words:

> Think what it would mean if even one-half the men and women who earn their daily bread in the field of zoology and nature study should elect to make this cause their own! And yet, I tell you that in spite of an appeal for help, dating as far back as 1898, fully 90 per cent of the zoologists of America stick closely to their desk-work, soaring after the infinite and diving after the unfathomable, but never spending a dollar or lifting an active finger on the firing-line in defense of wild life. I have talked to these men until I am tired; and most of them seem to be hopelessly sodden and apathetic.[3]

Troublesome, too, were aggressive attempts to weaken state game laws and to assault timber, mineral, water, and wildlife resources in national parks, forests, and wildlife refuges under cries of a national war emergency. These demands were outrageous enough in 1918 for Theodore Roosevelt to thunder at the American Game Conference in New York City:

> To the profiteering proposal of the Pseudopatriots, the Patriots for revenue only, that protection of wildlife in war time be relaxed, the united hosts of conservation reply: "You Shall Not Pass."

But Roosevelt died shortly thereafter, and the preservation cause suffered. By 1917, Shelford had observed a groundswell of interest among ESA members for preserving natural areas and suggested a committee to coordinate this. Immediately he found himself appointed chair of the Committee on Preservation of Natural Conditions by ESA president Ellsworth Huntington. Impressed by the prospects of the new committee, Huntington encouraged close attention to pending legislation and asked for a list of appropriate areas for preservation. "The more I think of the possibilities of the Ecological Society," Huntington wrote Shelford, "the more I am convinced that it is likely to become one of the strong forces in the scientific world. Those of you who first planned it certainly acted with wisdom."[4]

Shelford appreciated the accolade, but as usual fixed his attention to the task at hand. Beginning with a committee of twenty-five and the blessings of the society but precious little financial support, he set to work. Between 1917 and 1921 the committee increased its membership to more than fifty (society membership increased to over five hundred during this time) and identified about six hundred areas in North America that were "preserved or worth preserving." By far the majority of preserved areas lay in the national parks. Fortunately, since 1916 the fledgling National Park Service (NPS) had had effective leadership under its whirlwind director, Steven Mather. Conservation of scenery, natural objects, and wildlife were included in its charter; nevertheless, Shelford's committee would need to keep constant vigilance over the years to insure adherence to this charter. Committee members soon found they had an enormous educational job on their hands. They needed not only to enlist scientists, but also to lobby federal and state agencies, politicians, and the public, if they were going to succeed at preserving nature in the interest of biological research and the national heritage.[5]

Casting about for support, Shelford proceeded to weave a network of professional advisors and supporters. For example, Gifford Pinchot, who had become commissioner of forestry in Pennsylvania, supported the ESA's work and recommended it seek help from the National Research Council (NRC). He also suggested cooperation between these two organizations and the Society of American Foresters. Shelford eventually obtained a small grant of three hundred dollars from the NRC, which was used to produce a progress report in the summer of 1921.

This document was disarmingly frank. Shelford and his colleagues cited several reasons for the preservation of natural areas—scientific, recreational, aesthetic, and material. Understandably they emphasized the scientific. Natural areas, they stressed, are "living museums" whose value increases with time. The report explained that early action was required because of civilization's continuous and progressive impact. Halfhearted or tardy action would put in jeopardy the plants and animals on which the science of ecology depends. While ecologists could achieve some progress alone, Shelford's committee admitted, in the end, little could be done without public interest. Ideally, not only the federal government, but states, counties, cities, towns, and even colleges and universities needed preserves. The rallying cry for the committee, which distinguished its letterhead, thus became "An Undisturbed Area in Every Natural Park and Public Forest." To accomplish this goal, the committee planned to agitate for preservation; produce cogent arguments to answer the perennial question, Will it pay?; educate against roadside mowing and burning and swamp drainage outside natural preserves; solicit cooperation from state academies of science and natural history societies; and perhaps most important, provide scientific information about natural area preservation to individuals, organizations, and legislative bodies. The program was extremely ambitious, but Shelford was not daunted even by the challenge of securing areas in national forests and parks to be set aside for ecological research.[6]

Neither the Forest Service nor the National Park Service had a formal policy on wildlife preservation in natural areas in the early 1920s. Adequate ecological information had yet to reach these agencies and affect their management plans. Shelford became aware of the magnitude of this problem in 1921 when he represented the American Society of Zoologists at NPS director Steven Mather's first national conference on parks. Mather's heart was in the right place, but his ecological understanding of wildlife was rudimentary. In a letter to Charles Adams, Shelford reported on the meeting, writing, "Heavenly days! This crowd practically never heard of natural areas being of any use to science." He did record cautious optimism, though, adding "They welcome the idea of biological study as a further argument for natural tracts."

Here was an opportunity for biologists to organize—a favorite word in the 1920s—and provide a scientific basis for natural area preservation. The scientists were becoming active none too soon. Many of Shelford's colleagues were alarmed at the continuing acquisitive drive of water power interests for massive projects in national parks; if parks could be dammed and ditched, it was only a question of time before lumbering and hunting would also be allowed. Consequently, Shelford welcomed the chance to represent the AAAS on its conservation committee at a joint meeting with similar committees from the National Academy of Sciences and the NRC in New York during April 1921. The conferees agreed in fine progressive fashion that scientific research should be "brought to bear more effectively upon the problems of conservation." Soon the joint group officially became the Executive

Committee on Natural Resources, chaired by John C. Merriam, president of the Carnegie Institution. This high-level committee served as another forum for Shelford and his preservation committee, who wanted all the exposure they could get. In late 1923, however, Shelford resigned with mixed feelings from the general chair of the ESA preservation committee in order to spend more time finishing up *A Naturalist's Guide,* now five years in preparation.[7]

When Shelford and his colleagues were founding the ESA in 1914 and 1915, forest assistant Aldo Leopold worked in New Mexico for the United States Forest Service, and in his spare time, rounded up hunters from the Albuquerque area into game protection associations. A few years later, Leopold had risen to assistant district forester in the Gila National Forest, a former Apache battleground in New Mexico and Arizona. Leopold proposed that a protected wilderness area encompassing 700,000 acres of land with poorly accessible timber but abundant wildlife be established there. Arguing for wilderness preservation over the long term as the "highest use" for land, Leopold finally convinced his supervisor and got the first official American wilderness area approved in 1924. Five additional Forest Service tracts were so designated by 1925; however, the embryonic policy on designating wilderness areas only recommended that local forest officers consider wilderness values in their planning. Much was left to their discretion, far too much to satisfy preservationists.[8]

Henry Thoreau wrote most eloquently, "In Wildness is the preservation of the World," and, "Each town should have a park, or rather a primitive forest, of five hundred or a thousand acres, where a stick should never be cut for fuel, a common possession forever, for instruction and recreation." But neither Thoreau nor the preservation committee could have known how quickly a growing, more mobile American public would descend on the outdoors, filling up parks, campgrounds, and forests. In 1919, over seven hundred thousand people visited the national parks. During the twenties, the number of visitors passed two million while ten times as many visited national forests. People had more money, more leisure, more roads, and more cars. This was a time when eager and dedicated Forest Service and NPS workers competed to attract the recreation public, when the ESA was only one of a dozen organizations lobbying for wilderness areas, and when the complexity and enormity of the wildlife preservation idea perplexed the federal government. President Calvin Coolidge responded by appointing a committee of his cabinet to explore how a national policy of outdoor recreation could be encouraged and by calling a series of national conferences on outdoor recreation between 1924 and 1929. At the first conference in May 1924, 309 delegates from every state and Canada, including some from ESA, sought ways to coordinate the work of private and government groups and put forth resolutions on education, wildlife refuges, wetlands, indiscriminate predator control, and the need for improved state fish and game departments. Eventually almost all the resolutions were wholly or partially adopted. Implementation, unfortunately, was another matter.[9]

Taking heart from this increased national attention to matters of ecological interest, the ESA, through its preservation committee, moved resolutely ahead during the latter half of the twenties. They published A Naturalist's Guide; strongly recommended setting aside Glacier Bay Monument as a national park in one of the most effective preservation demonstrations ever; urged that Beckler Basin be retained as part of Yellowstone National Park; and argued against designating a poor quality site in Arkansas as a national park. Inevitably, greater involvement brought increased criticism. At ESA meetings in New York during December 1928, the preservation committee, through its chair W. G. Waterman, proposed that ESA members consider "whether or not it was the function of the Society to assist in the preservation of natural areas in view of the opposition and unfavorable publicity sometimes aroused." After a spirited discussion, most members affirmed that it was. The same question would arise several more times in the years ahead.[10]

Finding the work overwhelming and his knowledge of natural areas across the continent inadequate, Waterman resigned as chair of the ESA preservation committee in late 1929, after a year of relative inactivity. Shelford immediately appeared to chair a small committee with the charge to reorganize all ESA preservation activities during 1930. At first he tried combining the functions of the old preservation committee with the functions of a committee, consisting of Shelford, W. P. Taylor, and H. C. Oberholser, originally set up in 1926 to promote study of plant and animal communities. This did not work, as Shelford said, because "several men in state or federal government service were among the most enthusiastic workers in the combined committee and were either forbidden to lobby by law, or might readily be embarrassed by efforts of the chairman and secretary to influence government bureaus and legislative bodies." The dilemma was particularly acute in 1930 and 1931 when the ESA lobbied against predator control by the Bureau of Biological Survey. Consequently, in 1931 with society approval, they set up separate committees for preservation work. The Committee on the Preservation of Natural Conditions for the United States (and a similar one for Canada) became the action body; its duties included writing letters and resolutions to government bureaus and attending hearings. The Committee for the Study of Plant and Animal Communities, with a core advisory group of twenty to forty experts, local chapters organized under three regional chairs, and associated contributing societies, was meant to be a fact-finding body. Its letterhead read "A nature sanctuary with its original wild animals for each biotic formation."[11]

It will come as no surprise that Shelford was summarily elected chair of both new committees. He also served on the Wildlife Committee of the NRC from 1931 to 1935, chaired the Committee on Grasslands of the NRC from 1932 to 1939, and acted as a trustee of the watchdog National Parks Association (NPA) from 1930 to 1938. In addition, he served for a time in the early thirties with Charles Adams as one of only two Americans on the editorial board of the short-lived Russian *Journal of Ecology and Biocenology.*[12]

In May of 1930, three eager NPS workers loaded camping gear, collecting equipment, cameras, and assorted reference books into their sturdy field car and began a much-needed wildlife survey of national parks. Mammologist Joseph Dixon, ranger and scientific aide George Wright, and research associate Ben Thompson spent the next three summers on this project under the personal guidance of NPS director Horace Albright. All of their expenses were paid by Wright the first year; thereafter, federal appropriations covered about half. Their long-range objective was a wildlife management plan for the national parks; they no longer believed simple protection of animals was enough. The challenge as they saw it was to preserve and maintain the fauna in as natural a state as possible in the face of steadily increasing numbers of human visitors. The results of their work were two remarkably prescient reports issued in 1933 and 1935 that clearly show Shelford's influence and remain relevant today.[13]

Making his committee rounds in 1930, Shelford prepared for the trustees meeting of the NPA that December. The NPS was giving strong attention to the main scenic parks thanks to significantly increased appropriations, which were part of government attempts to combat the growing depression: Congress considered these funds a good investment, as they provided employment in the parks. Shelford knew, too, that President Hoover, a former president of the NPA; Secretary of the Interior Ray Wilbur; and NPS director Horace Albright were strong national parks supporters and that Wilbur and Albright were avowed wilderness advocates. Fueled by this climate of support and his own intense objections to predator control, Shelford was poised to scrutinize the current functions and uses of national parks, particularly in his role as a member of the NPA Preservation of the Primitive Committee, on which he served during the early thirties.

"There needs to be restoration of the primitive as well as protection of the primitive," Shelford wrote later in "strictly confidential" memo to his ESA study committee. His main concern was with the attitude of the men in charge of the parks. He complained, "They are thoroughly imbued with the prevalent agricultural idea (sense broad) that nature can be improved upon, and . . . with an ancient idea of a fixed balance in nature." To counteract this idea, Shelford proposed that "a study of the laws governing fluctuations in numbers [of prey] under first pristine and then modified conditions should throw much light on the validity of many if not all [predator] control measures now practiced." Gathering opinions from his ESA committee during 1931, Shelford drafted a policy statement for the ESA on nature sanctuaries in parks and forests. National parks were put first on the priority list of suitable places for sanctuaries because of their generally accepted function of preserving the primitive; national forests ranked second. Few existing or possible sanctuaries could be considered first class because only rarely were all large native animals present; nevertheless, each one should be large enough, most committee members believed, to encompass the home ranges of as many animal species as possible. Most important, sanctuaries needed to be ringed by buffer areas, where roaming animals would be protected and where experiments modifying the environment could be performed. Shelford's statement also proposed that only persons "conducting scientific, artistic or literary work of a serious nature" be admitted to designated research sanctuaries and that large carnivores be left alone where their presence "can be tolerated."[15]

The ESA approved these general principles on December 29, 1931, at its annual meeting in New Orleans. The next day it sponsored a special conference on nature sanctuaries on the Tulane University campus. Representatives from eight other societies and government agencies attended. They agreed with the ESA's basic position and offered additional suggestions.[16]

Then Shelford crafted a final ESA policy statement on nature sanctuaries that took him most of 1932 to complete. The finished statement was approved by the ESA in December at Atlantic City, published in April 1933, and mailed to federal agencies and the conservation commissions of thirty states. The National Parks Association quickly adopted the plan. The core of the statement was straightforward: whole communities are important, not only individual species. Proper preservation and administration of sanctuaries, the paper insisted, are dependent on knowledge of the structure and dynamics of these natural communities. For example, both the size and boundaries of sanctuaries should be set by the biological needs of the resident animals and plants, a concept still inadequately implemented in preserves, sanctuaries, and national parks today. Shelford was unequivocal in asserting the first priority: "to let natural areas alone" and allow nature to take its course. This meant a speedy end to indiscriminate control of predators and pests. The report's message was widely broadcast by ESA members to their many contacts.[17]

For a short while, Shelford's committees enjoyed some self-congratulation. Certainly, general recognition of the importance of natural areas had increased since the twenties, and any ecologist had to be impressed with the growing commitment of the NPS and the Forest Service to wilderness preservation. The NPS had even formed a wildlife division in 1931, with George Wright as chief. Yet animals and their needs required much more attention, particularly in national forests.

In the heady first hundred days of Roosevelt's New Deal, Shelford and the preservation committee directed a salvo of letters to federal agencies. These letters urged attention to the principles of nature sanctuaries and their means of providing scientists the "opportunity for continuous observation of the dynamics of nature over long periods." A letter arguing preservation was sent with a crisp new copy of *A Naturalist's Guide* to Franklin Delano Roosevelt's new Secretary of the Interior, Harold Ickes. Ickes replied that he appreciated the ESA's stand in championing primitive areas "where scientists may study virgin conditions" and thanked them for the book.[18]

Soon ecologists were hearing rumblings from Washington about reorganization. It was rumored that parks, forests, fisheries, and the Bureau of Biological Survey might be combined into a cabinet-level department of conservation or that the NPS might be subsumed by the Department of Agriculture. Shelford thought the latter move would jeopardize the preservation of natural sanctuaries in the parks and that parks were best kept under the Department of the Interior. Charles Adams was plainly worried, complaining to Shelford that *"economics* is certainly in the saddle now" and that he had "grave fears for the National Parks in the hands of Roosevelt, and his consolidation policies." The department of conservation idea had surfaced before in 1921 and 1927 and would linger for a few more years, absorbing the energies of countless Washington bureaucrats, a breed Shelford grumbled about along with "the preachers and those g.d. prohibitionists."[19]

Even before his election, Roosevelt picked conservation as an integral part of his relief and recovery plans for the nation. Soon after Roosevelt took office, Secretary Ickes boasted that the administration had prepared a comprehensive "twenty-five or fifty-year plan" for natural resources. Only seventeen days after his inauguration, Roosevelt proposed to Congress the creation of the Civilian Conservation Corps to scratch young, single men off welfare lists and put them to work in the forests. The agency was approved two weeks later. Shelford felt a surge of optimism for effective ESA action in concert with the government's conservation initiative.[20]

But Shelford had an even more immediate reason for celebration. Early in 1933 the first report on the vertebrate fauna in national parks by George Wright and his colleagues appeared. Their recommendations were clear-sighted and agreed with most of the ESA's ongoing concerns. Shelford took notice when he read, "Every species shall be left to carry on its struggle for existence unaided," and, "No native predator shall be destroyed on account of its normal utilization of any other park animal." He felt that even if only half the recommendations were followed, they would constitute a step forward for enlightened preservation in the national parks.

Shelford learned shortly thereafter that George Wright's wildlife division had been given responsibility for the NPS research reserve program. Wright immediately involved his staff in lengthy discussions on the need for and function of nature sanctuaries. In a series of memos written in 1934 and a final, long-term wildlife management report completed in 1935, they advised Arno Cammerer, the new director of NPS, that Shelford's ESA nature sanctuary plan be used as a guideline "to accord with the most advanced scientific thought on the subject." Wright and Ben Thompson reiterate the ESA principles:

> Under this scheme the whole of the park becomes a primitive area with the exception of certain fixed and well-defined areas to which developments must be limited. . . . For scientific study and to serve as control experiments, specific areas within the primitive area may be set aside as permanent or temporary research areas. . . . To make this program satisfactorily effective, the park should be surrounded by a buffer strip of the maximum width possible, in order to isolate it from external influences. Success of this measure must depend on whether adjacent lands are in public or private ownership and on the degree of cooperation which can be secured. . . .
>
> Fifty years from now we shall still be wrestling with the problems of joint occupation of national parks by men and mammals, but it is reasonable to predict that we shall have mastered some of the simplest maladjustments. . . .[21]

Less than a year after the 1935 wildlife management paper was published, George Wright was killed in an automobile accident. Yet due to his work and the influence of Shelford's committees, the NPS moved ahead, largely abandoning predator control by the late thirties, quietly setting aside some areas in the parks for preservation of and research on biotic communities, and giving at least nodding assent to the need for buffering park lands.[22]

Colleagues praised Shelford's work at winter 1933–34 ESA meetings in Boston, again approving the continuation of both the preservation and study committees and their activities. Shelford quickly requested the usual $150 from society dues, plus royalties from *A Naturalist's Guide,* to support his preservation work. But it was tougher now to get these funds, and he received less than he had hoped.

On the federal level it was a different story: newly created agencies poured out emergency appropriations for public works, unemployment relief, and the stimulation of economic recovery. Conservationists eagerly helped cut up the larger pie. Despite the best intentions, however, duplication of effort, interagency squabbles, and conflicting aims were widespread. Bureau of Biological Survey chief Jay "Ding" Darling's words at the time matched Shelford's sentiments: "The worst enemies of wildlife," he said, "are the Republicans and Democrats." Probably the most annoying were President Roosevelt's attempts to please everyone, although his interest in conservation was genuine and had been evident since his days as a state senator and governor of New York. With Roosevelt's urging the federal government bought up millions of acres of submarginal land from farmers across the nation and put them to use as wildlife propagation areas and waterfowl refuges. In time, the ESA preservation committee allied itself with Roosevelt's Committee on Wild-Life Restoration. Shelford himself suggested seven areas for purchase in early 1934, including Illinois River bottomland and bluffs near Lake Chautauqua, Illinois, which did eventually become a national wildlife refuge.[23]

Pushing sixty, Shelford kept a brutal pace between 1934 and 1938, and it caught up with him. He devoted about 70 percent of his university time to teaching, graduating eleven M.S. and five Ph.D. students. Summers he spent on the tundra, on Lake Erie, and in the West. During this time he also had partial responsibility for the zoology department. He labored on *Bio-Ecology* with Clements and chaired the university's Committee on Natural Areas, in addition to leading regional and national preservation work. His nerves and energies were stretched thin, and he found himself "not able to sleep for three nights" when things went awry.[24]

Shelford's troops had won some important battles, but these were eclipsed by what remained to be done. The issues multiplied rapidly: setting quality standards for national parks, designating parks in need of buffering, curbing aggressive predator control outside parks on both public and private land, and fighting the proposal to dig an irrigation tunnel under Rocky Mountain National Park all found places on Shelford's agenda. The Rocky Mountain tunnel unfortunately withstood the ESA's firm protest and won Secretary of the Interior Ickes's reluctant approval. It was completed in 1944.[25]

In Shelford's estimation, destruction of predators on range and forest land during 1935 was the worst ever. This disturbing development moved him to urge another round of ESA resolutions on all preservation issues. These were approved by his colleagues at winter 1935–36 meetings in St. Louis. Neither Shelford nor his committees had any illusions about the potential success of their recommendations: The replies they received were much as they expected. Acting chief of the Forest Service C. E. Rachford doubted whether big game could be provided with range lands at the magnitude suggested, but remarked that the "resolutions were received with considerable interest" and would "be given careful consideration." Secretary Ickes promised to "give all possible support." Bureau of Biological Survey chief Ira N. Gabrielson commented that some of ESA's suggestions had "definite possibilities" and that his bureau intended to follow preservation policies for the recently acquired Okefenokee Swamp. Shortly after the new chief of the Forest Service, Ferdinand Silcox, assumed office he claimed his bureau was trying to correct naive mistakes of the Civilian Conservation Corps, such as overeager brush clearing and drainage of wildlife habitat in marshes. "We are particularly sensitive to opinions of such agencies as the Ecological Society because the Society's membership is made up of thinking professionals," he wrote. National Park Service director Cammerer admitted that "few or none of the national parks are complete biological units," but assured the ESA that the NPS continued to discuss buffering and the possibility of enlarging park lands.[26]

This type of lobbying represented most of Shelford's contribution to the preservation committee in 1935; he left the rest of the work to secretary Robert Cahn. The press of his other work more than filled the gap, and in 1936 he decided to submit his resignation from the chairs of both the preservation and study committees when his terms expired that December. As it turned out, he continued to chair the study committee until May 1938, devoting his and the committee's energies during that time wholly to special grassland work. He successfully relinquished leadership of the preservation committee to Asa Weese in 1936.[27]

Shelford was troubled by the lack of a constitutionally established role, adequate financial support, and open recognition for preservation activities within the ESA, despite recurring votes at annual meetings in favor of the work. Until 1938 the society paid less than 30 percent of the total costs of both committees' work. From 1934 to 1938, in fact, money allocated to the preservation and study committees together usually totaled less than $100 each year, although Shelford maintained they needed $300 annually. In 1937 the society approved the establishment of a contributing membership for support of preservation work, but this was not advertised until 1944. Also in 1937, the suggestion (probably Shelford's) to allocate 35¢ from each member's dues to support preservation work was rejected; this would have yielded about $245 in 1938. Shelford pulled no punches, complaining to ESA President Robert Coker that the society's stress on annual meetings and journal papers added up to "an unvaried 17th century program" not "in keeping with modern life." He and like-minded colleagues believed that preservation activities were as important as other ESA activities and should be properly recognized as such by the society. Shelford considered it unfair to expect colleagues to shoulder preservation work when the job was "hidden away in the Society." Personally, he felt slighted because the preservation activities he conducted during the depression "at a heavy sacrifice" were so meagerly supported. "I am convinced," he wrote W. C. Allee, "that those who take part in the running of the society—rank and file who attend the business meetings and hold offices—are smugly conservative and unwilling to admit anything into the Society not characteristic of such organizations as the Society of Naturalists." He closed saying: "As [the society] exists, I am no longer interested and have reduced my membership to 'contributing' and whether or not I continue that, will depend on whether or not the committees for whom I intended the contribution get a fair portion of it." Shelford's donations were apparently distributed to his satisfaction because he subsequently increased his commitment to the "sustaining member" level.[28]

Shelford's unvarnished criticism ignited a controversy that would not be resolved until 1946. What demoralized him most was how easily the gains from his ESA preservation work could be lost. He believed the society had earned a unique leadership position through the efforts of the preservation and study committees: the ESA was widely respected for the rare virtue of basing its policies on scientific principles. He could only view the society's refusal to back preservation activities just when lasting success had become possible as utter foolishness. And so after turning over the study committee reins to Charles Kendeigh in May 1938, Shelford wearily reordered his work schedule, wrapped up *Bio-Ecology* for publication, and then succumbed to the fierce viral infection mentioned earlier that kept him in the hospital for weeks.[29]

Nothing better illustrates Shelford's lifelong affair with natural resources than his preoccupation with American ignorance and mistreatment of grasslands—those primeval seas of tall, mixed, and short perennial grasses that characterize central North America. In early pioneer days, big bluestem grass, with its dense sod and deep roots, towered 8 to 10 feet high; cattle could only be spotted by watching for telltale waves as the animals walked through the grass. Now, mostly only small clumps of the original tallgrass prairie remain, scattered along railroad right-of-ways, highways, and old fence rows or hidden away in crumbling cemeteries. Shelford's frequent published and unpublished reflections on the tragedy of the grasslands lovingly describe their early glories, from the enormous herds of bison and pronghorn that once ranged there to the prairie dogs, whose burrowing efficiently overturned and aerated shortgrass soil. His feelings about the human relationship with grasslands are more complex: He seems fascinated by the terror that prairie fires and howling winter storms inspired in pioneers. At the same time, he expresses sadness and disgust at the first settlers' scramble to turn the grass "wrong side up" and the subsequent damage that has been caused by overgrazing, mowing, plowing, irrigation, and drainage.[30]

Shelford believed that long-range policies on erosion, range depletion, water conservation, and wildlife biology must be ecologically based in order to succeed. He also stressed the importance of focusing on the three interacting elements of the Great Plains: the biotic community of animals and plants, the grassland habitat, and human beings. He further believed that the available base of knowledge and the fundamental research necessary to enlarge it, at the time, were "utterly inadequate" to foster the long-term health of the human and agricultural economy of the plains.[31]

If the grasslands themselves suffered from the influx of European settlers, the native plains animals fared even worse. (The fate of the buffalo is well known.) In the presettlement days of the grasslands, predators like the coyote, wolf, kit fox, bull snake, and owl helped keep the plant-eating pronghorn, bison, prairie dog, and rabbits in check. Settlers upset the balance by waging war on predators in defense of their livestock and poultry, redoubling their efforts when livestock losses increased due to overgrazing and range depletion as early as 1885. Attrition of predators resulted in larger populations of prairie dogs and other rodents that competed with livestock for grass. At the turn of the century, farmers began to demand poison control for rodents. By 1917 the Bureau of Biological Survey was fully engaged in the downward spiral of predator and rodent control. Increasingly, overgrazing by the protected livestock favored growth of broad-leaved plants and, thus, more abundant populations of the particular species of rodents and grasshoppers that fed on them.[32]

When the ESA study committee was organized in 1930, it designated a working group to deal with grassland problems in several states. Soon Shelford and his colleagues recognized an immediate need for setting aside grassland tracts for cooperative research: appropriate areas were disappearing fast. But buying land cost money, and cooperative research required a detailed plan. Shelford decided to present tentative plans for securing funds to his former professor, Frank Lillie, of Chicago, who had contacts with the NRC. Lillie recommended they request that the NRC form a special committee on the ecology of grasslands. This committee was approved in 1932 and placed under the NRC's Division of Biology and Agriculture. Shelford was appointed chair. Enthusiasm for the committee was helped no doubt by the increasing drought and intensified federal interest in the myriad issues involved.[33]

The committee's initial report in late 1933 estimated long-term costs of the proposed work at more than $1 million. Immediate cost projections for seven study centers to be assisted by local ESA committees in Arizona, Texas, Oklahoma, Nebraska, Illinois, North Dakota, and Saskatchewan included moneys for grassland acquisition totaling $91,000 at $10 to $75 per acre. In some of these study areas, no one yet knew how much virgin and salvageable prairie remained. Once pristine and more disturbed grassland remnants were identified and surveyed, they could be purchased and put to use for research on fundamental ecological questions. Some relevant research subjects had been pursued by individual committee members for years, including grassland root systems, animal grazing, animal fluctuations, prairie restoration, and physical factor variation. To gain a more complete picture, the committee proposed a well-integrated basic grassland study of both plants and animals—mammals, birds, and insects—across the various grassland habitats of North America. The trick would be to preserve enough tracts of relatively undisturbed native grasslands before they were seriously overgrazed or plowed under.[34]

An additional proposal was to set aside a very large grassland area as a national park or monument. Shelford is recorded as advancing this idea as early as 1931 (and he probably began much earlier). As it evolved, his plan called for a million acres, which would "preserve the original fuana in a natural state for posterity . . . while retaining historic conditions of the covered wagon days." Agreement with these stated goals was unanimous. Trouble arose with the suggestion that land be taken out of agricultural production for the sake of plants and animals that many people did not appreciate. Nevertheless, between 1932 and 1938, as the drought parched the land, Shelford's NRC grassland committee, his ESA committees, and the NPS painstakingly examined eleven areas of a million acres or more between southern North Dakota and north central Texas as candidates for a national grasslands monument. A tract in northwestern Nebraska and southwestern South Dakota was selected. The Department of the Interior requested transfer of this federal land for a grasslands monument without success. "Just as the matter was reaching the top levels in Washington," Shelford claimed, "the war broke out and the efforts gradually ceased."[35]

Equally unsuccessful were attempts to get money for support of the planned grassland study centers, despite annual appeals to the NRC. "It was therefore proposed," Shelford explained, "that a nonprofit corporation be organized . . . which could make direct application to granting bodies with the endorsement of the Division of Biology and Agriculture." The NRC gave its reluctant approval, and the Grassland Research Foundation was incorporated in 1939. In November of that year, Asa Weese was elected president and Martha Shackleford, treasurer. Shelford was named a director and immediately resigned as chair of the NRC Grassland Committee, which disbanded in 1943.[36]

The thirties gave way to the forties, the drought lessened and World War II heated up. Shelford, restless and lonely after Mabel's death, threw himself into his work as zoology chair and into his continuing crusade for nature preservation. He published an extensive list of nature reserves for the United States, Canada, and Mexico in 1941. In this way, he stayed in close contact with the ESA study and preservation committees, chaired now by Charles Kendeigh and Curtis Newcombe, respectively. The three men were increasingly concerned with both committees' activities in view of past and present criticism from the ESA executive committee (on which Kendeigh served in 1943). Since 1934, some officers had felt that the study and preservation committees dominated the society and therefore suggested variously that these committees should not receive outside funds, should not function during wartime, or should not function at all. On his own initiative and at his own expense, Shelford decided in the fall of 1943 to ask rank and file members their opinions about ESA work for the preservation of nature. ("It would have taken the Executive Committee five years to send out a questionnaire" was Shelford's caustic justification for acting alone.) He clipped a small ballot to a reprint of his article "Twenty-five-year Effort at Saving Nature for Scientific Purposes," originally published in *Science,* and mailed these to four hundred ESA members. He got back 373 ballots; among these 85 percent supported preservation work on par with annual meetings and journals and thought that other local and national societies should be allowed to contribute financial support specifically to preservation projects. Shelford estimated they could increase contributions to five or six hundred dollars annually with better support from the executive committee, which was not forthcoming. "There appeared," Charles Kendeigh said, "less hesitancy among the general membership for carrying on the work for preservation than among the officers of the Society."[37]

Alternatively, Shelford had for ten years considered forming a large union of societies interested in nature preservation, but he now gave up that idea. He preferred to encourage societies to affiliate themselves with and contribute to the ESA, while depending on dedicated professional ecologists within the ESA as the active core. He felt this group alone had the experience, scientific reputation, and sound conservation judgment needed to do the job. The union or council of organizations was suggested by others, as well, most notably Charles Adams, recently retired from the New York State Museum, and Robert Griggs, chair of the NRC Division of Biology and Agriculture and ESA president. They strongly questioned the nature preservation role of the ESA as it had evolved and called for centralized coordination of all conservation activities in the United States through a body separate from the ESA.[38]

Shelford had anticipated this move; so in early 1944, he drew up tactical plans for the looming battle over leadership of nature preservation in the United States. After conferring with Griggs in Washington, he wrote in an open letter to all ESA members that spring:

> The Ecological Society is not of the ordinary type, such as the majority which are affiliated with the AAAS. The fact that it has carried on this work, which fundamentally is concerned with the preservation of research materials for its members . . . is an indication of its unique character. . . . With the membership of the society strongly in favor of continuing the past program and twenty-seven years of experience as a basis for drawing up a definite basis of procedure and embodying it in the Constitution of the society for the guidance of incoming officers, it seems advisable to take immediate action in this direction.[39]

Soon after this, Charles Kendeigh, in consultation with Curtis Newcombe and several other colleagues, drew up a proposed article for the ESA constitution. The article stated that the ESA would maintain permanent coordinated committees for the study and preservation of nature; that these committees would be supported by 10 percent of society membership dues, plus ESA contributions, publication sales, and outside donations; and that they would be empowered to hold property and transact business. The article was submitted in preliminary form for comments to Robert Griggs and William Dreyer, secretary-treasurer of ESA, in July 1944. Griggs instructed that the proposed article be presented for society consideration at the annual ESA business meeting in Cleveland on September 13, but promised that the society's executive committee would preview it on September 11.

Griggs believed the question to be whether ESA was, or should be, "different from other scientific societies." Should the society continue to take direct action for the preservation of nature? From his vantage point as president, Griggs reported to Charles Adams, "There is a general feeling that this is the time to settle it." Adams replied diplomatically, "Shelford has done a lot of good work for the Society," qualifying his support with the comment, "25 years have not been enough to convince Shelford that the Ecological Society does not have the money to *finance* his program." Nor did Adams think preservation activities should be written into the ESA constitution. Shelford wrote Griggs in August saying simply, "The Society should put this [preservation] work on a thoroughly organized basis or discontinue it." And so the lines were drawn.[40]

What happened next angered Shelford and dumbfounded his supporters: at the ESA business meeting in Cleveland that September, the executive committee recommended that the preservation committee be abolished. At the very least, Shelford and his supporters had expected the executive committee to arrange for discussion, allowing Kendeigh, Newcombe, and "other people doing the work" a chance to express their views. Moreover, anticipating debate, Kendeigh's and Newcombe's committees had worked out a revised statement to be included in the constitution, which they were prepared to present at the business meeting as a last resort. It read simply: "The Society shall maintain permanent committees for the study and preservation of nature." All other provisions for financing and administration would be proposed as bylaws. Successful passage of this statement, they felt, would at least "insure the perpetual maintenance of this necessary work by the Society."[41]

The root of opposition to direct action in nature preservation lay in the executive committee and among a number of past presidents who advised the committee. These men did not believe it proper for a scientific society to act as a pressure group—even in as important a cause as preservation of natural areas. "They believed they shouldn't get mixed in politics," Shelford complained.[42]

Instead, this group, which included Griggs and Adams, supported the conservation council idea. A motion passed at the Cleveland business meeting directed the incoming 1945 ESA officers to organize such a council—eventually called the Natural Resources Council. The ESA, then, as a council member, would only give scientific advice, while designated pressure groups represented on the council would take political action. (As it turned out, the Natural Resources Council proved unwieldy and lacked a definite commitment to direct action; Shelford, Kendeigh, Newcombe, and their supporters consequently lost interest in it before the end of 1945.)

Recommendations from the executive committee did not necessarily reflect the will of the members. After much discussion at the Cleveland business meeting and urging from Shelford, it was decided to hold a referendum by mail on the fate of the preservation committee and, thus, the future of direct action by the society. In the meantime, Shelford girded himself for action, writing to Charles Adams of his concern over the "dictatorship of conservation activities" that appeared to be developing and identifying the chair of the NRC Division of Biology and Agriculture in Washington as the culprit. Adams reported Shelford's comments to Griggs, who replied, "I knew of course . . . that Shelford would attack with all means at his disposal." In a later letter to Adams, Griggs wrote more forcefully: "I think you are right that we have one man only with whom to deal and that he will not be diverted or stopped by anything short of the clear-cut decision which he asked for."[43]

Once the problem was clearly defined, Shelford set a firm course. As usual, his viewpoint was practical and grassroots. In fact, he enjoyed fracases, controversies, and intrigue when an issue was worth the fight. In a short article appearing in *Science* in the late fall of 1944, while he was on sabbatical leave, Shelford addressed the conservatism of scientific societies that refuse to apply their scientific principles and the inevitable consequences of such refusal. He closed saying;

> Agencies representing special fields of knowledge, some of it technical, can not make presentations through another less scientific agency. To minimize misconstructions and misrepresentations, public application of scientific principles and the needs of future research should be urged by the specialists themselves. Human society, which supports research, will hold scientific men and the societies which they constitute responsible for failure to urge the application of their knowledge directly and simply whenever it is in the interest of society to do so. No scientific society devoted to research should fail in fulfilling this obligation.[44]

Continuing the private side of his battle, Shelford declared to Charles Adams: "It is my opinion that if the Committee on Preservation is discontinued, it will very likely wreck the cooperation which has been built up with local societies, etc. They are interested in preservation and not in study."[45]

Early in 1945, Albert Hazen Wright, an eminent zoologist from Cornell, wrote Shelford that he was distresed about current happenings and that he agreed with Shelford's *Science* article. Wright had served earlier on the now defunct NRC Committee for the Preservation of Natural Conditions, of which he reported:

> Whenever there was a disposition on the part of that committee to accomplish something and not sit on ten haunches awaiting something that mighty Washington might put in our laps, we would get a hush-hush from fearful people. Time and time again individuals in the Research Council would try to sit on us and say we should not be aggressive, independent. We had a committee of ten men who in no way were in government service and therefore could be independent. . . .
>
> Now in the light of the passing of that committee of the National Research Council, imagine my surprise at finding much the same forces trying to do much the same sort of thing for the committees of the Ecological Society of America. I do not want everything stemming from Washington. The sticks once in awhile have ideas and know the facts better than the city streets.[46]

Wright had put his finger on another real problem in his last sentence—the failure of some ESA members to understand all the facts. Even people on the executive committee were guilty of this. Alfred Redfield, president of ESA in 1945, for example, thought the study committee was concerned simply with ecological research; he was not aware of its role as a supplier of vital information for the potential action of the preservation committee. In fact, both committees were needed for preservation tasks. Unsuccessfully, Shelford requested more time to clarify these points. Eventually, however, the executive committee withdrew its recommendation that the preservation committee be abolished, recommending instead that it become a fact-finding body only, effectively duplicating what the study committee had been doing for many years. The executive committee called this a "redirection" and "strengthening" of preservation efforts. Shelford called it foolishness. These attempts to clarify the issues, and argue the wording of the referendum statements, continued into May of 1945. Redfield finally called a halt to the matter in a letter to Shelford: "I think the discussion of the statement has gone as far as is profitable. I want to express my appreciation of your frankness in presenting your point of view with which I am afraid I have not always been in agreement."[47]

Shelford was not finished by any means. Six weeks before the referendum he sent out a private letter to many ESA members, for which he expected to be "expelled from the society." After summarizing events since his private ballot in 1943, Shelford got to the heart of his concern. He claimed an attempt was being made to emasculate the preservation committee, abolish the ESA's role as a leader in nature preservation, and centralize conservation activities in Washington. These ends were assisted, he suggested, by the striking overlap of senior officials from the NRC's Division of Biology and Agriculture with ESA officers since 1936. "It is my impression," he said, "that this interlocking has been brought about by a desire of some persons in the Ecological Society to further grants for research."[48]

The following excerpts from replies to his letter prove that Shelford was not without support:

> I am really concerned about the situation wherein everybody seems to be definitely committed to the idea that you can find all the facts you want but you simply must not do anything about them.

> I think the Society should be free at any time legislation is justified by scientific knowledge, to make itself felt in no uncertain way.

> The well-known pressure groups frequently make such nuisances of themselves that what they have to say is discounted and at times their motives are also suspect. These are two charges that could not be leveled against the Ecological Society.

> When I was at Cleveland I was amazed at the secrecy with which the Executive Council was surrounded and the fear [that] various members of the Society had of even approaching the Executive Council. It seemed to me that there was a large amount of foggy understanding of the aims and purposes of the Committee on Preservation of Natural Conditions.

> Dear Shelford: You're right.[49]

In July 1945 the society voted by mail on the following amendment to the bylaws defining the duties of the preservation committee:

> It shall encourage the preservation of natural conditions by providing information and advice to those interested in securing sound legislation for this purpose, but shall not have authority to take direct action designed to influence legislation on its own behalf.

Direct action was defined as presenting resolutions or taking part in "political, pressure group, or propaganda activity." Yet supplying information or advice on the ecological implications of activities related to preservation was allowable, and the "privilege of the Committee to ask the Society to take direct action" was not restricted.[50]

The amendment was approved 213 to 115. "The vote was undoubtedly influenced," opined Kendeigh, "by the prestige of the Executive Committee, especially among members whose interests were not directly involved, in the same way as the larger response with strikingly opposite results was affected by Shelford in his earlier [1943] questionnaire." For Shelford it was a stinging defeat, but he was not seriously discouraged. He quickly busied himself with plans for an independent preservation organization.[51]

In December 1945, Shelford sent a personal check for three hundred dollars to Harold Hefley of Texas Technological College to be used "for the primary purpose of forming an organization to carry on the kind of work formerly done under the auspices of the Ecological Society of America." Hefley was designated secretary-treasurer of a floating preservation committee. Within a few weeks, Hefley sent a letter endorsed by fourteen ecologists, including four past presidents of ESA, and a draft constitution for an "Ecologists' Union" to four hundred supporters of the old preservation committee. Shelford and Hefley felt they could realistically expect two to four dozen interested people to join them. Word of their endeavor spread rapidly: Weese wrote to Shelford, "Evidently the animals are becoming stirred up." In early March 1946 Hefley reported a "vigorous, enthusiastic and favorable response," on the strength of which he proclaimed the founding of the Ecologists' Union. Eighty-three ecologists became charter members.[52]

Next the fate of the ESA preservation committee had to be decided. Neither Shelford, Newcombe, nor Kendeigh thought the committee could function effectively if it could not take autonomous action. At the ESA business meeting on March 29, 1946, in St. Louis, Newcombe recommended that his committee be abolished; his recommendation was approved. Kendeigh resigned from the chair of the study committee, which remained alive.

That same week saw the first meeting of the embryonic Ecologists' Union, also in St. Louis. Its objective was the "preservation of natural biotic communities, and encouragement of scientific research in preserved areas." Charles Kendeigh was commissioned as general chair until decisions about a constitution, officers, and a board of governors were settled. Kendeigh and Newcombe again found themselves chairing study and preservation committees, but under new colors. Shelford started to breathe easier.[53]

Membership continued to increase, reaching 158 by December 1946. At the Boston meeting that month, a board of governors that included Shelford was approved. The Ecologists' Union seized upon many of the issues the ESA had previously addressed, vigorously lobbying Congress and making its new presence felt. During 1947 the union involved itself in a drive for an international park on the Minnesota-Canada border, in strong opposition to the transfer of western grazing lands from federal to state or private control, and in the perennial pleading for the creation of a grassland preserve. An important step toward maturity occurred in December 1947 at the Chicago meeting: a permanent constitution was adopted, and Lee Dice of the University of Michigan and Asa Weese were elected the first president and vice-president, respectively. Membership increased to 191 people. Two years later under Weese's presidency, the union boasted 294 members, and Shelford had been named a patron.[54]

This relatively rapid increase in membership came with the addition of scientists who were not strictly ecologists; and vice-president George Fell was anxious to increase the rolls even faster by taking in nonscientists with "varied talents, occupations, and personalities to contribute their efforts to the organization." Fell, a botanist, had taken courses in animal ecology at Illinois under Shelford and Kendeigh. He teamed up with board member Richard H. Pough, of the American Museum of Natural History, to urge the union to expand, or even affiliate with a larger group. Fell had tentative plans for a "Nature Conservancy," modeled somewhat after the recently formed organization of the same name in England. With his wife, Barbara, George Fell developed a high-priority list of one hundred natural areas that they felt must be preserved—but who would buy them?[55]

The organization that would eventually acquire and assist in the preservation of several million acres of natural areas with the help of its celebrated, multimillion-dollar revolving capital fund was born September 11, 1950, in Columbus, Ohio, when the Ecologists' Union changed its name to The Nature Conservancy. Stanley Cain, of the

University of Michigan, was elected president; and George Fell, vice-president. Shelford and Richard Pough served on the board of governors. The group's objectives remained the same, differing little from those of the small group of twenty-five commissioned by ESA president Ellsworth Huntington back in 1917.

During the academic year 1964–65, when Shelford was in his eighty-eighth year, he received in his mail a copy of a page from the University of Illinois President's Report. Below penciled congratulations from university president David D. Henry, it read:

Nature Conservancy Honors Accomplishments of Professor Shelford

The Nature Conservancy, a national organization devoted to the preservation of natural areas of the United States, honored Dr. Victor E. Shelford, professor emeritus of zoology, at its annual meeting [on August 22, 1964] on the Urbana-Champaign campus.

Professor Shelford was cited for his 20 years as chairman of the Ecological Society's Committee on the Preservation of Natural Conditions, his establishment in Trelease Woods of the first University ecological research area in America, his [participation in the] founding of the Nature Conservancy, and for his scholarly writings.

The Conservancy now has more than 6000 members.

In 1989, The Nature Conservancy listed more than 535,000 members and 300 corporate associates, managed a national system of 1,000 nature sanctuaries, and operated 54 field offices and regional chapters. Since 1951, it has participated in the preservation of almost four million acres of land and water in the United States, the Virgin Islands, Canada, the Caribbean, and Latin America. Current projects include training and assistance in ecosystem preservation in Colombia, a state heritage program, special work in wetlands conservation, and aggressive work for long-term protection of endangered species and natural communities, including restoration of tallgrass prairie. The Nature Conservancy has become the leader in preserving diverse portions of the natural world throughout the Western Hemisphere.[56] Shelford would be immensely pleased.

7

ENDINGS
1946–1968

During the late forties and early fifties, the United States sought to resolve the conflicts between postwar idealism and reality in the midst of a population explosion and a remarkable outburst of prosperity. As soon as ration books, khakis, Navy blues, and civil defense helmets were put away, Americans quickly took up private interests again. Although housing was desperately short, most people had jobs. Despite their rising incomes, many Americans took some time to believe fully that the depression was behind them. Thousands of veterans descended on college campuses, delighting their instructors with their earnest thirst for education. In 1948, Americans were shocked by the Berlin blockade, spry Harry Truman's smashing upset of Thomas E. Dewey, and zoologist Alfred C. Kinsey's remarkable new book on human sexual behavior. A year later, the State Department reported that China had gone Communist, and President Truman announced tersely, "We have evidence an atomic explosion occurred in the USSR."[1]

Except for an occasional "holy mackerel" or "heavenly days" in response to all this change, Shelford ignored it in favor of his own research plans and activities. He now occupied Vivarium 203A, furnished with a desk, swivel chair, and small typewriter table. On one corner of his desk stood an old Spencer dissecting microscope issued him in 1917 and beside it, a more recently acquired Leitz microscope.

He greatly appreciated the vivarium space, given the arrival of three more grandchildren at home between 1945 and 1949. Yet he was not happy about his compulsory retirement and once complained, according to Illinois zoologist Donald Hoffmeister, that "his status was not emeritus, but rather demeritus." He still considered himself active in every way, and so did others. "I always think of you as young, as I knew you," wrote Shelford's old Chicago mentor, Charles Child, from Stanford. "To find you have been retired is a surprise, but we all come to it. I am glad you can keep working."[2]

Truly, Shelford loved working and usually admired evidence of it anywhere. But it was too much when he spied termites busily tunneling into his shrubs, trees, and even the porch steps of his Urbana house. So he embarked on his own experimental termite control program. He sprayed these animals with chlordan and noted high mortality. Then he applied 1 percent aqueous chlordan to the soil near his house foundation, porch footings, and chimney base. Deciding to determine the continuing effects of this single chlordan application, he compared termites exposed to treated soil with a control group of termites in untreated soil each year for five years. Chlordan toxicity persisted during the five-year period, indicated by significantly higher termite paralysis and subsequent mortality in chlordan-treated soil. This project inaugurated a period of seven years from 1949 to 1956, during which he published sixteen papers (only five on termites). He was well into his seventies when he finished.[3]

Naturally, in 1947 he found it difficult to give up the chair of the university's Committee on Natural Areas and Uncultivated Lands, a position he had held tenaciously since 1930. He served so long because he believed the committee's mission to be absolutely vital to ecological research at Illinois. He fought constantly for more authority, while opposing the control of woods and fields by the university physical plant, an office that Shelford firmly believed was simply meddling in matters it did not adequately understand. High on the committee's priority list since the mid-thirties had been the designation of natural areas to be used for research and teaching in the biological and soil sciences. In the early forties the committee supported a plan to connect Trelease and Brownfield woods, east of Urbana, along the west branch of the Salt Fork River, a corridor of almost 1,000 acres; by 1946 they had reduced the plan to 200 acres. At that time, Robert Allerton, of

Monticello, Illinois, gave the university several thousand acres of second-growth floodplain forest and a small portion of virgin upland on both sides of the Sangamon River, 1,500 acres of which were to be used for education and research. Shelford, who had been developing plans for studies on the effect of solar radiation on living organisms, pushed hard for the creation of a research facility in the proposed Robert Allerton Park. He hoped also to establish correlated studies on campus and at Trelease and Brownfield woods. To accomplish this, Shelford suggested to Carl Hartman, chair of zoology and physiology, that they obtain a hefty quarter-million-dollar, long-term grant. Robert Allerton Park became a reality, but the solar radiation research facility never materialized because both Shelford and Hartman retired without convincing anyone else to pick up the project.[4]

In the summer of 1948, Shelford drove east to attend his niece Dorothy Shelford's wedding to Carl Parmelee in Elmira, New York. A snapshot shows him, a snappily dressed professor in a three-piece suit, standing at ease by his big Buick, not looking his seventy-one years. Yet his feelings did not match his demeanor. Shelford estimated that the value of his pension had been cut by inflation about 27 percent since his retirement two years earlier, and the fact lay like a thorn in his side. By 1951, the reduction amounted to 44 percent for all University of Illinois pensions granted since 1940. Plainly, retired academic people were hurting. Predictably, Shelford began agitating for just treatment of university emeriti immediately after retirement. In 1946 his report to colleagues showed that about two-thirds of Illinois emeriti were serving in scholarly and other professional capacities, largely without remuneration. He noted in his report five years later that some emeriti were drawing pensions as low as $95 per month, while monthly state welfare payments were set at $125. In 1951 he helped generate a petition, signed by seventy-two Illinois emeriti, requesting cost-of-living adjustments to pensions. University president George Stoddard suggested in reply that the committee of emeriti work with the Illinois State Pension Laws Commission to get approval for pension reform. Sadly, four years later in 1955 the commission still disapproved of their plan for cost-of-living increases. With no choice but to adapt to his small income, Shelford pared down his society memberships and journal subscriptions, sold off some books that he felt others could profitably use, and put himself in trim for unfinished research and writing.[5]

Of immediate interest to Shelford were the voluminous quantitative population data for resident and seasonal forest animal species that he and his students had collected from Trelease Woods since 1933. When graphed, the abundance of spiders, chinch bugs, squirrels, and birds, for example, showed striking cyclic fluctuations over a thirteen-year period. There were very few data sets like this in existence, and it still fascinated Shelford to sort out and identify the chief environmental factors behind the cycles. He had no doubt that experiments should concentrate on certain sensitive times, such as the breeding period and the early growth of young animals and plants. A case in point was the chinch bug. Bug population increases in Trelease Woods and the upper Mississippi Valley dating back to the nineteenth century were correlated with relatively narrow limits of solar ultraviolet light and optimum moisture. Together, Shelford believed these conditions provided an effective reproductive stimulus for the bugs. He argued similarly for quail (*Colinus virginianus*) data from Illinois and other midwestern states and showed that population of antelope (*Antilocapra americana*) in Yellowstone Park and prairie chicken (*Tympanuchus*) in Illinois correlated with moisture levels and the duration of sunshine during the preceding mating season. The data suggested that sunlight and moisture affect the number of young born; the quality of vegetative cover; and, in the antelope, milk production, as well.[6]

Yet Shelford quickly discovered two serious obstacles to further progress. First, biologists needed more frequent on-site measurements of solar radiation, moisture, temperature, and other environmental characteristics from habitats where the populations of interest actually lived. Second, the often outmoded architectural and landscape design of biology buildings and their crowded, shaded surroundings made it impossible for biologists who worked with plants and animals other than "fungus, cockroach, and white rats" to carry out laboratory and outdoor controlled experiments effectively, especially when solar radiation was to be measured. This was true for the vivarium, and even the Illinois Natural History Survey, housed on campus, had no space or facilities to "tie a fox out-of-doors," Shelford quipped.[7]

Searching for a remedy, Shelford bristled at the opinion of university officials—including the physical plant—that "all work on live animals can be done away from campus and the instruction laboratory." He replied that if the university did not develop integrated facilities to support modern ecological work on campus, a "million dollars in special laboratories and equipment will be spent two miles out, and another quarter-million per ten years in extra assistance, transportation, and inconvenience." Saddened and angered by the growing tendency around the nation to provide less space for the study of living things, Shelford lamented, "Clearly, the architects, campus planners, and the test tube biologists are quite willing to decide many things they know nothing about."[8]

Marshaling his forty-five years of experience, he decided to design his own campus complex for the life sciences. His plan called for small, glass-roofed experimental houses and kennels, cages, gardens, and ponds. One full acre of land was to be cleared to receive unobstructed sunlight year-round and the main building would be located so as not to shade the smaller research facilities. The entire grounds would cover about nine acres. Shelford published a short, descriptive paper, in which he provided diagrams and outlined his rationale for the life science complex, with the hope that some college or university would build one. His own university did not take advantage of his work. Yet he had made an important proposal for furthering fundamental animal population studies and had focused attention on what is now known as photobiology. In 1953 he received the Nash Conservation Award for this paper.[9]

Eighteen years after Shelford's death, a copy of a letter written by him in 1955 and apparently never shown to anyone turned up in the vivarium files. It read:

> To whom it may concern:
>   This is written without malice toward any individual but in protest against certain administrative policies of the University of Illinois notably in connection with the Physical Plant and its operations. The writer is constrained to state that none of his property, books, papers, maps, or equipment housed in any University building at the time of his death, shall be given to the University of Illinois library or any department. However, my executors may give such articles as are not desired or claimed by the members of my family, to my colleagues in the field of animal ecology or Zoology.[10]

Like most people, Shelford thrived on praise for a job well done, with the caveat that it not be excessive. He received with great pleasure the encomium given in September 1955 at an ESA banquet in East Lansing, Michigan, which summed up his tremendous achievements:

> Ecology is one of the more recent sciences, and that part devoted to animals traces its origin to a period within the life span of many of us. In spite of the youthfulness of animal ecology, it is one of the most active divisions of zoology. Much of the development and even much of the present activity and scope of modern ecology can be traced to the work of Victor E. Shelford. . . . Dr. Shelford is the father of modern animal and bioecology, and gave it the impetus which has enabled it to reach its present state. . . . His keen mind has enabled him to explore the various avenues of approach to ecology and to turn readily from one approach to another as he saw fit. . . . With retirement, Dr. Shelford has continued to devote his time to ecological research and is still a familiar figure wherever ecologists meet. . . . All ecologists owe an appreciation to Dr. Shelford for the contributions he has made to animal ecology.[11]

Shelford, however, was not one to allow even well-deserved praise to distract him. He renewed his efforts to finish his book, *The Ecology of North America,* and by mid-December he thought he was almost there. Early in 1956 he sent the manuscript to the Macmillan Publishing Company. Nearing eighty, Shelford was still erect and vigorous, still keeping up with the literature, still writing and studying in the vivarium, and still driving his Buick. He even got into the field to study a bit of remnant prairie in northern Illinois. The ecologist, Richard Brewer, a graduate student at Illinois during the late fifties, recalls that most students knew Shelford as "that quiet man with the glasses." He had not given up the occasional beer at Bidwell's and the attendant opportunity to deliver a broadside on conservative Eisenhower Republicans or to criticize the Nature Conservancy for not moving fast enough with preservation work. Returning with Brewer from a meeting on Nature Conservancy business in the late fifties, Shelford remarked, "Near as I can tell, they're turning into another g.d. Audubon Society." He felt then that empire-building had become a higher priority than preservation, but by the early sixties The Nature Conservancy really hit its stride as an agent for preservation.[12]

At home, Victor still enjoyed carpentry and house repairs. His grandchildren got their share of his attention when he could tear himself away from his writing: they saw he was dead serious about that. "Grandpa was a stern man," his granddaughter Betty remembers, "but we had fun . . . when he played Santa at Christmas or when he made believe he was a big bear." Teenaged Betty was the oldest grandchild, and Victor took pride in her being much like himself—competitive and persistent. The same was true for his youngest grandchild, Mary, who began competitive swimming at seven. Victor also continued to socialize with friends and to attend fall receptions for new faculty. On his eightieth birthday, Lois surprised him by inviting in the neighbors for cake and ice cream. Victor was by then old enough to joke about meeting his Maker, but he was not too old to keep up with his ongoing projects.[13]

He had brought a few things to a close, though. The year before (1956), he had gone expectantly to the joint meeting of the ESA and the American Institute of Biological Sciences (AIBS) in Storrs, Connecticut. The Nature Conservancy was holding its meeting at Storrs, too. At The Nature Conservancy conference, Shelford met with retiring president Richard Pough and his successor, botanist Dick Goodwin; got filled in on recent land acquisitions of more than 5,000 acres; and genuinely enjoyed the sense of dedication and urgency shown by the members. The ESA and AIBS meetings were a far different matter. Although he heard a fine paper on radioecology by Stan Auerbach and then ran into Nathan Riser, another former student from Illinois, he declared, "This is the last meeting I shall attend. None of my friends are at any of the meetings now. They're all gone."[14]

Seeing he would be so near, Victor had planned a side visit with his cousin, Hilda Tillman, in upstate New York. He took the train to Albany and then traveled by bus westward to Oneonta, where Hilda and her husband met him. From there they drove over to the Tillman's summer house on Goodyear Lake about 25 kilometers south of Cooperstown. Hilda thought Victor looked remarkably fit; it had been about twenty years since she had seen him. They reminisced about Chemung, the old Shelford farm, and their uncle, William Rumsey, with whom Shelford had stayed when he was a student at West Virginia at the turn of the century. They also talked of Shelford's impending book, and he promised to send them a copy when it was published. This was his last visit to the country of his boyhood.[15]

That fall Shelford was stunned when Macmillan rejected *The Ecology of North America*. The book would cost too much to publish and attract too small a market wrote the publishers with regret. Shelford gathered up the manuscript and submitted it to Ronald Press. It came back with another rejection in June 1958. He was told that Ronald Press very much appreciated considering this voluminous work (it ran well over a thousand manuscript pages) by an eminent ecologist, but that the manuscript was too long and needed a "more meaningful structure."[16]

Now Shelford really turned cantankerous, as well he might, given the forty-two years he had spent on the work. He sought the advice of his Illinois colleague, Charles Kendeigh. For a while they considered breaking the massive work into several parts, with one volume by Shelford and his friends and former students, Clarence and Marie Goodnight, tentatively titled *Ecology below the Mexican Border*. They gave up that idea when the University of Illinois Press came through with an offer. Colleagues and graduate students helped trim the manuscript under the able direction of Charles Kendeigh. Kendeigh recounts his participation in the project:

> I agreed to revise the manuscript and see it through to publication only after I got assurance from the UI Press that it would be accepted. Shelford wanted me to put my name on the title page but I refused. The book was the culmination of his life's work and besides I did not agree fully with some things in it.[17]

The agreement with Illinois Press in 1959 required Shelford to contribute several thousand dollars to match a similar amount from the press. The Illinois Foundation seemed a good bet for additional support. Even the chief potential obstacle proved benign: "I discovered to my dismay," Shelford said in a later interview, "that the head of the foundation was the same man I had quarreled with in public about faculty salaries. Fortunately he helped support the book anyhow."[18]

If Shelford ever entertained thoughts of giving up on something, it might have been this book. Kendeigh sensed as much, particularly when Shelford suffered from mounting high blood pressure in 1959 just before the Illinois Press deal was made. On his desk at the vivarium, Shelford kept the motto, "I am old and have had many troubles, but most of them never happened." Increasingly it gave him pause.[19]

During that time Shelford found a constructive outlet for his frustration in the Grassland Research Foundation. He had been on the board of directors off and on since the foundation was formed in 1939. After almost twenty years, it still had little success in attracting support for long-term research and preservation of grasslands. In 1958 at the age of eighty, Shelford assumed the presidency. The foundation could claim a roster of 250 members, but not much action. Shelford first resigned from the board of directors and then drew up a streamlined set of bylaws for foundation approval. He also persuaded the officers and directors to protect the foundation's endowment by investing in United States securities and proposed that if the foundation should fail, all endowment funds would go to the Oklahoma Academy of Science to stimulate grassland research. "Under no circumstances should the funds be allowed to go into the hands of an organization east of the Mississippi River or west of the Rocky Mountains," Shelford stipulated.[20]

Nevertheless, the foundation did not prosper. By 1959 membership had dropped by half, and two years later Shelford reported that the foundation was "bogged down again." He did not believe there was enough interest to sustain the organization and suggested that any interested people join The Nature Conservancy. Yet the matter dragged on, and in 1963 Shelford threatened to "demand the return of $210 which I gave to [the foundation] in order to keep it alive," if the members could not agree to disband. Shelford's money amounted to about 11 percent of the total endowment that reverted to the Oklahoma Academy of Science when the Grassland Research Foundation was legally dissolved in 1966.[21]

During 1961 Shelford readied his book for publication. Likewise he put the finishing touches on his last paper, which dealt with the important role of physical factors during sensitive periods in the life histories of plants and animals. He took great pride in keeping up with his field at eighty-four. His biggest disappointment was not having his wife with him after retirement. His loneliness, though, made him even more self-reliant. As "independent as a hog on ice" is how he often described himself. He took interest, too, in young John Kennedy's presidency: he was curious to see how the Democrats would handle the accumulated problems of the previous turbulent eight years.

That fall he arranged a trip to Washington, D.C., to visit his son, John, and to deliver a paper at AAAS meetings in late December, giving lie to his resolve about meetings a few years back. Then early in December while at supper in a restaurant at Green and 6th streets in Urbana, he suffered a stroke and wound up in the hospital for a few days. His physician said he had most certainly had hypertension for many years. (Later Shelford admitted he regretted never having regular checkups). Nevertheless, he recovered well and doggedly insisted on going to Washington but agreed to skip the AAAS meetings. So he took his last train trip with his sixteen-year-old grandson, Shelford Bennett—two Shelfords traveling on the old man's favorite conveyance.[22]

Almost one year later Shelford had a second stroke at home. Initially he could not speak, but again he recovered nicely in the succeeding months. Yet he was perceptibly weaker, needing both rest and his cane more. Still, nothing short of collapse could have spoiled his triumph in seeing *The Ecology of North America* published in 1963. Just shy of fifty summers had rolled by since he announced to that seminar group at Puget Sound his intention of writing a treatise on the natural communities of North America. Now in his eighty-sixth year, he had tangible evidence of his life's work.

The time was opportune for a book like his: since the fifties, the news had been filled with stories of nuclear fallout, pesticides, space exploration, and population growth. Shelford realized $1300 in royalties during the first eight months alone. The book sold for ten dollars and was favorably reviewed. "He was pleased with the way the book was received," his daughter, Lois, remembers. "It was even on sale in one of our department stores." Despite its popular success, the book is not for the unattentive reader. It is a lengthy, well-illustrated synoptic description of the principal biomes and their distinctive plants and animals, climate, soils, and topography from Alaska and northern Canada south to lower Central America and the larger islands of the West Indies. Shelford's attractive promise to reconstruct the ecological conditions of primeval North America prior to European colonization helped sales, no doubt, but was understandably only partially realized. What the book did well was present a snapshot of the continent through the lens of a man who had studied most of it diligently. It provided standards for checking the health of nature. Consequently, besides delighting the curious layperson, the book has served over the years as a reference for ecologists, ornithologists, anthropologists, wildlife biologists, ichthyologists, herpetologists, botanists, behaviorists, soil scientists, foresters, entomologists, range and refuge managers, and park workers—exactly the audience for which Shelford wrote the book.

Shelford was arguably the only person of his time with the experience and the audacity to write this book, this encyclopedic natural history of an entire continent. Only one who had tramped the dunes and forests with Cowles and Child, written and tussled with Clements, peered at specimens with Davenport, worked with Forbes, listened to Charles Whitman, and read Brehm and Semper could have undertaken such a work; and, only a full-sighted man with a keen eye for the landscape and the physical stamina of a draft horse could have carried it through.[23]

Shelford lived from day to day after the strokes, enjoying simple pleasures and creature comforts. On the whole, he had come to terms with his life and gained a measure of contentment. As the hectic schedules and worries of bygone days dropped away, he gradually slipped into a comfortable routine: listening to the radio, watching television, reading, chatting and comparing obituaries with cronies who stopped by, taking short walks, and lunching out several times a week with his son-in-law, Edmond Bennett. He still went regularly to fall receptions on campus for new faculty members. He also managed to keep abreast of such modern developments as the space program, which he supported because it increased knowledge and understanding of the world. He did not believe, however, that space should be pursued at the expense of critical environmental needs. For him the plight of the natural world remained foremost.

In the summer of 1966, Shelford fractured his pelvis when he fell trying to turn a water valve in his cellar. He recovered and learned to walk well again. In 1967, he stumbled on his front steps and smashed a femur, for which he gained a metal pin in his leg. Afterward he required a walker and wheelchair for extra support, but he could still walk without them for short distances if he had to. That September he eagerly put his mobility to test at a faculty reception: University of Illinois president David Henry had arranged a special celebration for Shelford's ninetieth birthday, and he could not cut the cake properly sitting down. He wrote a note to President Henry later:

I want to thank you and your beloved wife for the birthday cake that you gave me on my birthday, with appropriate ceremonies. The cake was excellent, and tasted as good on the inside as it looked on the outside. I appreciate it very much.[24]

Victor needed more and more rest, but according to his daughter, "his mind was still sharp though his body gave out." Zoologist Hurst Shoemaker regularly cut his hair, and Charles Kendeigh occasionally stopped by to chat. He was surprised by a visit from his nephew Harry Shelford and his wife, who traveled from Dundee, New York, and found Victor looking unexpectedly frail.

Occasionally, Shelford reminisced about the people and places of his life: the magnificent Indiana dunes and tiger beetles playing at the water's edge; his snug laboratory in Hull Zoology Building at Chicago and the excitement of the early days in animal ecology; his young wife and small children; the Chemung fields and forests where his fascination for the outdoors began; his father, mother, and brothers; and even early boyhood hikes on the hilly road to Oak Hill School.[25]

In 1968, The Ecological Society of America honored Shelford as Eminent Ecologist of the year. When called on to say a few words at the Urbana ceremony, Shelford was overcome with emotion and could not speak. Old friends and colleagues greeted him in his wheelchair, and he missed recognizing only a few on sight.

In December of that year, Shelford eagerly watched television coverage of Apollo 8, the first mission to send humans to the moon. The day after Christmas he told Lois he felt very hot and restless. She took him to Mercy Hospital later that afternoon, fully expecting him back home in a few days. The next day, December 27, she visited him in the hospital; his breathing was shallow and troubled. He died suddenly at 5:30 P.M. of uremia and pneumonia. He never did see the dramatic picture from the lunar horizon of Earth hanging 111,550 miles out in space, surrounded by inky blackness, with its lifegiving land and water partially hidden by wispy clouds. This vision of the planet in its wholeness symbolized Victor Shelford's life's work, and neither his nor any other ecologist's words could ever match it.[26]

Epilogue

Midmorning on Monday, December 30, 1968, three days after Shelford's death, a small memorial service was held for him in the Mittendorf Chapel in Champaign. Family members and close friends made up the congregation, and the pastor of Wesley United Methodist Church in Urbana, Rev. Joseph N. Peacock, gave the eulogy:

> We are gathered to celebrate the long and productive life of Victor Ernest Shelford. Few men are granted so long a span of years, even fewer to be so immensely productive through their life. . . . Nature was Victor Shelford's domain. [Although he] did not theologize much about nature and his relationship to it, he did absorb himself religiously and with joyful abandon to its understanding. . . . Especially we are thankful today for [his] lifetime of devotion to teaching and to his students; for his love of nature and his efforts to preserve and keep it whole. . . . We thank [the Lord] for his devotion to family, his absorption in the community, and for all the great gifts in his life.

Victor was buried in Urbana's Eastlawn Cemetery beside Mabel.

Eight months later, *Time* magazine presented its readers with a story on ecologists, the "new Jeremiahs," and ran photographs of a few prominent North Americans: Eugene Odum's picture appeared along with Barry Commoner's. The article, which called 1969 the "year of ecology," marked the popular beginnings of the environmental movement of the seventies, an explosion of public concern the likes of which Shelford and his generation of colleagues could only have dreamed. Soon ecologists were pushed willy-nilly into unfamiliar limelight, with much more expected of them than they could, or would, deliver. Few people could yet tell an ecologist from an environmentalist, and fewer knew that ecology as such had been around for more than three-quarters of a century. Astute people, though, noticed how uncommonly strange the aggregate principles and prescriptions of the nature doctors appeared alongside the beliefs, dreams, and behavior of humans beings in modern-day society. Today awareness of environmental problems is widespread, and ecology is gaining stature and authority as a road to planetary health and safekeeping.

If Victor Shelford were here now, with his dedication, his tenacity, with all his medals and scars, he would perhaps recognize a likeness of himself in the words of Robert Frost:

> They would not find me changed from him they knew,
> Only more sure of all I thought was true.

Appendix 1

DOCTORAL THESES SUPERVISED

BY VICTOR SHELFORD

1912–1942

University of Chicago

Allee, Warder Clyde, "The Effect of Dissolved Gases on the Behavior of Isopods" (1912).

University of Illinois

Andrews, Harry Lee, "An Ecological Study of Living Forms in the Kelp Beds of Monterey Bay and Carmel Bay, California, with Suggestions as to the Hydroclimatic Influences" (1938).

Bird, Ralph Durham, "Biotic Communities of the Poplar Savanna of Central Canada" (1929).

Blake, Irving Hill, "A Comparison of the Animal Communities of Coniferous and Deciduous Forests" (1925).

Cahn, Alvin Robert, "An Ecological Study of Certain Southern Wisconsin Fishes" (1924).

Dexter, Ralph Warren, "The Marine Communities of a Tidal Inlet at Cape Ann, Massachusetts: A Study in Bio-Ecology" (1938).

Dirks, Jane Claire, "Comparison of Douglas Fir–Hemlock and Oak-Hickory Biotic Communities" (1941).

Eddy, Samuel, "A Study of Fresh-water Plankton Communities" (1930).

Fautin, Reed Winget, "Biotic Communities of the Northern Desert Shrub Biome in Western Utah" (1941).

Gersbacher, Willard Marion, "The Development of Stream Bottom Communities in Central Illinois" (1932).

Hayward, Charles Lynn, "Biotic Communities of Mt. Timpanogos and Western Uinta Mountains, Utah" (1942).

Jewell, Minna Ernestine, "Effects of the Hydrogen Ion Concentration and Oxygen Content of Water upon Regeneration and Metabolism in Tadpoles" (1918).

Johnson, Maynard Stickney, "Activities and Distribution of Certain Wild Mice in Relation to Biotic Associations" (1925).

Jones, Sarah Elizabeth, "Ecological Studies on Forest Invertebrates" (1938).

Kendeigh, Samual Charles, "The Role of Temperature and Other Environmental Factors in the Life of Birds" (1930).

Powers, Edwin Booth, "The Influence of Temperature and Concentration on the Toxicity of Salts to Fish" (1918).

Rasmussen, Daniel Irvin, "Biotic Communities of the Kaibab Plateau" (1932).

Roberts, Tilden Wirt, "Light and Certain Endogenous Factors as Regulators of Community Activity for the Crayfish, *Cambarus virilis* Hagen" (1942).

Roney, Harland Burr, "The Effect of Temperature and Light on Oxygen Consumption and Rate of Development of *Helisoma*" (1938).

Shackleford, Martha Wheatley, "Animal Communities of an Illinois Prairie" (1927).

Smith, Vera Grace, "Animal Communities of the Deciduous Forest Succession" (1927).

Townsend, Myron Thomas, "Hibernation in Certain Cold-Blooded Animals" (1925).

Twomey, Arthur Cornelius, "The Bird Population of an Elm-Maple Forest with Special Reference to Food, Territory and Seasonal Variations" (1937).

Weese, Asa Orrin, "A Study of the Animal Ecology of an Illinois Elm-Maple Forest" (1922).

Wells, Morris Miller, "The Relation of Fishes to Ions in Their Natural Environments" (1915).

Appendix 2

STUDENTS COMPLETING A MASTER'S THESIS
UNDER VICTOR SHELFORD
1909–1947

University of Chicago

1909   Isely, Frederick B.

1912   Norcross, Katherine

1914   Phipps, Charles F.

University of Illinois

1915   Chenoweth, Homer E.

1920   Young, Nellie

1921   Leonard, Veda F.

1926   Hyde, Arthur S.

1927   Savage, John R.

1929   Rice, Lucille
       Rutherford, Harriet
       Stein, Hilda A.

1930   Firkins, Curtis J.
       Heck, Florence A.

1931   Goff, Carlos C.
       Stewart, Lyle F.

1932   Beall, Geoffrey

1932   Carpenter, John R.
       O'Donnell, Donald J.
       Olson, Sigurd F.

1933   Dawson, Emily S.
       Gearhart, Harry E.

1934   Allen, Katherine G.

1935   Dunlap, Mary M.
       Lindeborg, Robert G.
       Miller, Lawrence F.
       Plaster, Helen L.
       Steel, Wade A.

1936   Costley, Richard J.
       Kanatzor, Charles
       Rush, John M.

1937   Black, Charles T.
       Martin, Dorothy L.
       Stevenson, Clarence A.

1938   Harper, Marguerite
       Salisbury, Douglas H.

1939   Koestner, Joseph

1939	McKean, Russel R.	1941	Yapp, Robert G.
	Ostendorf, Marie	1942	Thompson, Donald R.
	Schupp, Alice L.	1943	Tucker, Marie
	Williams, Carl E.		
	Wright, Bertrand A.	1945	Sparkman, Drew
1941	Flori, Beatrice M.	1946	Degani, John G.
	Graff, Blanche A.		Mackenthum, Kenneth M.
	Hanson, Hugh	1947	Auerbach, Stanley I.

Chronology of the Life of Victor Shelford

1877   Born on September 22 in Chemung, New York, to Alexander Hamilton Shelford and Sarah Ellen Rumsey Shelford.

1884–1894   Attended Oak Hill School, Chemung, New York.

1894   Taught in Chemung County schools.

1895–1897   Attended Cortland Normal and Training School, Cortland, New York.

1896   Received third grade teaching certificate from the state of New York.

1897–1899   Taught in Chemung County schools.

1898   Entered Waverly High School in Tioga County, New York.

1899   Graduated from Waverly High School on June 21.

     Entered West Virginia University as a special student in October.

1900   Appointed tutor in zoology at West Virginia University.

1901   Entered the University of Chicago on September 30.

1903   Received the S.B. degree from Chicago with honors in zoology on June 16.

1907   Received the Ph.D. degree *summa cum laude* from Chicago on June 11, with a dissertation titled, "The Life-Histories and Larval Habits of the Tiger Beetles."

     Elected to Phi Beta Kappa.

     Married Mary Mabel Brown in Chicago on June 12.

     Appointed associate in zoology at the University of Chicago in July.

1908   Conducted research work on tiger beetles in European museums from January through March.

1909   Appointed instructor in zoology at the University of Chicago as of July 1.

1912   Daughter, Lois, born on May 13.

1913   *Animal Communities in Temperate America* published.

     Son, John, born on July 28.

1914   Appointed assistant professor of zoology at the University of Illinois.

1914–1929 Served as biologist in charge of the research laboratories for the Illinois Natural History Survey.

1914–1930 In charge of marine ecology research at Puget Sound Biological Station, Washington, during alternate summers.

1915 Elected first president of the Ecological Society of America.

1920 Appointed associate professor of zoology at the University of Illinois.

1926 *A Naturalist's Guide to the Americas* published.

1927 Appointed professor of zoology at the University of Illinois.

1929 *Laboratory and Field Ecology* published.

1939 *Bio-Ecology,* coauthored with Frederic Clements, published.

1939–1940 Served as acting chair of the Department of Zoology at the University of Illinois.

1940 Wife, Mabel, died of malaria in El Salvador on August 17 at age sixty-four.

1940–1941 Chaired Department of Zoology at the University of Illinois on formal apointment.

1946 Instrumental in formation of the Ecologists' Union.

Named emeritus professor by the University of Illinois.

1950 Founding of The Nature Conservancy on September 11.

1961 Suffered a stroke in December.

1962 Suffered a second stroke, also in December.

1963 *Ecology of North America* published.

1966 Fractured hip but recovered well.

1967 Fractured a femur.

1968 Designated Eminent Ecologist by the Ecological Society of America in September.

Died on December 27 at age ninety-one of uremia and pneumonia.

Abbreviations

RC/	Author's interview
RCC/	Author's correspondence
VES-PP	Victor E. Shelford personal papers*
UIA-VES	University of Illinois Archives, Victor E. Shelford Papers
UIA-HBW	University of Illinois Archives, Henry B. Ward Papers
UIA-AGV	University of Illinois Archives, Arthur G. Vestal Papers
UIA-WML	University of Illinois Archives, Wilbur M. Luce Papers
UIA-CZ	University of Illinois Archives, Charles Zeleny Papers
UI–LA&S, D	University of Illinois, Liberal Arts and Sciences, Dean's Office
UI–Sen.Inq.	University of Illinois, Senate Inquiry, Educational Organization and Procedures, 1925–26
UI–Bd. of Tr.	University of Illinois Board of Trustees
VES–UI Acad. Appt. F.	Victor E. Shelford, University of Illinois, Academic Appointment File
UI-Al. F.	University of Illinois Alumni File
UIA-NHS	University of Illinois Archives, Natural History Survey Subject File
WMUA-CCA	Western Michigan University Archives, Charles C. Adams Papers
ECA-WCA	Earlham College Archives, Warder C. Allee Papers
HIA-DSJ	Hoover Institution Archives, David Starr Jordan Papers
UWy-CC	University of Wyoming, American Heritage Center, Frederic Clements Collection

*Lois Shelford Bennett graciously allowed me to examine countless documents and photographs of her father's, which are herein denoted as Victor E. Shelford personal papers.

ABBREVIATIONS

APS-CBD   American Philosophical Society, Charles B. Davenport
Papers

UCA-FRL   University of Chicago Archives, Frank R. Lillie Papers

Victor Shelford is referred to by the initials V. E. S. throughout.

Notes

PROLOGUE

1. Shelford, *Animal Communities in Temperate America* (1913); Shelford, *Biol. Bull.* 14, no. 1 (1907), 9–14; Shelford, *J. Linn. Soc. Lond. Zool.* 30 (1908), 157–84; University of Chicago, *Register of Doctors of Philosophy* (1927), 102; Cittadino, *Studies in History of Biology* 4 (1980), 171–98; Tobey, *Saving the Prairies.*

2. McIntosh, *The Background of Ecology* (1985), 23–27; Egerton, "Ecological Studies and Observations before 1900" in Taylor and White (eds.), *Issues and Ideas in America* (1976), 339–42; Cravens, *The Triumph of Evolution* (1978), 18–33; Allen, *Life Science* (1975), 1; Tobey, *Saving the Prairies* (1981), 24.

CHAPTER I. THE MAKING OF AN ECOLOGIST

1. Shelford, "Notes on the Rumsey Family" (1949), reprinted from *The Independent Republican*, Goshen, New York; Heidgerd and Shoemaker, *The Schoonmaker Family*, pt. 1 (1974), 7.

2. Shelford, "Memorandum" (1944), mimeo.; RC/Dorothy Parmelee 7/13–14/ 1981; RC/Lois Bennett 8/16–22/1981.

3. Shelford, "Memorandum" (1944), mimeo.; VES-PP; author's observations 7/ 14/1981. Phoebe Shelford's maiden name was also Shelford; she and Eli were first cousins.

John Shelford III's immigration to California in 1855, with his wife and four children, gave rise to the "California Shelfords" with whom Victor visited years later during some of his western field trips. Eli Shelford's house (later Alexander's) burned down in 1944. The fire consumed everything, including copies of Victor's books given to his youngest brother, Wiley. The farm was worked until 1945 by Wiley's sons, Harry and Donald. Succession has now claimed a good portion of the land. Thomas Shelford's house has been restored and is now owned—as is the Shelford farm—by Thomas's great-granddaughter, Mrs. Hope Wohnus Perry. The earlier Eli Shelford house, where Victor was probably born and lived for a short time, no longer stands.

4. VES-PP; RCC/Lois Bennett 5/23/1981; RC/Lois Bennett 8/16–22/1981; RC/ Clarence and Marie Goodnight 6/17/1983; Langdon, *The Chemung Historical Journal* (1979); RCC/Martha Squires 5/14/1981.

5. VES-PP; author's observations 7/14/1981; Lois Bennett to Joy Elliott 9/28/

1971 (courtesy of Lois Bennett); RC/Dorothy Parmelee and George Wohnus 7/14/ 1981; RCC/Clarence and Marie Goodnight 5/14/1981; RC/Lois Bennett 8/16/1981; RC/Drew Wetzel 11/15/1981; RCC/Hilda Tillman 2/3/1982.

6. Commager, *The American Mind* (1950) 48, 50, 52; Faulkner, *Politics, Reform, and Expansion* (1959), 141; RC/Lois Bennett 8/22/1981; VES-PP.

7. Adams, *The Education of Henry Adams* (1918), 127; VES-UIAcad. Appt. F.; RCC/Robert Checca 12/3/1981; Miller, *The Academy System* (1969), 131; Rogers, *Oswego* (1961), 313, 58–59, 65; Park, *Cortland* (1960), 21–22, 86.

8. Rogers, *Oswego* (1961), 16–17; Park, *Cortland* (1960), 24; RCC/Robert Checca 12/3/1981; Francis J. Cheney to Whom It May Concern 7/26/1897, VES-PP; VES-UI Acad. Appt. F.

9. RCC/William Gillespie 7/2/1981; RCC/Lois Bennett 5/23/1981; Towner, *Our County*, pt. vii (1892), 21; VES-PP; RCC/John Brisbane 4/24/1981.

10. *National Cyclopaedia of American Biography*, vol. 25 (1936), 401–2, vol. 1 (1898), 279–80, and vol. 11 (1901), 376–77.

11. Osborn, *Fragments*, pt. 1 (1937), 306; Strausbaugh, *Castanea* 3 (1938), 53–55; RCC/William Gillespie 7/2/1981; Lois Bennett to Joy Elliott 9/28/1971; VES-PP; Guthrie (ed.), *Arboretum Newsletter* 11, no. 1 (1961). The Rumsey Trail was formally dedicated and opened to the public on May 6, 1961. The trail is close to Morgantown but gives the illusion of remoteness. It winds through scenic Hidden Hollow and includes some of the more interesting plants to be found in the West Virginia University Arboretum.

12. RCC/John Brisbane 4/27/1981; *American Men of Science*, vol. 6 (1938), 740; John Johnston to Whom It May Concern 9/30/1901, VES-PP; V. E. S. to Henry B. Ward, UIA-HBW, box 7; V. E. S. to Ecology Club, University of Illinois, 5/22/1957 (RCC/Richard Brewer 1/12/1983).

13. *American Men of Science*, vol. 9 (1955), 223; *Who Was Who*, vol. 5 (1973), 150; West Virginia University Catalogue, 1900–1903, 191; Edwin Copeland to Whom It May Concern 6/18/1901, VES-PP; Edwin Copeland to Jerome Raymond 3/3/1901, VES-PP.

14. VES-PP; J. R. Day to V. E. S. 4/19/1901, VES-PP; *American Men of Science*, vol. 3 (1921), 290; R. Cobb to V. E. S. 6/20/1901, VES-PP; George Cernan to V. E. S. 7/ 18/1901, UIA-VES, box 1.

15. *National Cyclopaedia of American Biography*, vol. 25 (1936), 402; Storr, *Harper's University* (1966), 75; Evans and Evans, *William Morton Wheeler* (1970), 72–73; taped interview with V. E. S. by M. Brichford, 3/24/1965, UIA-VES, box 2; VES-PP; George Vincent to V. E. S. 10/4/1901, VES-PP.

16. Storr, *Harper's University* (1966), 324; Transcript of V.E. Shelford's undergraduate work, University of Chicago; "Circular," University of Chicago, 1902–3; VES-PP. Later, during his graduate studies, Shelford audited courses with Lillie in physiology of development and vertebrate embryology (transcript of V.E. Shelford's graduate work, University of Chicago.)

17. Transcript of V.E. Shelford's undergraduate work, University of Chicago; RC/ Lois Bennett 8/17–22/1981; VES-PP; Lois Bennett to Joy Elliott 9/28/1971; RCC/

David Williams 12/2/1981; Riddle, *Biog. Mem. Nat. Acad. Sci.* 25 (1949), 78; *Who Was Who* (1950), 345.

18. Davenport, *Science* 14, no. 348 (1901), 317–23; transcript of V.E. Shelford's undergraduate work, University of Chicago; Riddle, *Biog. Mem. Nat. Acad. Sci.* 25 (1949), 81; *Bot. Gaz.* 33, no. 5 (1902), 400; Davenport, *Decennial Publications of the University of Chicago, The Biological Sciences* 10 (1903), 155–76; Davenport, *Science* 8, no. 203 (1898), 685–89. Davenport's early study of animal ecology at Cold Spring Harbor included a brief gross comparison of the brackish sand beach fauna there with the sand beach fauna from Lake Michigan near Jackson Park, Chicago. Davenport also made some remarks on the preadaptation of animals to particular habitats and the success of these animal species if the appropriate habitats were "found." Shelford did not cite Davenport's 1903 paper until more than two decades later (Shelford and Towler, *Publ. Puget Sound Biol. Sta.* 5 (1925), 33–73).

19. Shelford, *Ill. Biol. Monogr.* 3, no. 4 (1917), 6, 13, 46–47, and *passim;* transcript of V. E. Shelford's undergraduate work, University of Chicago; VES-PP; Sarah Ellen Shelford to V. E. S 7/15/1903, VES-PP; Mabel Brown to V. E. S 7/24/1903 and 9/7/1903, VES-PP; President W. R. Harper to V. E. S 9/15/1903, VES-PP.

20. Newman, *Bios* 19, no. 4 (1948), 218, 220–21; "Circular," University of Chicago, 1903–7, *passim;* Shelford, *J. Morphol.* 3, no. 4 (1917), 613; Shelford, *Ill. Biol. Monogr.* 3, no. 4 (1917), 11. Charles Whitman was the first director of the Marine Biological Laboratory at Woods Hole (1888–1908).

21. Tansley, *J. Ecol.* 28 (1940), 450–52; Hyman, *Biogr. Mem. Nat. Acad. Sci.* 30 (1957), *passim;* Oppenheimer, *Essays* (1967), 16–17; Hyman, *Science* 121, no. 3151 (1955), 717–18; transcript of V.E. Shelford's graduate work, University of Chicago; "Circular," University of Chicago, 1903–7, *passim;* Shelford, *Ill. Biol. Monogr.* 3, no. 4 (1917), 11; Shelford, *J. Morphol.* 22, no. 3 (1911), 613. Shelford said (at the age of seventy-nine) that he had taken a course with Child in the spring of 1902 (*Bull. Ecol. Soc. Amer.* 37, no. 1 [1956], 33); however, Shelford's undergraduate transcript shows no biological science course for spring 1902. Child's natural history interests are illustrated by his presentation of a paper titled "Litoral [sic] Fauna of Pacific Grove, California" before a meeting of the American Society of Zoologists at the University of Chicago on April 1, 1905 (*Science* 21, no. 544 [1905], 853). Child taught graduate courses in regeneration and cytology, both of which Shelford audited as a graduate student (transcript of V.E. Shelford's graduate work, University of Chicago).

22. Transcript of V.E. Shelford's graduate work, University of Chicago; "Circular," University of Chicago, 1903–4, 113; Cook, *Cowles Bog* (1980), 11–13, 15–20; Tansley, *Ecology* 16, no. 3 (1935), 284; Cowles, *Bot. Gaz.* 31, no. 2 (1901), 73; Cowles, *Science* 19, no. 493 (1904), 879; taped interview with V. E. S. by M. Brichford 3/24/1965, UIA-VES, box 2. At the age of eighty-eight, Shelford said that the development of his interest in ecology was a gradual process (taped interview with V. E. S. by M. Brichford 3/24/1965, UIA-VES, box 2). My interpretation of the evidence is that his early developing interest ignited after close contact with Cowles.

23. Shelford, *Ill. Biol. Monogr.* 3, no. 4 (1917), 38, 42, 116; Shelford, *J. Linn. Soc. Lond. Zool.* 30 (1908), 160, 164; Kwiat, *Entomol. News* 16, no. 4 (1905), 128.

24. *J. New York Entomol. Soc.* 14, March (1906), 5–8; Horn, *Deutsche Entomologische Zeitschrift,* suppl. to vol. 2 (1905); Shelford, *Ill. Biol. Monogr.* 3, no. 4 (1917), 38, 42. The world list of Cicindelidae stands somewhere near 1300 species; there have been perhaps fewer than 100 species described since the early 1900s. North American species (including those found in Panama and the West Indies) total 192, 147 of which belong to the genus *Cicindela* (RCC/Gary Dunn 8/13/1982).

25. VES-PP; Roethele, *The Nature Conservancy News* 30, no. 6 (1980), 13–14; Cowles, *Bot. Gaz.* 31, no. 3 (1901), 174–75, 177.

26. Tobey, *Saving the Prairies* (1981), 102, 107–8; Cowles, *Bot. Gaz.* 31, no. 2 (1901), 81; Cowles, *Science* 19, no. 493 (1904), 881, 884; Sears, *The Living Landscape* (1966), 77; Cowles, *Bot. Gaz.* 31, no. 3 (1901), 177. Cowles's pioneering efforts have more recently been examined further. Radiocarbon and tree ring dating were applied to successional stages at Lake Michigan dunes. The oldest dunes (approximately twelve thousand years) still had black oak associations with low soil fertility and pH, presaging less favorable conditions for succession toward beech-maple forest, which is found in moist lowlands. Thus succession proceeds to a variety of destinations, depending on a complex of biotic and abiotic factors (Olson, *Bot. Gaz.* 119, no. 3 [1958], 125–70). Cowles would be delighted.

27. Shelford, *Biol. Bull.* 21, no. 3 (1911), 130; Mayer and Wade, *Chicago* (1969), 242–44; taped interview with V. E. S. by M. Brichford 4/1/1965, UIA-VES, box 2.

28. Sears, *The Living Landscape* (1966), 80; Drude, "The Position of Ecology" in Rogers (ed.) *Congress of Arts and Sciences, Universal Exposition* (1906) 179, 187–88; Shelford, *Biol. Bull.* 14, no. 1 (1907), 9–14. Since Shelford's pioneering tiger beetle studies, microhabitat distribution and the life cycles of species have been little studied, although the beetles are quite well known taxonomically. Recent studies in Nebraska, Missouri, Kansas, Oklahoma, and in the Indiana Dunes, however, support Shelford's general conclusion that different species of *Cicindela* occupy distinct microhabitats and show highest activity and abundance during different seasons. (Willis, H. L. *The Univerisity of Kansas Science Bull.* 47, no. 5 [1967], 145, 212–16, 217, 219, 306; Knisley C. B. *Proc. Indiana Acad. Sci.,* 88 [1979], 212, 215, 216). I recently (1983) visited the southern end of Lake Michigan to explore Shelford's early collecting areas. Some of his original study sites in northwestern Indiana are now occupied by residential developments and steel plants. Others, including the Indiana Dunes State Park and the more recently developed Indiana National Lakeshore, are still choice areas for collecting tiger beetles and for finding the plants and animals associated with particular lakeshore successional stages.

29. Shelford, *J. Linn. Soc. Lond. Zool.* 30 (1908), 157–84; University of Chicago, *Register of Doctors of Philosophy* (1927), 102; transcript of V. E. Shelford's graduate work, University of Chicago; Shelford, *Bull. Ecol. Soc. Amer.* 37, no. 1 (1956), 33–34; VES-PP. The University of Chicago Library's copy of Shelford's Ph.D. thesis is a bound reprint of the published Linnaean Society paper cited above (RCC/Douglas Sprugel 2/24/1981; RCC/Leigh Van Valen 5/22/1981); in the paper, Shelford acknowledges his debt to the "Staff of Zoology," (p. 180). Elsewhere (Lillie, *J. Morphol.* 22, no. 1 (1911), xlv-xlvi), Shelford is described as a student of Charles Whitman. I

interpret this description to be related to Whitman's position as head of the department—a quite powerful position at Chicago, autocratically benevolent in Whitman's example. On tape (with Maynard Brichford 3/24/1965) Shelford simply said "Whitman approved my thesis." Shelford's graduate transcript shows his final examination was passed Wednesday, May 15, 1907, in zoology and botany, *summa cum laude*, and is signed by C. O. Whitman. Shelford's fields of study are listed as "Zoology (Evolution and Field Zoology) and Botany (Plant Ecology)," in Whitman's writing. In line with my interpretation of scientific influences on Shelford, Sprugel (*Bull. Ecol. Soc. Amer.* 61, no. 4 [1980], 198–99) indicates the important roles of Cowles and Child on Shelford. I would also add Charles Davenport, not however, in the way described by Brewer (*Occasional Papers of the C. C. Adams Center for Ecological Studies*, no. 1 [1960], 7).

30. Shelford, *J. Linn. Soc. Lond. Zool.* 30 (1908), 157, *passim*, 179; Haeckel, *Wonders of Life* (1904), 95.

31. VES-PP; RC/Lois Bennett 8/17/1981; Sarah Ellen Shelford to V. E. S 6/19/1907, VES-PP.

32. VES-PP; transcript of V. E. Shelford's graduate work, University of Chicago; University of Chicago Annual Register, 1907–8, 351; Harry Shelford to V. E. S 10/29/1907; RC/Lois Bennett 8/16/1981; VES-PP.

33. RC/Lois Bennett 8/22/1981; Mabel Shelford to Dr. and Mrs. Issac Brown and Walter Brown 12/27/1907; VES-PP Mabel Shelford to Brown family 12/29/1907 and 1/2/1908, VES-PP.

34. VES-PP; Shelford, "Memorandum" (1944), mimeo.; Lois Bennett to Joy Elliott 9/28/1971. Henry Dickens was an orphan who was raised by the first John Shelford (1769–1840) and his second wife, Nancy Ruff; he married into the Shelford family (Shelford, "Memorandum" [1944], mimeo.).

35. VES-PP; Mabel Shelford to Brown family 1/15/1908, VES-PP; Shelford, *Ill. Biol. Monogr.* 3, no. 4 (1917), 8, 9, 11, 12.

36. VES-PP; Mabel Shelford to Brown family January 1908, VES-PP; Mabel Shelford to Florence Shelford 1/28/1908, VES-PP.

37. VES-PP; Mabel Shelford to Mrs. Isaac Brown 2/12/1908 and 2/21/1908, VES-PP.

38. VES-PP; Mabel Shelford to Walter Brown 3/13/1908, VES-PP; Mabel Shelford to Brown family 3/4/1908 and 3/10/1908, VES-PP; Mabel Shelford to Mrs. Isaac Brown 3/26/1908, VES-PP.

39. Burnham (ed.), *Science in America* (1971), 271; Shelford, *J. Morphol.* 22, no. 3 (1911), 552n; Shelford, *J. Linn. Soc. Lond. Zool.* 30 (1908), 157, 180.

CHAPTER 2. CHAMPION OF ANIMAL ECOLOGY

1. Shelford, *Biol. Bull.* 21, no. 1 (1911), 9–10.

2. Shelford, *J. Morphol.* 22, no. 3 (1911), 552n; Shelford *Biol. Bull.* 21, no. 1 (1911), 11, 12; Shelford, *J. Morphol.* 22, no. 3 (1911), 553, 591 (word order changed),

596, 602. For a discussion of the revolt of young biologists of the early twentieth century against speculative morphological, evolutionary, and phylogenetic work of the nineteenth century, see Allen, *Life Science in the Twentieth Century* (1975), 8–10.

3. Taped interview with V. E. S. by M. Brichford 3/24/1965, UIA-VES, box 2; Kleinschmidt, *Neue Deutsche Biographie* (1955), 569–70; Thomson, "Introductory Essay" in Brehm, *From North Pole to Equator* (1895), xxv-xxxi; Möbius, *Die Auster (The Oyster)* (1877), 723; Semper, *Animal Life* (1881), *passim;* Howard, *Biograph. Mem. Nat. Acad. Sci.* 15 (1932–34), *passim.*

4. Cowles, *Amer. Nat.* 42 (1908), 265; Cowles *Am. Nat.* 43 (1909), 357. There had been tension between the newer physiological point of view and the older natural history approach since the latter part of the nineteenth century. Botanists felt that tension directly, as plant ecologists employed physiology to elucidate their understanding of plants in nature (Ganong, *Science* 19, no. 482 (1904), 494; Cittadino, *Studies in the History of Biology* 4 (1980), 171–81, 192–94; Farber, *Journal of History of Biology* 15, no. 1 (1982), 145–52).

5. Shelford, *J. Morphol.* 22, no. 3 (1911), 554, 593–94, 611; Shelford, *Biol. Bull.* 23, no. 6 (1912), 334–35. No doubt Shelford felt pressure to pursue experimental work during his years at Chicago. Increased prestige and wider career opportunities typically awaited the people who did so (Cravens, *The Triumph of Evolution* [1978], 29–34; McIntosh, *The Background of Ecology* [1985], 23–24, 68.)

6. Shelford, *Biol. Bull.* 23, no. 6 (1912), 335, 354; Shelford, *J. Morphol.* 22, no. 3 (1911), 584, 587, 590, 598, 602, 613.

7. Shelford, *Biol. Bull.* 21, no. 1 (1911), 11, 30; Shelford, *Biol. Bull.* 23, no. 6 (1912), 333, 354. Ecologists do not use the word *mores* anymore, but Shelford had anticipated an idea that would appear in expanded form six decades later with evolutionary connections and implications for ecological succession: the life history strategies of species (McIntosh, *The Background of Ecology* [1985], 87–88).

For a review of ecological succession, including comments on the importance of ecosystem and community processes versus species population processes, see McIntosh, "The Relationship between Succession and the Recovery Process" in Cairns (ed.) *The Recovery Process in Damaged Ecosystems* (1980), 11–62 (especially 43–47).

8. Shelford, *Biol. Bull.* 21, no. 1 (1911), 11–18, and *passim.* Since Shelford's early work on streams, ecologists have employed several factors to predict stream faunas, e.g. gradient, width, erosion, and drainage area. These factors are interrelated and all include some measure of stream size (Sheldon, *Ecology* 49, no. 2 [1968], 197; Barila *et al., J. Appl. Ecol.* 18 [1981], 130). Ecologists today, however, do not consider succession vis-à-vis geological base leveling.

9. Shelford, *Biol. Bull.* 21, no. 3 (1911), 136, 149, and *passim;* Shelford, *Biol. Bull.* 22, no. 1, (1911), 34; Cowles, *Bot. Gaz.* 51, no. 3 (1911), 171; Cowles, *Bot. Gaz.* 31, no. 3 (1901), 147. Shelford was ably assisted in his pond work by several graduate students at Chicago. One of these students was Warder Clyde Allee.

10. Shelford, *Biol. Bull.* 22, no. 1 (1911), 32–33.

11. Shelford, *Biol. Bull.* 23, no. 2 (1912), 60, 93, and *passim.* Much evidence is available for a higher correlation in the distribution of forest insects, spiders, birds, and

mammals to the physiognomy of plants, rather than to the presence of particular plant species (MacMahon, "Successional Processes" in West *et al.* (eds.), *Forest Succession* [1981], 301).

12. Shelford, *Biol. Bull.* 23, no. 2 (1912), 94, and *passim*. Recent work also shows marked changes in species composition and relative abundance of bird species in the same five plant stages Shelford studied (Van Orman, M.S. thesis, Western Michigan University, Kalamazoo [1976]). Ecologists have since learned more about the role of animals in the ecology and development of soils. Arthropod species of the forest floor fragment leafy and woody litter, transport detrital and fecal material in the soil profile, graze on microbial decomposer populations, and assist in some nutrient cycling. The changes in dominant soil arthropod species as plant succession proceeds are not yet clarified (Seastedt, *Annu. Rev. Entomol.* 29 [1984], 25–46; Usher *et al.*, *Pedobiologia* 23 no. 2 [1982], 126–44; Wallwork, *Annu. Rev. Entomol.* 28 [1983], 109–30).

13. Shelford, *Biol. Bull.* 23, no. 2 (1912), 93; Shelford, *Biol. Bull.* 23, no. 6 (1912), 359, 362, 363. Interested readers should refer to Shelford's *Animal Communities in Temperate America* (1913) for a listing of animal communities (pp. 39–41) and a diagram of suggested successional stages (pp. 311–13). Much of the terminology, e.g. strata, association, formation, did not originate with Shelford, although he used it to illustrate the Lake Michigan communities. Shelford's stress was on the mores—a word he did suggest. Ecological terminology would become more complex in a few decades. During the period from 1907 to 1912, it was exciting to deal with sand dunes and forests near Lake Michigan. The community structure and dynamics were striking, and clear to experienced observers—they would not be as clear in other situations in the future.

Shelford taught a course in experimental behavior and ecology at Chicago during 1913, the forerunner of a course in physiological ecology he taught at Illinois beginning in 1915 (University of Chicago Annual Register, 1912–13, 271). To better prepare himself for teaching and for his research plans, Shelford audited courses in physical chemistry and physiological chemistry at Chicago during the winter of 1913 (transcripts of V. E. Shelford's graduate and post-graduate work, University of Chicago).

The five papers on succession appeared in a seventeen-month period between June 1911 and November 1912. *Biological Bulletin*, where Shelford published, was a journal started by experimentally inclined biologists at Woods Hole. The managing editor during 1911–12 was Frank Lillie.

14. VES-PP; RCC/Margaret Fallers and Lorna Straus 12/17/1982 and 12/21/1982; University of Chicago Annual Register, 1907–8 to 1910–11, *passim; Science* 32, no. 827 (1910), 633; *Science* 32, no. 833 (1910), 859. Shelford contributed to instruction by mail in the correspondence study department of University Extension beginning when he was a graduate student in 1905 and continuing through the academic year 1913–14. He offered individual instruction in general biology, general zoology, general morphology and natural history of the invertebrates, advanced animal ecology, and economic zoology. Extension activities, and particularly correspondence study, were major interests of President Harper who believed in bringing the university "into direct contact with human life and activity" (University of Chicago Annual Register, 1906–7

to 1912–13, *passim;* Storr, *Harper's University* [1966], 197). Some of Shelford's regular courses were also considered part of the two-year curriculum offered to students of Rush Medical College, with which the university was affiliated (RCC/Daniel Meyer 2/10/1983).

15. Shelford, *Ill. Biol. Monogr.* 3, no. 4 (1917), 6, 41, 54, 112, 116; VES-PP; V. E. S to C. C. Adams 10/7/1910, WMUA-CCA, 1910 folder. The Shelfords visited with sons and daughters of John Shelford III and their families in San Francisco, on the Russian River, and in the Sacramento Valley (Shelford, "Memorandum" [1944], mimeo.).

16. Sarah Ellen Shelford to V. E. S and Mabel Shelford 1/29/1911, VES-PP; Alexander Shelford to V. E. S and Mabel Shelford 2/16/1911, VES-PP.

17. Sarah Ellen Shelford to V. E. S and Mabel Shelford 4/9/1911, VES-PP; Wiley Shelford to V. E. S and Mabel Shelford 4/9/1911, VES-PP. Letters to Shelford from his mother during these years typically included news from home about farming matters, mortgage foreclosures, deaths, illnesses, and local social gatherings and meetings. His father's letters were shorter and generally referred to weather and farm chores. Victor's parents were Methodists, other family members Baptists. Sarah Ellen is described by living family members as a "very sweet, hardworking, patient woman" and as a woman who had a knack for "getting people to work for her" when they visited the Shelford home (VES-PP; RCC/Lois Bennett 6/3/1982; RC/Lois Bennett 8/17/1981 and 8/21/1981; RCC/Hilda B. Tillman 2/3/1982).

18. VES-PP; V. E. S to C. C. Adams 10/17/1910, WMUA-CCA, 1910 folder; Lois Bennett to Joy Elliott 9/28/1971.

19. Newman, *Bios* 19, no. 4 (1948), 225–26; University of Chicago Annual Register, 1910–11, 358; Shelford, *Bull. Ecol. Soc. Amer.* 37, no. 1 (1956), 33.

20. Newman, *Bios* 19, no. 4 (1948), 226, 235; University of Chicago Annual Register, 1911–12, 357, 359–60, and (1907–8 to 1912–13), *passim.*

21. VES-PP.

22. Allee, *The Social Life of Animals* (1958), 5–6; Shelford, *J. Ecol.* (1915), 3–4; W. C. Allee to V. E. S 2/6/1911; VES-PP. W. C. Allee taught school before going to Earlham College at age nineteen. He graduated in 1908. After receiving his Ph.D. at Chicago, he spent a year as instructor of botany at Illinois and then filled a series of positions before returning to Chicago in 1921, where he remained until 1950. He then served at the University of Florida until his death in 1955. Allee was a renowned contributor to animal ecology and behavior, including group behavior in humans, and was a leader in the "Ecology Group" at Chicago during the 1930s and 1940s. The group embraced "organicism," believing there was a tendency in nature for evolution toward cooperation, e.g. colonies, flocks, tribes, cities, and finally world economies. After World War II the group disbanded (Schmidt, *Biogr. Mem. Nat. Acad. Sci.* 30 [1957], *passim;* Worster, *Nature's Economy* [1977], 326–31). Allee and four midwestern colleagues wrote the monumental *Principles of Animal Ecology* (1950).

23. W. C. Allee to V. E. S 2/6/1911, VES-PP; Allee, *The Social Life of Animals* (1958), 6; Allee and Tashiro, *J. Anim. Behav.* 4 (1914), *passim;* Shelford, *J. Ecol.* 3 (1915), 5.

24. Shelford and Allee, *J. Exp. Zool.* 14, no. 2 (1913), 208 and *passim;* Shelford, *Science* 48, no. 1235 (1918), 225–30; Shelford and Allee, Science 36, no. 916 (1912), 76. Biologists have modified Shelford and Allee's gradient tank to provide a steeper gas concentration gradient, believing this allows for a sharper fish preference. More shallow gradients—similar to Shelford and Allee's—are also more difficult to reproduce accurately. A criticism of steeper gradients is that they are not common in nature (Larrick *et al., Hydrobiologia* 61 (1978), 262–63). Many other complex refinements of Shelford and Allee's gradient tank have been made (Cherry and Cairns, *Water Res.* 16, no. 3 (1982), 263–301).

25. Shelford, *Animal Communities in Temperate America* (1913), 34; Shelford, *Biol. Bull.* 25, no. 2 (1913), *passim;* Shelford, *J. Anim. Behav.* 4 (1914), 39. In another 1914 paper (one of the more dense he wrote), Shelford argues for a better understanding of response phenomena in sessile and motile animals and plants. He discusses these in reference to theories of natural selection, adaptation, and the germ plasm—subjects he typically avoided. His argument closes with a discussion of biological science research strategy and priorities, emphasizing the need for a diversity of approaches and the importance of combining results from different investigations with a view to broader generalizations. In effect, the paper defends Shelford's method in physiological animal geography and makes a pitch for getting physiology out-of-doors (Shelford, *Amer. Nat.* 48 [1914], 641–74).

26. Shelford, *Biol. Bull.* 26, no. 5 (1914), *passim;* Shelford, *J. Ecol.* 3, no. 1 (1915), *passim.*

27. *Science* 38, no. 976 (1913), 314; *Science* 29, no. 1009 (1914), 660; *Science* 37, no. 965 (1913), 977; V. E. S to C. C. Adams 6/9/13, WMUA-CCA, 1913 folder; Engel, *Sacred Sands* (1983), 153–54, 318n. 44; V. E. S to C. C. Adams 2/14/1913, WMUA-CCA, 1913 folder; V. E. S to C. C. Adams 10/11/1913, WMUA-CCA, 1913 folder; C. C. Adams to S. A. Forbes 7/23/1913, WMUA-CCA, 1913 folder.

In 1909, the year after Charles Adams was hired by Stephen Forbes as an animal ecologist at Illinois, Henry B. Ward arrived at Illinois as the new chair of zoology. Within only a few months, Adams and Ward clashed, and Adams began a long correspondence with Charles Davenport, recounting suspicions that Ward was working against him and asking for advice. Davenport suggested Adams improve his communication with Ward and show the University of Illinois why "it should be unwilling to lose him" (C. C. Adams to C. B. Davenport 12/23/1909, C. B. Davenport to C. C. Adams 7/8/1910, C. C. Adams to C. B. Davenport 9/23/1910, all WMUA-CCA, appropriate year folders). The Illinois plant ecologist, Arthur Vestal, in a seminar at Champaign on 5/22/1957, said simply "H. B. Ward drove off Adams" (RCC/Richard Brewer 1/12/1983). Henry B. Ward was not an easy man to work for.

28. Shelford, *Animal Communities in Temperate America* (1913); Adams, *Guide to the Study of Animal Ecology* (1913); Shelford, *Science* 39, no. 1007 (1914), 580–81. Charles Adams's *Guide to the Study of Animal Ecology* grew into a book from what was planned as a a section of a report on cooperative ecological work between the Illinois State Laboratory of Natural History and members of the Ecological Survey Committee of the Illinois Academy of Science. In 1911, Adams, Forbes, and Shelford were committee members

(Adams, *Guide to the Study of Animal Ecology* [1913], vii; *Science* 33, no. 852 [1911], 670).

29. Adams, *Guide to the Study of Animal Ecology* (1913), 134; Shelford, *Animal Communities in Temperate America* (1913), 10, 20, and *passim*.

30. Elton, *Animal Ecology* (1962), xviii; Elton, *The Ecology of Animals* (1960), 30; Shelford, *Animal Communities in Temperate America* (1913) vi, 1, 13–15, 70–72, 87–90, 116–17, 153–55, 166–68; Pianka, *Evolutionary Ecology* (1978), 237–70; P.P.C., *Entomol. News* 25 (1914), 82–86, UIA-VES, box 3; W.L.M., *The Auk* 31 (1914), 120–23, UIA-VES, box 3; S. A. Forbes to V.E.S. 11/4/1913, VES-PP; V. E. S to S. A. Forbes 11/13/1913, UIA-NHS.

31. Shelford, *Animal Communities in Temperate America* (1913), 6; Shelford, *J. Morphol.* 22, no. 3 (1911), 606n; Elton, *The Pattern of Animal Communities* (1966), 33.

32. Elton, *The Pattern of Animal Communities* (1966), 34–35, 37; Summerhayes and Elton, *J. Ecol.* 11, no. 1 (1923), 232, 283; Elton, *Animal Ecology* (1927), 55–70. For a discussion of Charles Elton's contributions see D. L. Cox (1979) "Charles Elton and the Emergence of Modern Ecology," Ph.D. dissertation, Washington University, St. Louis.

33. V. E. S to C. C. Adams 10/11/1913, WMUA-CCA; R. H. Wolcott to V. E. S 3/27/1914, VES-PP. W. C. Allee commented to Thomas Park in the late 1930s, "Shelford had been 'encouraged' to leave on the grounds that if he stayed at Chicago there would be no promotion to tenure" (RCC/Thomas Park 5/18/1983). Frank Lillie wrote Shelford in mid-1914, saying: "I do not need to tell you again how sorry we are to lose you from the Department. But it would have been unwise to have remained, and would no doubt have been interpreted by the authorities as sign of weakness on your part." (F. R. Lillie to V. E. S 7/13/1914, UIA-VES, box 1). Adding to the dismal scene for Shelford at Chicago was the low number of advanced students in zoology—the fewest in many years. Shelford had only four students, as did Lillie and Tower. Strong had three, although Child and Newman had many undergraduate students in their invertebrate and elementary zoology courses. The depression also contributed to the problem. (V. E. S to C. C. Adams 2/14/1913, WMUA-CCA, 1913 folder).

Robert H. Wolcott was an enthusiastic field naturalist with a friendly personality and wide contacts. He was an authority on water mites and the birds of Nebraska. He received his M.D. degree in 1893 but never practiced. He originally came to the University of Nebraska at the urging of H. B. Ward, chair of zoology. Wolcott remained at Nebraska for forty years. It is probable that his influence was important for Shelford's long summer connection at Puget Sound Biological Station where Wolcott was a staff member (Ward, *Science* 79, no. 2054 [1934], 422–23).

34. V. E. S to C. C. Adams 5/19/1914, WMUA-CCA, 1914 folder; J. P. Goode to K. C. Babcock 4/25/1914, VES–UI Acad. Appt. F.; H. C. Cowles to K. C. Babcock 4/21/1914, VES–UI Acad. Appt. F.

35. H. B. Ward to K. C. Babcock 5/1/1914, VES–UI Acad. Appt. F.; S. A. Forbes to K. C. Babcock 5/12/1914, VES–UI Acad. Appt. F.; taped interview with V. E. S. by M. Brichford 3/24/1965, UIA-VES, box 2; S. A. Forbes to C. C. Adams 6/26/1908, WMUA-CCA, 1908 folder; Ward, *Science* 71, no. 1841 (1930), 380; RCC/Richard Brewer 1/12/1983.

36. "Memorandum Regarding Victor E. Shelford by K. C. Babcock and revised by S. A. Forbes and H. B. Ward," 5/18/1914, VES–UI Acad. Appt. F.; K. C. Babcock to E. J. James 5/26/1914, VES–UI Acad. Appt. F. In fact, during 1914–15, Shelford would receive (unknown to him) money from the state laboratory originally designated for a librarian's salary (taped interview with V. E. S. by M. Brichford 4/1/1965, UIA-VES, box 2). Morris M. Wells was Shelford's first doctoral student at Illinois, completing his degree in 1915. He served as an instructor at the University of Chicago from 1915 to 1919 and then founded General Biological Supply House (Turtox) in 1919 (*American Men of Science* [1921], 727). Wells was one of the earliest workers to study the effect of carbon dioxide on fish (Wells, *Biol. Bull.* 25, no. 6 [1913], 323–47).

37. K. C. Babcock to V. E. S 5/27/1914 and 6/1/1914, VES–UI Acad. Appt. F.; V. E. S to C. C. Adams 5/19/14, WMUA-CCA, 1914 folder; C. C. Adams to A. G. Vestal 5/27/1914, UIA-AGV, box 2; *Science* 39, no. 1013 (1914), 785; V. E. S to H. B. Ward 6/30/1914, UIA-CZ, box 6; E. J. James to V. E. S 6/13/1914, VES–UI Acad. Appt. F.

38. V. E. S to E. J. James 6/24/1914, VES–UI Acad. Appt. F.; H. B. Ward to V. E. S 6/20/1914 and V. E. S to H. B. Ward 6/30/1914 (two letters), UIA-CZ, box 6; author's observations 8/18/1981; University of Illinois Register, 1914–15 through 1945–46; V. E. S to C. Zeleny 7/25/1915, UIA-CZ, box 5. As far as I can determine, the vivarium was first occupied during February 1916 (RCC/Maynard Brichford 9/14/1983). On May 5, 1983, the building was formally dedicated as the Victor E. Shelford Vivarium. Shelford's daughter, Lois Bennett, and his grandson, Shelford Bennett, were guests of honor. I presented an afternoon address titled "Victor E. Shelford: The Roots and Making of a Pioneer Ecologist."

39. Shelford and Powers, *Biol. Bull.* 28 (1915), 332–33 and *passim;* Powers, *Biol. Bull.* 27, no. 4 (1914), 177–200. Edwin B. Powers was a Texan who received his A.B. at Trinity University, Texas, and his M.S. at Chicago (1913). He was a fellow at Illinois from 1915 to 1917 and received his Ph.D. degree under Shelford at Illinois in 1918 with concentration in ecology and biochemistry. His dissertation was titled "The Influence of Temperature and Concentration on the Toxicity of Salts to Fish." He spent several summers at Puget Sound Biological Station between 1919 and 1927 and from 1925 through 1947 was professor of zoology and head of the department at the University of Tennessee. During his career, he followed and expanded on his earlier interests in fish behavior, physiology, and toxicology and in the physiochemical relationships of natural waters. Powers is perhaps best known for his classic paper on the toxicity of salts, acids, drugs, etc., to the goldfish and the theoretical relationship between survival time and the concentration of toxic substances (*American Men of Science* [1949], 1982; Powers, *Ill. Biol. Monog.* 4 [1917], 127–93.)

40. F. R. Lillie to V. E. S 7/13/1914, UIA-VES, box 1; VES-PP.

CHAPTER 3. PROFESSOR AT ILLINOIS

1. Clayton, *The Illinois Fact Book* (1970), 42, 44; Tingley, *The Structuring of a State* (1980), 141–42; *Science* 40 no. 1043 (1914), 925.

2. University of Illinois Register, 1914–15 through 1940–41; UI–Bd. of Tr. report, 1916; Van Cleave, *Bios* 18, no. 2 (1947), 81–82, 84–88.

3. VES-PP; Adams, *Amer. Mus. J.* 7 (1917), 491–94. For a discussion of the application of scientific and technical principles to resource conservation in the early 1900s, see Hayes, *Conservation and the Gospel of Efficiency: The Progressive Conservation Movement* (1959).

4. Warren, *Biology and Water Pollution Control* (1971), 6; Shelford, *Bull. Illinois State Lab. Nat. Hist.* 11 (1917), 381. Not until the passage of the 1956 Water Pollution Control Act did the United States government gain the means for effective action in water pollution abatement and control.

5. Shelford, *Bull. Illinois State Lab. Nat. Hist.* eleven (1917), 381, 387, 406–7; Shelford, *Sci. Monthly* 9 (1919), 97; RCC/John Savage 8/29/1983. The indifference, even attraction, of fish to toxic solutions was later verified by other work (Jones, *J. Exp. Biol.* 25, no. 1 [1948], 22–34; Jones, *Fish and River Pollution* [1964], 144–51). The use of preference and avoidance tests on aquatic animals increased during the 1970s and early 1980s, e.g. studies of the behavior of animals in thermal and waste effluents in mixing zones of aquatic habitats. There now remains the task of increasing industrial and regulatory interest in this subject (Cherry and Cairns, *Water Res.* 16, no. 3 [1982], 264, 293).

6. Shelford, *Sci. Monthly* 9 (1919), 122 and *passim;* Shelford, *Geogr. Rev.* 9 (1920), *passim;* Shelford, *Publ. Puget Sound Biol. Sta.* 2, no. 39 (1918), 97, 103–4; V. E. S to S. A. Forbes 6/8/1918, UIA-NHS, Forbes Papers.

The Miles acid process for treating raw sewage was a method for removing bacteria and thickening the sludge by decreasing water content. The method probably went out of use in the 1940s (RC/Nancy Kinner 9/12/1983; Babbitt, *Sewage* [1932], 507).

7. V. E. S to D. S. Jordan 5/30/1917, HIA-DSJ, box 20, folder 2; D. S. Jordan to V. E. S 6/16/1917, UIA-VES, box 1; RCC/Stanley Auerbach 1/24/1984; RCC/Lois Bennett 2/19/1984; Senator R. LaFollette to V. E. S 11/7/1917, UIA-VES, box 1. The petitions Shelford refers to are those opposing the war. They were probably generated after the emergency convention of the Socialist Party held in St. Louis in April 1917 (Shannon, *The Socialist Party in America* [1955], 93–97.

8. Link, *American Epoch,* vol. 1 (1967), 234; Perrett, *America in the Twenties* (1982), 31; Dulles, *Twentieth Century America* (1972), 250–54.

9. Perrett, *America in the Twenties* (1982), 9–11, 101–2, 337, 373, 488–91; Lois Bennett to Joy Elliott 9/28/1971, Lois Bennett's personal papers; RC/Lois Bennett 8/17–22/1981; RCC/J. Savage 8/29/1983; RC/Dorothy Parmelee 7/13/1981; RCC/Dorothy Parmelee 9/7/1981. Shelford's father, Alexander, died June 22, 1922; his mother, Sarah Ellen, died November 14, 1924. Victor's parents, brothers, his Shelford grandparents, and some dozen other relatives are buried in Riverside Cemetery overlooking the Chemung River on old Route 17, a short distance westward from the junction with Snell Road (the Henpath).

10. RC/Lois Bennett 8/17–22/1981; Lois Bennett to Joy Elliott 9/28/1971, Lois Bennett's personal papers; author's observations 8/22/1981; RCC/Lois Bennett 10/29/1981 and 2/19/1984; Shelford, *The Ecology of North America* (1963), vii; Shelford, *A Naturalist's Guide* (1926), vii, 3, 14, 85.

11. Perrett, *America in the Twenties* (1982), 117, 118, 120, 122; Link, *American Epoch,* vol. 2 (1967), 326–29.

12. Shelford, *Bull. Illinois Nat. Hist. Survey* 16, no. 5 (1927), 311, 315, 317; V. E. S to S. A. Forbes 7/6/1917, UIA-NHS, Forbes Papers; V. E. S to S. A. Forbes 10/16/ 1918, UIA-NHS, Forbes Papers.

13. Shannon, *The Socialist Party in America* (1955), 87, 122–25; J. C. Fetterman to V. E. S 9/9/1920, UIA-VES, box 1; V. E. S to S. A. Forbes 9/10/1920, UIA-NHS, Forbes Papers; S. A. Forbes to V. E. S 9/10/1920, UIA-NHS, Forbes Papers.

14. Shelford, *Trans. Ill. State Acad. Sci.* 13 (1920), 259, 260–61; Shelford, *Bull. Illinois Nat. Hist. Survey* 16, no. 5 (1927), 318, 332, 351–53, 359, 419; Krogh, *Zeitschrift für Allgemeine Physiologie* 16 (1914), 163–177.

15. Shelford, *Bull. Illinois Nat. Hist. Survey* 16, no. 5 (1927), 313, 319–23; Shelford, *Ecol. Monogr.* 4 (1934), 492; Hagley, *Can. Entomol.* 105 (1973), 1085; Reidl, Croft, and Howitt, *Can. Entomol.* 108, no. 5 (1976), 449. The higher abundance of codling moths during dry, hot weather appears to be due not only to better larval survival, but also to increased egg laying by moths under those conditions. In addition, pheromone (chemical signal) traps have been used to trap male moths flying about just before females lay eggs. The number of moths trapped was then used to predict the date of egg hatching; this was fairly accurate for the first generation with the help of Shelford's data (Hagley, *Environmental Entomology* 5, no. 5 [1976], 967–69; Reidl, Croft, and Howitt, *Can. Entomol.* 108, no. 5 [1976], 449–60). A recent study involved examination of codling moth developmental rates on apples at constant temperatures (Rock and Shaffer, *Environ. Entomol.* 12, no. 3 [1983], 831–34).

16. Shelford, *Bull. Illinois Nat. Hist. Survey* 19, article 6 (1932), *passim.*

17. *Science* 47, no. 1210 (1918), 247–48; *Science* 49, no. 1256 (1919), 99; *Science* 51, no. 1313 (1920), 218; Shelford, *J. Econ. Entomol.* 19, no. 2 (1926), 259–61; G. A. Dean to V. E. S 11/28/1923 and 12/10/1923, UIA-VES, box 2; E. W. Ball to V. E. S 2/ 9/1924, UIA-VES, box 2; E. W. Ball to V. E. S 2/15/1924, UIA-VES, box 2.

18. Taped interview with V. E. S. by M. Brichford 3/24/1965, UIA-VES, box 2; RCC/Vera Smith Davidson 4/13/1984; RCC/Lena Feighner 8/8/1983, 2/26/1984, and 4/11/1984. Beginning in 1924, Shelford brought his whole family along by train to Friday Harbor. During the late twenties their train included a private Pullman car for the use of Shelford's students descending on Puget Sound Biological Station to take his marine ecology course. Shelford had a lively interest in railroads and "had a drawer full of up-to-date time tables." He traveled very often by train to lectures and meetings and to visit relatives. (RCC/Lois Bennett 5/31/1985 and 7/27/1986).

19. Shelford, *Publ. Puget Sound Biol. Sta.* 7 (1929), *passim;* Shelford and Gail, *Publ. Puget Sound Biol. Sta.* 3, no. 65 (1922), 144, 145, 169; Holmes, "Solar Radiation" in Hedgpeth (ed.), *Treatise on Marine Ecology,* vol. 1 (1957), 110; Shelford and Kunz, *Ecology* 10, no. 3 (1929), 308.

20. Saffo, *Bio Science* 37, no. 9 (1987); Hellebust, "Light: Plants" in Kinne (ed.), *Marine Ecology,* vol. 1, pt. 1 (1970), 149–50; Shelford and Gail, *Publ. Puget Sound Biol. Sta.* 3, no. 65 (1922), 145, 148, 170–71, 174; RCC/Vera Smith Davidson 4/13/1984. Later work in Hood Canal, a connector to Puget Sound, verified the depths of algal

distribution reported by Shelford and Gail (Philips and Fleenor, *Pac. Sci.* 24 [1970], 275–81).

21. Shelford and Kunz, *Transactions Wisconsin Academy of Sciences, Arts and Letters* 22 (1926), 283, 288, and *passim;* Knudsen, Conseil Internat. pour l'Exploration de la Mer, Pub. de Circ. 76 (1922), 14–16; Shelford, *Publ. Puget Sound Biol. Sta.* 7 (1929), 162, 165, and *passim.*

22. Shelford and Towler, *Publ. Puget Sound Biol. Sta.* 5 (1925), 43–44; Shelford, *Ecology* 7, no. 3 (1926), 389; Wennekens, Ph.D. dissertation, University of Washington (1959); Clements, *J. Ecol.* 5 (1916), 120–21. A decade later Shelford said that although ideally communities could be considered on a physiological basis, a serious lack of "knowledge of physiology of environmental relations" precluded practical implementation (Shelford, *Ecology* 13, no. 2 [1932], 114–15).

23. Shelford and Towler, *Publ. Puget Sound Biol. Sta.* 5 (1925), 66 and *passim.*

24. VES-PP; RCC/W. M. Gersbacher 10/16/1981.

25. Shelford *et al., Ecol. Monogr.* 5 (1935), 251, 252, 265–72, 328; Thorson, "Bottom Communities" in Hedgpeth (ed.), *Treatise on Marine Ecology,* vol 1. (1957), 518.

26. F. R. Lillie to V. E. S 7/13/1914, VES-PP; UI–Sen. Inq., 1925–26. Shelford's salary doubled to $5000 by 1928 when he was the second highest paid member of the department behind H. B. Ward at $6500. Shelford retired with a salary of $6300 in 1946 (UI–Bd. of Tr. transactions, 1930 and 1946).

27. UI–Sen. Inq., 1925–26; University of Illinois Register, 1914–15 through 1945–46; "Shelford's Courses: 1917–18," mimeo., ECA-WCA. For the interested reader, especially for former Illinois students, the courses had the following numerical designations in the order mentioned: Zoology 11, 9, 109, 110, 111, and last, 121C, 125, or 120 depending on the year. From 1936 to 1942, Shelford also taught Zoology 19, Wildlife Management, with Charles Kendeigh.

28. Allee *et al., Principles of Animal Ecology* (1950), 55, 57–60; A. S. Pearse to V. E. S 3/15/1943, UIA-VES, box 1; Elton, *Animal Ecology* (1927), 188.

29. VES-PP; RCC/Vera Smith Davidson 4/13/1984; V. E. S to H. B. Ward 6/3/1929, courtesy of Charles Kendeigh; RCC/John Savage 8/29/1983; RC/Charles Kendeigh 8/21/1981; *Daily Illini,* 11/22/1929, 4; VES-PP.

30. RCC/W. M. Gersbacher 10/16/1981; RC/Norman Meinkoth 7/8/1981 and 8/13/1981.

31. VES-PP; RCC/Jane Dirks-Edmunds 3/8/1982.

32. RC/Charles Kendeigh 8/21/1981; RCC/Vera Smith Davidson 4/13/1984; RC/Clarence Goodnight 6/17/1983; RCC/Mrs. Daniel Rasmussen 7/12/1981; VES-PP; RCC/James Carson 12/1981; RCC/Vera Smith Davidson 4/13/1984; RCC/Martha Shackleford 11/30/1981; V. E. S to David Kinley 2/20/1928, UIA-NHS, Forbes Papers.

33. Shelford's statistical time reports of his university work, 1920–29 (from Charles Kendeigh); V. E. S to H. B. Ward 2/23/1928; UIA-NHS, Forbes Papers; University of Illinois Register, 1927–28; V. E. S to H. B. Ward 2/15/1929; UIA-NHS, Forbes Papers, taped interview with V. E. S. by M. Brichford 4/1/1965, UIA-VES, box 2; RC/Lois Bennett 8/17/1981. In 1928–29, besides professors Ward, Shelford, Zeleny, and

Van Cleave, the zoology faculty also included associate professor Waldo Shumway (vertebrate embryology), assistant professors Lyell Thomas (general zoology and helminthology), Alvin Cahn (field ecology with Shelford), and Leverett Adams (vertebrate zoology and comparative anatomy) and associates Frank Adamstone (general zoology, embryology, cytology, and histology) and Richard Kudo (protozoology) (University of Illinois Register, 1928–29; Van Cleave, *Bios* 18, no. 2 [1947], 87–88).

34. Kofoid, *Ecology* 11, no. 3 (1930), 609–11; Elton, *J. Ecol.* 19 (1931), 216–17; RCC/Curtis Newcombe 8/20/1981; W. C. Allee to V. E. S 7/22/1929, VES-PP; Cook *Ecology* 11, no. 3 (1930), 611–14.

35. At a 1933 Ecological Society of America symposium in Chicago, Shelford made some relevant remarks about misplaced faith in the importance of controlled laboratory experiments unless the investigator continuously put to test laboratory results by adequate observations in natural habitats (Shelford, *Ecol. Monogr.* 4 [1934], 491–93).

CHAPTER 4. BIO-ECOLOGY

1. Burgess, "The Ecological Society of America" *in* Egerton (ed.), *History of American Ecology* (1977), 7; Shelford, *Ecology* 19, no. 1 (1938), 165–66; V. E. S to C. Davenport 11/7/1916, APS-CBD; *J. Ecol.* 5 (1917), 119–28; M. T. Shelford to V. E. S 12/16/1916, UIA-VES, box 1. Faith Shelford Wohnus received her M.D. degree in 1918 from New York Medical College and Hospital for Women. She served as College Physician at Adelphi College in Garden City, New York, from 1930 to 1949 (RCC/ Helen Stephens 2/22/1984). Melvia T. Shelford, Ph.D., D.D., served nearly fifty years as a minister and was dean of the National Bible Institute in New York City from 1922 to 1926 (*New York Times,* 9/16/41, 23).

2. Shreve (ed.), *Bull. Ecol. Soc. Amer.* 1, no. 1 (1917), 1; VES-PP; *New York Times,* 12/27/16, 5; *Science* 45, no. 1149 (1917), 1.

3. *New York Times,* 12/22/16, 1; *New York Times,* 12/27/16, 5; *New York Times,* 12/ 23/16, 1; *New York Times,* 12/27/16, 1; *New York Times,* 12/28/16, 6.

4. *J. Ecol.* 5 (1917), 120–21.

5. Shelford, *Ecology* 12, no. 3 (1931), 456; A. G. Vestal to V. E. S 9/16/1912, UIA-AGV, box 2; RC/Charles Kendeigh 8/20/1981.

6. Vestal, *Bull. Illinois State Lab. Nat. Hist.* 10 (1913), 13; Vestal, *Amer. Nat.* 48 (1914), 430, 442, 444; Evers, *Trans. Illinois State Acad. Sci.* 57, no. 2 (1965), 77–79; A. G. Vestal to C. C. Adams 12/6/1911, WMUA-CCA, 1911 folder; F. E. Clements and Shelford, *Bio-Ecology* (1939), 6; V. E. S to F. E. Clements 11/10/1937, UWy-CC, box 122.

7. E. S. Clements, *National Cyclopedia of American Biography,* vol. 34 (1948), 266; Ewan, *Dictionary of Scientific Biography,* vol. 3 (1971), 317; Schantz, *Ecology* 26, no. 4 (1945), 317–18; Pool, *Ecology* 35, no. 2 (1954), 110; Pound, *Ecology* 35, no. 2 (1954), 112; Tobey, *Saving the Prairies* (1981), 59; E. S. Clements, *Adventures* (1960), 102 and *passim;* A. G. Vestal to Ecology Club, University of Illinois, 5/22/1957 (RCC/Richard Brewer 1/12/1983); RCC/Charles Kendeigh 5/15/1984; RCC/Lois Bennett 7/26/1984.

8. E. S. Clements, *National Cyclopedia of American Biography,* vol. 34 (1948), 266–67; Ewan, *Dictionary of Scientific Biography,* vol. 3 (1971), 317; E. S. Clements, *Adventures* (1960), 14–16, 144, 224 and *passim; Carnegie Institution Washington Yearbook,* no. 14 (1916), 24; *Carnegie Institution Washington Yearbook,* no. 15 (1917), 21.

9. Schantz, *Ecology* 26, no. 4 (1945), 318; E. S. Clements, *Adventures* (1960), 224 and *passim;* E. S. Clements, *National Cyclopedia of American Biography,* vol. 34 (1948), 266.

10. F. E. Clements, *Research Methods* (1905), 10, 16, 18; F. E. Clements, *Carnegie Institution Washington Yearbook,* no. 21 (1923), 355; F. E. Clements, *Carnegie Institution Washington Yearbook,* no. 16 (1918), 304, 306; F. E. Clements, *Carnegie Institution Washington Yearbook,* no. 17 (1919), 287.

11. F. E. Clements, *Carnegie Institution Washington Yearbook,* no. 17 (1919), 288; F. E. Clements, *Carnegie Institution Washington Yearbook,* no. 18 (1920), 336–38; F. E. Clements, *Carnegie Institution Washington Yearbook,* no. 19 (1921), 360; F. E. Clements, *Carnegie Institution Washington Yearbook,* no. 20 (1922), 408.

12. VES-PP; UIA-VES, box 1, folder 1920–23; *Science* 58, no. 1489, suppl. (1923), x.

13. F. E. Clements, *Carnegie Institution Washington Yearbook,* no. 19 (1921), 361; F. E. Clements, *Carnegie Institution Washington Yearbook,* no. 21 (1923), 355–56; F. E. Clements, *Carnegie Institution Washington Yearbook,* no. 23 (1924), 267. Charles T. Vorhies received his Ph.D. degree from Wisconsin in 1908. He was professor of entomology at Arizona from 1918 to 1936, during which time he worked with Frederic Clements on Carnegie Institution projects concerning birds, mammals, and insects. He completed his academic career as professor of economic zoology at Arizona from 1936 until his death (*American Men of Science,* 6th ed. [1938], 1474). Walter P. Taylor received his Ph.D. degree from the University of California in 1914. He served as a biologist with the United States Fish and Wildlife Service from 1919 to 1935, as senior biologist for the Cooperative Wildlife Research Unit at Texas A&M from 1938 to 1948, and as professor of zoology at Oklahoma A&M from 1948 to 1951. He was president of the Ecological Society of America in 1934. Taylor was well known for his work in wildlife management and conservation and for his studies of mammal grazing in grasslands (*American Men of Science,* 10th ed. [1961], 4404).

14. Shelford and Towler, *Publ. Puget Sound Biol. Sta.* 5 (1925), 66–67; F. E. Clements, *Carnegie Institution Washington Yearbook,* no. 24 (1925), 329; F. E. Clements and Shelford, *Bio-Ecology* (1939), 2. I have reason to believe that Shelford stated as early as 1924 that progress in animal ecology depended on employing concepts from plant ecology, although I cannot document the statement. In any event, Clements was appreciative of Shelford's early acceptance of these concepts and the biotic community viewpoint (Phillips, *J. Ecol.* 23, no. 2 [1935], 501).

15. VES-PP; RCC/Lois Bennett 7/26/1984 and 8/24/1984; F. E. Clements to V. E. S 10/4/1925, UWy-CC, box 113; F. E. Clements, *Carnegie Institution Washington Yearbook,* no. 25 (1926), 367–68. Shelford's many field trips to Colorado resulted in a small mountain lake at 11,000 feet being named after him. Shelford's personal papers contain an illustrated flier from Rocky Mountain Biological Laboratory and a note that

Lake Shelford is located near Crested Butte, Colorado (Gunnison County), but I have not been able to verify the exact location of this lake.

16. F. E. Clements, *Carnegie Institution Washington Yearbook*, no. 26 (1927), 335; A. G. Vestal to Ecology Club, University of Illinois, 5/22/1957 (RCC/Richard Brewer 1/23/ 1984); F. E. Clements, *Carnegie Institution Washington Yearbook*, no. 23 (1924), 266; F. E. Clements, *Carnegie Institution Washington Yearbook*, no. 24 (1925), 337–40; F. E. Clements, *Carnegie Institution Washington Yearbook*, no. 26 (1927), 336. Asa O. Weese received his Ph.D. at Illinois under Shelford in 1922 with a dissertation titled "A Study of the Animal Ecology of an Illinois Elm-Maple Forest." He took up his position as professor of zoology in 1924 at the University of Oklahoma, where he remained until his death. His primary interest was in biotic communities and succession, especially among grassland insects. He also taught the marine ecology course at Puget Sound in 1925 and 1929 and was president of the Ecological Society of America in 1931 (*American Men of Science*, 9th ed. [1955], 1198; Richards, *Science* 124, no. 3220 [1956], 477).

17. F. E. Clements, *Carnegie Institution Washington Yearbook*, no. 26 (1927), 305–37.

18. F. E. Clements, *Carnegie Institution Washington Yearbook*, no. 26 (1927), 335.

19. *American Men of Science* (1965), 420; Bird, *Ecology* 11, no. 2 (1930), 362–63, 369, 383, 406, 410–11, 423; F. E. Clements to V.E.S. 3/6/1929, UWy-CC, box 116; F. E. Clements to V.E.S. 4/30/1929 and 12/8/1929, UWy-CC, box 116.

20. Shelford, *Ecology* 12, no. 3 (1931), 456.

21. Shelford, *Ecology* 12, no. 3 (1931), 455, 456, 459–61, 465, and *passim*.

22. F. E. Clements to V.E.S. 4/20/1930 and 7/19/1930, UWy-CC, box 116; V.E.S. to F. E. Clements 5/5/1930 and 7/7/1930, UWy-CC, box 116.

23. Phillips, *J. Ecol.* 19, no. 1 (1931), 1, 19, 20, 23, and *passim;* Shelford, *Ecology* 12, no. 3 (1931), 456; RCC/Charles Kendeigh 10/23/1984. In 1935 Phillips agreed fully with Clements and accepted biotic communities as organisms (Phillips, *J. Ecol.* 23, no. 2 [1935], 497–98). Some eighty-seven letters between Shelford and Clements from the University of Wyoming's Clements Collection contain no reference to Clements's complex organism concept.

24. V. E. S to F. E. Clements 11/11/1930, UWy-CC, box 116.

25. F. E. Clements to V. E. S. 3/4/1931 and 5/2/1931, UWy-CC, box 117; F. E. Clements, *Carnegie Institution Washington Yearbook*, no. 30 (1931), 275; V. E. S. to F. E. Clements 3/21/1931, UWy-CC, box 117; VES-PP; V. E. S to F. E. Clements 4/21/ 1933, UWy-CC, box 118. Eventually Shelford and Clements applied their biome concept and successional terminology to the sea in *Bio-Ecology,* but these have not stood the test of time and further work.

26. *Science* 73, no. 1890, suppl. (1931), 13–14; Ellis, *A Nation in Torment* (1970), 453; *Science* 75, no. 1931, suppl. (1932), 8; F. E. Clements to V. E. S. 11/30/1931, 12/ 14/1931, 12/22/1931, and 1/2/1932, UWy-CC, box 117; V. E. S. to F. E. Clements 12/15/1931 and 12/24/1931, UWy-CC, box 117.

27. F. E. Clements and Shelford, *Bio-Ecology* (1939), 20; Shelford, *Ecology* 13, no. 2 (1932), 112, 118, and *passim*.

28. V. E. S. to F. E. Clements 12/24/1931, UWy-CC, box 117; F. E. Clements to V. E. S. 12/14/1931 and 1/2/1932, UWy-CC, box 117. *Bio-Ecology* covered the grass-

land biome in greatest detail; freshwater and marine communities were given only preliminary treatment (F. E. Clements and Shelford, *Bio-Ecology* [1939], 249–50).

29. Ellis, *A Nation in Torment* (1970), 179; McElvaine, *The Great Depression* (1984), 49–50; RCC/Lois Bennett 2/19/1984.

30. V. E. S. to F. E. Clements 3/20/1933, 3/31/1933, and 4/21/1933, UWy-CC, box 118.

31. F. E. Clements to V. E. S. 4/10/1933 and 5/6/1933, UWy-CC, box 118.

32. F. E. Clements to V. E. S. 4/10/1933 and 7/27/1933, UWy-CC, box 118; Shelford and Olson, *Ecology* 16, no. 3 (1935), 394; Tobey, *Saving the Prairies* (1981), 180–84; F. E. Clements and Shelford, *Bio-Ecology* (1939), 355–58.

33. F. E. Clements to V. E. S. 5/6/1933 and 5/17/1933, UWy-CC, box 118; V. E. S. to F. E. Clements 5/12/1933, UWy-CC, box 118. Shelford apparently wrote out a tentative list of criteria for the biome concept and sent a copy to Clements early in 1933, but I have not been able to find it (F. E. Clements to V. E. S. 5/6/1933 and V. E. S. to F. E. Clements 5/12/1933, UWy-CC, box 118).

34. Pruitt, *Boreal Ecology* (1978), *passim;* Cowles, *Bot. Gaz.* 31, no. 2 (1901), 81. William S. Cooper also commented in 1913 on the mosaic nature of the climax forest of Isle Royale, Michigan (Cooper, *Bot. Gaz.* 55, no. 1 [1913], 43–44).

35. V. E. Shelford's class roll book, 1942–46, courtesy of Charles Kendeigh; Whittaker, *Ecol. Monogr.* 23, no. 1 (1953), *passim;* Whittaker, *Northwest Sci.* 25 (1951), 17–31. While Robert Whittaker pursued community work in the Great Smokey Mountains during the late 1940s, John Curtis and his students at the University of Wisconsin independently came up with community data supporting the idea of a vegetation continuum similar to Whittaker's gradient. Whittaker was also influenced by Arthur Vestal at Illinois, who by the 1940s had changed his previous associational view, rejected Clementsian ecology, and come to support the ideas of Henry A. Gleason of the New York Botanical Gardens. Gleason's individualistic, or population-centered, concept of plant ecology was presented in 1917 and 1926 and was addressed later by both Whittaker and Curtis. Actually, Forrest Shreve described the vegetation continuum even before Gleason (*Vegetation of a Desert Mountain Range* [1915], 88–112, and *passim*). Similar ideas appeared in France (Lenoble) and Russia (Ramensky) during the latter 1920s (Whittaker in Jensen and Salisbury, *Botany: An Ecological Approach* [1972], 689–91; Curtis and McIntosh, *Ecology* 32 [1951], 476–96; Gleason, *Bull. Torrey Bot. Club* 53 [1926], 7–26. Gleason, *Bull. Torrey Bot. Club* 44 [1917], 463–81; Whittaker, *Ecol. Monogr.* 23, no. 1 [1953], 45).

36. F. E. Clements, *J. Ecol.* 24, no. 1 (1936), 273, 280, and *passim;* F. E. Clements and Shelford, *Bio-Ecology* (1939), 235; Weaver and F. E. Clements, *Plant Ecology* (1929), 53–54. Both the organismic views of Clements with their modern holistic derivatives and the individualistic population-centered views of Gleason still figure prominently in current concepts of succession and the ecological theory (McIntosh in Cairns, *The Recovery Process in Damaged Ecosystems* [1980], 18–23, 43–54; McIntosh in West *et al., Forest Succession* [1981], 22–23).

37. F. E. Clements, *J. Ecol.* 24, no. 1 (1936), 271; F. E. Clements and Shelford, *Bio-Ecology* (1939), 241–43.

38. Shelford and Olson, *Ecology* 16, no. 3 (1935), 376, 378, 382, 384, and *passim;* Weaver and F. E. Clements, *Plant Ecology* (1929), 425. Clements also displayed some ambivalence over the subclimax and climax roles of paper birch, black spruce, aspen, and larch (Weaver and F. E. Clements, *Plant Ecology* [1929], 432–33).

39. Shelford and Olson, *Ecology* 16, no. 3 (1935), 379, 380, 382, 394, 396, 398, 399, and *passim;* V. E. S. to F. E. Clements 7/28/1935, UWy-CC, box 120.

40. F. E. Clements, *Carnegie Institution Washington Yearbook,* no. 32 (1933), 205; F. E. Clements to V. E. S. 1/25/1935 and 6/7/1935, UWy-CC, box 120; E. S. Clements's diary for 9/19/1934, "Colorado to Urbana and return," UWy-CC, box 162; E. S. Clements's diary for 9/27/1936, "Champaign, Illinois," UWy-CC, box 162.

41. V. E. S to F. E. Clements 3/26/1935 and 7/28/1935, UWy-CC, box 120. In Shelford's defense concerning "dragging his feet" during the period from 1935 to 1938, 70 percent of his university time was devoted to teaching, 15 percent more than he had spent a decade earlier (Shelford's statistical time report of his university duties, 1924–28, courtesy of Charles Kendeigh).

42. F. E. Clements to V. E. S. 4/15/1935 and 6/7/1935, UWy-CC, box 120; Tobey, *Saving the Prairies* (1981), 200–201; F. E. Clements, *J. Ecol.* 24, no. 1 (1936), 256; F. E. Clements, *Carnegie Institution Washington Yearbook,* no. 30 (1931), 267; Weaver and F. E. Clements, *Plant Ecology* (1929), 412–16.

43. Egler, *Ecology* 32, no. 4 (1951), 677; F. E. Clements and Chaney, *Carnegie Institution Washington Supplementary Publications,* no. 24 (rev. ed.) (1937), 51–52; F. E. Clements to "Billy" (?) 1/27/1937, UWy-CC, box 122. F. E. Clements to V. E. S. 12/19/1936, UIA-VES, box 1.

44. Shelford, "The Physical Environment" in Murchison (ed.), *A Handbook of Social Psychology* (1935), 567; F. E. Clements and Shelford, *Bio-Ecology* (1939), 2, 24; F. E. Clements to "Billy" (?) 1/27/1937, UWy-CC, box 122.

45. Tansley, *Ecology* 16, no. 3 (1935), 284–85, 304, and *passim.*

46. Phillips, *J. Ecol.* 19, no. 1 (1931), 1–24; Phillips, *J. Ecol.* 22, no. 2 (1934), 554–71; Phillips, *J. Ecol.* 23, nos. 1 and 2 (1935), 210–46, 488–508; Tansley, *Ecology* 16, no. 3 (1935), 285–86; Tobey, *Saving the Prairies* (1981), 167.

47. Tansley, *The British Islands,* vol. 1 (1953), vi, 221–26; Tansley, *Ecology* 16, no. 3 (1935), 294–95. Evidence for the early decimation of British forests includes the importation of timber into Britain in the eleventh century and extensive imports at the end of the thirteenth and fourteenth centuries. Except for the Highlands, a shortage of timber in Scotland was felt a century earlier than in England. The seventeenth century marks the time of exhaustion of the last forest reserves and the beginning of serious planting of trees (Tansley, *The British Islands,* vol. 1 (1953), 181–84, 188).

48. Tansley, *Ecology* 16, no. 3 (1935), 296–97, 299–300, 305.

49. F. E. Clements to A. G. Tansley 4/28/1935, UWy-CC, box misc.; Shelford's statistical time report of his university duties during 1936, courtesy of Charles Kendeigh; V. E. S to F. E. Clements 2/5/1937, UWy-CC, box 122; G. Laing to V. E. S 4/24/1937, UWy-CC, box 122. Shelford said that he and Clements could not take criticism of chapter 1 by the referee "very seriously," because, "Chapter 1 was read by him [Shelford believed the reader was W. C. Allee] about three years ago when

separated from the rest of the text and praised very highly" (V. E. S to G. Laing 4/27/1937, UWy-CC, box 122). During Clements's fall 1936 visit with Shelford in Urbana, the two men held a frank discussion of ecology and its problems and promises at the Wednesday afternoon Ecology Club meeting on October 7. The students were thrilled and had vivid memories of the experience long after (A. L. Soderwell to J. Dirks-Edmunds 10/18/1936, courtesy of Jane Dirks-Edmunds).

50. V. E. S to G. Laing 4/27/1937, UWy-CC, box 122; F. E. Clements to V. E. S 5/3/1937, UWy-CC, box 122. Clements's symposia contributions were part of the one hundredth AAAS meetings, held June 21–26, 1937. He delivered two papers: "Climatic Cycles and Human Populations," a consideration of plant cover as related to erosion, (with ESA) and "Investigations on the Influence of Environment on Expression in Plant Species" (with the Botanical Society of America) (*Science* 86, no. 2218 [1937], 8; *Science* 86, no. 224 [1937], 132, 140).

51. V. E. S to F. E. Clements 7/23/1937, UWy-CC, box 122; F. E. Clements to V. E. S 7/27/1937, UWy-CC, box 122; E. S. Clements, diary for 10/19/1937, "Washington, D.C., Mostly about Dr. John Philips [sic]," UWy-CC, box 162.

52. F. E. Clements and Shelford, *Bio-Ecology* (1939), vi; V. E. S to F. E. Clements 11/10/1937, UWy-CC, box 122.

53. F. E. Clements to V. E. S 11/27/1937, UWy-CC, box 122. For an analysis of the rise and decline of the American school of grassland ecology and its relationship with fundamental Clementsian ecology, see Tobey, *Saving the Prairies* (1981), particularly chapter 7.

54. V. E. S to F. E. Clements 12/1-2/1937, UWy-CC, box 122.

55. Allee, *Ecology* 20, no. 3 (1939), 418–21; Carpenter, "The Biome" in Just (ed.), *Am. Midl. Nat.* 21 (1939), 75–91; Elton, *J. Anim. Ecol.* 9, no. 1 (1940), 151–52; RC/Clarence Goodnight 6/17/1983; RCC/Clarence Goodnight 12/8/1984; RCC/Lois Bennett 8/24/1984.

56. Kofoid, *Bio-Abstracts* 13 (1939), 1249; Hutchinson *Ecology* 21, no. 2 (1940), 267–68; *Bird Lore* 42 (1940), 203; *The Quarterly Review of Biology* 15, no. 1 (1940), 77–78; Elton, *J. Anim. Ecol.* 9 (1940), 148–49; F. E. Clements to V. E. S 4/13/1940, VES-PP; V. E. S to F. E. Clements 4/18/1940, VES-PP; M. Matheson to V. E. S 5/22/1958, VES-PP. In late 1941 and early 1942, Shelford was one of eight ecologists to whom Raymond Lindeman sent copies of his revised manuscript, "The Trophic-Dynamic Aspect in Ecology." This would be his classic paper serving as an impetus for later studies of energetics in natural communities (Lindeman, *Ecology* 23 [1942], 399–418; R. E. Cook, *Science* 198, no. 4312 [1977], 24). More recently, it has come to light that the Russian ecologist V. V. Stanchinskii presented in 1931 an equation for the annual energy balance in an ecological community, based in part on his studies of energy flow between trophic levels in a steppe grassland environment (Weiner, *Isis* 75, no. 279 [1984], 686–88).

CHAPTER 5. ITINERANT ECOLOGIST

1. Taped interview with V. E. S. by M. Brichford 3/24/1965, UIA-VES, box 2.
2. RCC/Eugene Odum 10/26/1981.

3. RCC/Jane Dirks-Edmunds 3/8/1982.

4. RCC/Lena Feighner 4/8/1983, 2/26/1984, and 4/13/1984.

5. RC/Ralph and Drew Sparkman Wetzel 11/15/1981; RCC/Mrs. Daniel Rasmussen 7/12/1981; RCC/Jane Dirks-Edmunds/1985; RCC/Arthur Twomey (tape) 10/12/1981.

6. RCC/Curtis Newcombe 11/22/1982; RCC/Jane Dirks-Edmunds 3/8/1982.

7. RC/Clarence and Marie Goodnight 6/17/1982; RCC/Beatrice Flori 7/21/1984; RC/Drew Sparkman Wetzel 11/15/1981; RCC/Jane Dirks-Edmunds 3/8/1982.

8. RCC/C. Lynn Hayward 9/21/1981.

9. RCC/Edward Baylor October 1981.

10. Kendeigh, *Bull. Ecol. Soc. Amer.* 49, no. 3 (1968), 100; RCC/Clarence Goodnight 5/14/1981; RCC/Stanley Auerbach 11/21/1986.

11. RCC/Curtis Newcombe 8/20/1981.

12. VES-PP; taped interview with V. E. S. by M. Brichford 4/1/1965, UIA-VES, box 2.

13. Shelford, *Ecology* 35, no. 2 (1954), 128.

14. Shelford, *Ecology* 35, no. 2 (1954), *passim;* RCC/Arthur Twomey (tape) 10/12/1981; RCC/Jane Dirks-Edmunds 3/8/1982; VES-PP.

15. RCC/Arthur Twomey (tape) 10/12/1981.

16. Lois Bennett to Joy Elliott 9/28/1971; Shelford, *Ecology* 24, no. 4 (1943), 472, 476, and *passim;* RCC/Arthur Twomey (tape) 10/12/1981; Shelford and Twomey, *Ecology* 22, no. 1 (1941), 47.

17. RCC/Arthur Twomey (tape) 10/12/1981; Shelford and Twomey, *Ecology* 22, no. 1 (1941), 47.

18. Shelford and Twomey, *Ecology* 22, no. 1 (1941), *passim;* Shelford, *Ecology* 24, no. 4 (1943), 476 and *passim;* Shelford, *Auk* 62 (1945), 592–96; VES-PP. Subsequent research on tundra lemmings showed that the causes of three-to-six-year population cycles remain controversial, although the abundance of predators such as birds and weasels appears closely linked to the abundance of lemmings and other microtine rodents. Variability of population cycles suggests a number of factors may be involved, including temperature, snow cover, nutrition, predation, and endrocrine hormones (Batzli in Golley *et al.* (eds.) *Small Mammals* [1975], 247, 267; Stenseth, *Oecologia* 33, no. 2 [1977], 166–67; Batzli in Bliss *et al.* (eds.), *Tundra Ecosystems* [1981], 379, 384).

John and Lois Shelford both graduated from the University of Illinois in 1934, John with a degree in general engineering and Lois with a degree in Spanish (*The Illio* [1934], 102). Lois subsequently completed three years (1935–38) of graduate work at the University of Chicago in Russian, German, Swedish, Greek, and Latin (Lois Shelford to C. C. Adams 3/26/1938, WMUA-CCA, Shelford correspondence).

19. VES-PP; Shelford and Twomey, *Ecology* 22, no. 1 (1941), 47; RCC/C. Lynn Hayward 9/21/1981; RCC/James Carson 12/4/1981; *Science* 77, no. 2006 (1933), 558; taped interview with V. E. S. by M. Brichford 3/24/1965, UIA-VES, box 2; Van Cleave, *Bios* 18, no. 2 (1947), 89–90.

From the mid 1930s continuing into the 1940s, there were obvious differences of opinion and style among professors Shelford, Shumway, and Van Cleave. Some of the rocky times were residual from the Ward era at Illinois and some were related to their close work on the department executive committee from 1935 to 1938. As to the well-known running feud between Shelford and the university physical plant—this was eternal.

S. Charles Kendeigh received his A.B. and A.M. degrees from Oberlin College and his Ph.D. degree from Illinois in 1930. His Ph.D. thesis was titled "The Role of Temperature and Other Environmental Factors in the Life of Birds." After six years (1930–36) on the faculty at Case Western Reserve, he returned to Illinois, proceeding through the academic ranks to professor. He had been professor emeritus since 1973. Much of his research related to vertebrate physiological ecology—focusing especially on birds, population census and dynamics, community classification, general conservation, and the preservation of natural areas. He succeeded Shelford as animal ecologist at Illinois and became mentor to Eugene Odum, Robert Whittaker, forty-nine other doctoral students, and sixty-five master's students. He was a founder of the Animal Behavior Society and served as president of the Wilson Ornithological Society from 1943 to 1945 and of the Ecological Society of America in 1951. He was selected as Eminent Ecologist by the ESA in 1978 (Muller *et al., Bull. Ecol. Soc. Amer.* 59, no. 4 [1978], 168–69).

20. RCC/Ralph Dexter 10/30/1981; RCC/Jane Dirks-Edmunds 3/8/1982; RC/ Charles Kendeigh 8/18/1981.

21. RC/Clarence and Marie Goodnight 6/17/1983; Kendeigh, *Ill. Biol. Monogr.* 50 (1979), acknowledgments, 2.

22. Kendeigh, *Ill. Biol. Monogr.* 50 (1979), 2–5, 86; Kendeigh, *Bull. Ecol. Soc. Amer.* 49, no. 3 (1968), 98; Shelford, *Ecol. Monogr.* 21, no. 1 (1951), 184, 186, and *passim.* The extreme drought of the early 1930s probably acted as one impetus for Shelford to begin formal, long-term population studies in what was then called University Woods. By the summer of 1934, herbs had died, the ground was almost bare, and many trees had completely lost their leaves by August. University Woods was finally soaked by rain for the first time in three years on May 3, 1935, but the drought returned again in August (Shelford, *Ecology of North America* [1963], 50; *Science* 82, no. 2120 [1935], 8). Additional studies began in Brownfield Woods (60 acres, 2.4 kilometers northwest of Trelease Woods) in 1949 and in Funk Forest (60 acres, 80 kilometers west northwest of Urbana) in 1954 and continued through 1971. Sampling for invertebrate species in ground, herb, and shrub levels of all forests was carried out one to three times per month depending on location and season (Kendeigh, *Ill. Biol. Monogr.* 50 [1979], 3, 5, 22–24).

23. RCC/Eugene Odum 10/20/1981; Allee *et al., Principles of Animal Ecology* (1950), 58–60; Shelford, *Laboratory and Field Ecology* (1929), 63; Shelford and Eddy, *Ecology* 10, no. 4 (1929), *passim;* Shelford, *Ecology* 11, no. 1 (1930), 235–37; Shelford, *Ecol. Monogr.* 4 (1934), 491–93.

24. VES-PP.

25. VES-PP; Merriam, North American Fauna, no. 3 (1890), 1–2; Kendeigh, *Ecology* 35, no. 2 (1954), 160, 163, 169; Sterling, *Last of the Naturalists* (1977), 231, 232; Shelford, *The Wilson Bulletin* 44 (1932), 155 and *passim.*

26. RC/Charles Kendeigh 3/20/1981; RC/J. "Jake" Weber 5/6/1983. During the thirties, Shelford smoked cigarettes but later gave them up. He smoked, he said, "to help smoking students feel at ease" (RCC/Lois Bennett 2/9/1987).

27. RCC/Eugene Odum 10/20/1981; RCC/Jane Dirks-Edmunds 3/8/1982.

28. Shelford, "The Physical Environment" in Murchison (ed.), *A Handbook of Social Psychology* (1935), 567–72.

29. V. E. S to R. D. Carmichael 10/18/1939, courtesy of Charles Kendeigh.

30. RCC/James Carson 12/4/1981; Shelford and Boesel, *Ohio J. of Sci.* 42, no. 5 (1942), 182; VES-PP; RCC/Curtis Newcombe 8/20/1981.

31. RC/Dorothy Parmelee 8/13/1984; RCC/Dorothy Parmelee 7/12–14/1981; RC/ Faith Hallock 8/13/1984; RCC/Dorthy Parmelee 3/17/1982; RCC/Paul Shelford, Jr. 9/ 3/1982; RC/Donald Shelford 7/15/1981; RCC/Lois Bennett 2/9/1987.

32. RC/Charles Kendeigh 8/20/1981; RCC/Lois Bennett 5/31/1985; Shelford, *The Ecology of North America* (1963), 406, 421; Minter, *The Chagres* (1948), 383. Barro Colorado Island Biological Station, at the time Shelford was there, was administered through the Institute for Research in Tropical America, supported by the National Research Council. John Shelford was married on June 20 just prior to the Panama trip; he received an M.S. in Engineering from Cornell and later served as an officer in the Navy during World War II and then as a civilian employee with the Department of the Army.

33. Minter, *The Chagres* (1948), *passim;* Shelford, *The Ecology of North America* (1963), 406–9, 412–19; RCC/Lois Bennett 8/24/1984; RC/Lois Bennett 8/22/1981 and 7/18/1985. In the early 1920s Mabel Shelford had an acute influenza infection leaving her with heart damage and a need for digitalis from time to time.

34. RC/Lois Bennett 8/17/1981; RCC/Lois Bennett 8/24/1984 and 5/31/1985; RCC/William Fierke, Office of Admissions and Records, University of Illinois, 10/12/ 1981; RCC/Hugh Hanson 1/18/1982; Shelford's statistical time report for his university duties 1940–41, courtesy of Charles Kendeigh; VES-PP.

35. Link, *American Epoch,* vol. 3 (1967), 552–56; Watters, *Illinois in the Second World War,* vol. 1 (1951), 8, 135, 165, 409, 411; Willard, *Science* 95, No. 2467 (1942), 372–73; Van Cleave, *Bios* 18, no. 2 (1947), 92; UIA–LA & S, D, departmental and subject file, 1943–44, box 33, University of Illinois Register, 1945–46; RCC/William Fierke, Office of Admissions and Records, University of Illinois, 10/12/1981.

36. RCC/Lois Bennett 8/24/1984; RCC/Hugh Hanson 1/18/1982; RCC/Henry Siebert 9/29/1981; VES-PP. During World War II Shelford eventually obtained a "T certificate" from the Office of Defense Transportation, allowing the purchase of gas for research field trips. Also, in 1942 Shelford set up Animal Ecology Field Studies, Inc., a corporation designed to provide transportation and equipment to students and staff on a cost basis, to secure and care for parcels of land, and to encourage field instruction and research. Students were "requested" to become corporation members for twenty-five or fifty cents per year.

37. RCC/James Carson 12/4/1981; Lois Bennett to Joy Elliott 9/28/1971; RC/ Norman Meinkoth 8/13/1981; RC/Ralph and Drew Sparkman Wetzel 11/15/1981; RC/Clarence and Marie Goodnight 6/17/1983; RCC/Stanley Auerbach 1/24/1984; RC/ Lois Bennett 8/17/1981; VES-PP; RCC/Lois Bennett 2/9/1987.

38. RCC/Hugh Hanson 1/18/1982; RCC/Henri Siebert 9/29/1981; RC/Norman Meinkoth 7/8/1981 and 8/13/1981; RCC/Jane Dirks-Edmunds 3/8/1982 and 2/6/1985; RC/Drew Sparkman Wetzel 11/15/1981; RCC/Stanley Auerbach 1/24/1984; RCC/ Emily Dawson Stephan 7/25/1984. Stanley Auerbach received his B.S. (1946) and M.S.

(1947) degrees at Illinois and his Ph.D. (1949) at Northwestern University. Since 1954 he has been associated with the Oak Ridge National Laboratory in Oak Ridge, Tennessee, serving from 1972 to 1986 as director of the environmental sciences division and most recently as senior staff advisor to the division. He has contributed to ecosystem analysis both at Oak Ridge and as the director of the Eastern Deciduous Forest Biome Project through the International Biological Program from 1968 to 1976. He has helped mold public policy on radiation ecology, nuclear energy, and hazardous waste disposal. During the 1971−72 term he was president of the Ecological Society of America, and in 1986 he received the society's Distinguished Service Citation (*American Men and Women of Science* [1982], 196, and [1986], 204; *Bull. Ecol. Soc. Amer.* 67, no. 1 [1986], 44−45).

39. V. E. Shelford's class roll book 1942−46, courtesy of Charles Kendeigh; RCC/ Stanley Auerbach 1/24/1984 and 11/21/1986; Shelford, *J. Morphol.* 22, no. 3 (1911), 555; Tobey, *Saving the Prairies* (1981), 180−84. Shelford mentioned evolution as such only in some very early papers (e.g. Shelford, *J. Morphol.* 22 [1911], 551−618; Shelford, *Amer. Nat.* 48, no. 575 [1914], 641−74). There and elsewhere he referred to the importance of environmental factors for influencing physiological and behavioral responses of organisms. Shelford's stance on the notion of inheritance of acquired characteristics, however, is not clear. Certainly he was not strongly neo-Lamarckian in the same sense that Clements was.

40. Taped interview with V. E. S. by M. Brichford 4/1/1965, UIA-VES, box 2; RCC/Drew Sparkman Wetzel 10/26/1984; UI−LA&S, D, departmental and subject file, 1943−44, box 33.

41. RCC/Drew Sparkman Wetzel 10/26/1984; RCC/Donald Shelford 4/17/1985; RCC/Lois Bennett 2/9/1987, UI−LA&S, D, departmental and subject file, 1943−44, box 33; Lois Bennett to Joy Elliott 9/28/1971; VES-PP; Shelford, *The Ecology of North America* (1963), *passim*.

42. RCC/Edward Baylor 10/1981; RC/Drew Sparkman Wetzel 11/13/1981.

43. M. T. McClure to A. C. Willard 1/6/1944, UI−LA&S, D, departmental and subject file, 1943−44, box 33.

44. UIA-VES, box 1; RCC/Lois Bennett 5/23/1981; Carl Hartman to M. T. Mc-Clure 5/1/1945, VES−UI Acad. Appt. F.

45. R. E. Kunkel to V. E. S 7/9/1946; RCC/Stanley Auerbach 1/24/1984 and 2/28/ 1984; VES-PP; RCC/Stanley Auerbach 11/21/1986.

46. RCC/Stanley Auerbach 1/24/1984; RCC/Jane Dirks-Edmunds 3/8/1982.

47. RCC/Vera Smith Davidson 4/12/1984; RCC/Stanley Auerbach 1/24/1984.

48. RCC/Stanley Auerbach 1/24/1984; RC/Dorothy Parmelee 8/13/1984; RCC/ Donald Shelford 3/1984 and 4/17/1985.

49. VES-PP; RC/Norman Meinkoth 7/8/1981; RCC/Stanley Auerbach 1/24/1984.

CHAPTER 6. PRESERVING NATURE

1. Robert Wolcott to V. E. S 3/27/1914, VES-PP; V. E. S to Robert Wolcott 4/8/ 1914, VES-PP; Robert Wolcott to V. E. S 4/24/1914, VES-PP.

2. Shelford, *Ecology* 19, no. 1 (1938), 165; Cowles, "A Proposed Ecological Society" 9/20/1915, UIA-AGV, box 2; ESA, announcement of formation, 2 pp., UIA-AGV, box 2; VES-PP; Forrest Shreve to V. E. S 3/4/1916, UIA-VES, box 1. The twenty-two present at the 1914 Philadelphia meeting were as follows: C. C. Adams, H. H. Bartlett, F. H. Blodgett, W. L. Bray, C. T. Brues, W. A. Cannon, H. C. Cowles, A. P. Dachnowski-Stokes, R. F. Griggs, J. W. Harshberger, A. F. Hill, O. E. Jennings, D. T. MacDougal, Z. P. Metcalf, G. E. Nichols, R. C. Osburn, A. S. Pearse, H. L. Shantz, V. E. Shelford, F. Shreve, N. Taylor, and R. H. Wolcott (Shelford, *Ecology* 19, no. 1 [1938], 165).

3. Shelford, "Conservation of Wildlife" in Parkins and Whitaker (eds.), *Our Natural Resources and Their Conservation* (1936), 488; O'Riordan, *Journal for American Studies* 5, no. 2 (1971), 157; Udall, *The Quiet Crisis* (1963), 133; Nash, *Wilderness and the American Mind* (1967), 143–45, 152–53, 160, 180–81; Worster (ed.), *American Environmentalism* (1973), 1–9; Matthiessen, *Wildlife In America* (1959), 191, 195; Sumner, *Science* 54, no. 1385 (1921), 39–43; Hornaday, *Wildlife Conservation* (1914), 184.

4. Trefethen, *Crusade for Wildlife* (1961), 205–8; Bates, *Mississippi Valley Historical Review* 44, no. 1 (1957), 49–50; Shankland, *Steve Mather* (1951), 202–6; Shelford, *Naturalist's Guide* (1926), 3; Ellsworth Huntington to V. E. S 3/17/1917, UIA-VES, box 1.

5. Shelford, *Science* 51, no. 1317 (1920), 316–17; V. E. S to C. C. Adams 1/21/1922, UIA-VES, box 1; ESA, Committee on Preservation of Natural Conditions, *Preservation* (1921), 9, 23, 25, 31, 32; Shankland, *Steve Mather* (1951), 101.

6. Gifford Pinchot to V. E. S 4/15/1920, UIA-VES, box 1; C. E. McClung to V. E. S 12/17/1920, UIA-VES, box 1; ESA, Committee on Preservation of Natural Conditions, *Preservation* (1921), *passim*. In 1921, the ESA preservation committee had four joint chairs with Shelford as senior chair. Duties were divided up as follows: Shelford took on research and publication; R. B. Miller, an Illinois State Forester, handled publicity and state organization; F. B. Sumner, of the Scripps Institution in La Jolla, organized research interests; and C. F. Korstian, of the United States Forest Service in Ogden, Utah, was responsible for natural areas in national forests (ESA, Committee on Preservation of Natural Conditions, *Preservation* [1921], 31–32).

7. Ise, *Our National Park Policy* (1961), 320; Robinson, *The Forest Service* (1975), 229; Shankland, *Steve Mather* (1951), 270; V. E. S to C. C. Adams 1/21/1922, UIA-VES, box 1; Shelford, *Science* 53, no. 1375 (1921), 431; *Science* 53, no. 1358 (1921), 4; *Science* 53, no. 1379 (1921), 521; *Ecology* 5, no. 2 (1924), 209. The AAAS representatives to the Executive Committee on Natural Resources besides Shelford were Henry S. Graves, former chief, United States Forest Service; Barrington Moore, president, ESA; and Isaiah Bowman, American Geophysical Union (*Science* 53, no. 1381 [1921], 550–51).

8. Nash, *Wilderness and the American Mind* (1967), 183; Ise, *Our National Park Policy* (1961), 643; Robinson, *The Forest Service* (1975), 157. A high-level, more permanent, true wilderness preservation policy was not adopted by the Forest Service until 1939 (Robinson, *The Forest Service* [1975], 158).

9. Thoreau, *Excursions* (1893), 275; Torrey and Allen (eds.), *The Journal of Henry David Thoreau*, vol. 12 (1906), 387; Swain, *University of California Publications in History* 76 (1963), 131; Foresta, *America's National Parks* (1984), 25−27, 29, 30−32; Trefethen, *Crusade for Wildlife* (1961), 242−47; Perrett, *America in the Twenties* (1982), 431; Ise, *Our National Park Policy* (1961), 641; *Ecology* 6, no. 2 (1925), 186−87. The period from 1921 to 1933 is not generally thought of as a noteworthy phase of the conservation movement (see Swain, *University of California Publications in History* 76 [1963], 1−221). For Shelford, the preservation committee, and the ESA as a whole, this period was important as a time when a group of scientific professionals developed a federal, state, and private network and operating procedures and policies for the preservation and study of natural areas.

10. Park, *Ecology* 18, no. 2 (1937), 306; Shelford, ESA, "The Work of the Society's Standing Committees" (1937), mimeo., UIA-VES, box 1; Weese, *Ecology* 10, no. 2 (1929), 259. Copies of *A Naturalist's Guide,* published in 1926, sold very well; by late 1926, twelve hundred copies had been sold (R. S. Gill to C. C. Adams 11/19/1926, WMUA-CCA, 1926 folder). It was one of forty books from the United States selected by the American Library Association for a 1926 list of six hundred notable books published that year (Park, *Ecology* 18, no. 2 [1937], 306).

11. V. E. S to C. C. Adams 2/27/1931, WMUA-CCA, 1931 folder; V. E. S to ESA preservation committee 3/2/1930, UIA-VES, box 1; Kendeigh, "The Fight to Preserve Natural Areas," unpublished memoirs, 5−7. During the period from 1931 to 1936, the three regional chairs of the ESA study committee serving under Shelford were C. F. Jackson, University of New Hampshire; Z. P. Metcalf, North Carolina State College; and W. S. Cooper, University of Minnesota.

12. In 1934, Shelford contributed an article to the Russian journal, *Problems of Ecology and Biocenology,* which succeeded the earlier *Journal of Ecology and Biocenology,* after the original journal's principal editor, the ecologist Vladimir V. Stanchinskii, was purged in the Cultural Revolution of 1928−32 (Shelford, *Problems of Ecology and Biocenology* 1 [1934], 3−11; Weiner, *Isis* 75, no. 279 [1984], 684−96).

13. Wright *et al.,* Faunal Series, no. 1 (1933), iv, 2−5, 8−10; Ise, *Our National Park Policy* (1961), 593; Wright and Thompson, Faunal Series, no. 2 (1935), 203.

14. Weese, *Ecology* 12, no. 2 (1931), 429; Ise, *Our National Park Policy* (1961), 325−26, 354; Emerson, *Ecology* 13, no. 2 (1932), 203.

15. V. E. S to ESA study committee 12/1931, UIA-VES, box 1; V. E. S to ESA study committee 12/29/1931, UIA-VES, box 1. Over the years, national parks were generally more closed to commercial use and development and safer from boundary changes than were national forests. One matter that bedeviled Shelford and his preservation colleagues was the fact that wildlife conservation on national forest and Bureau of Land Management lands had been the shared responsibility of the states (regulation of hunting and fishing and conservation) and the federal government (management of the habitat) (Ise, *Our National Park Policy* [1961], 646; Robinson, *The Forest Service* [1975], 228, 231).

16. Emerson, *Ecology* 13, no. 2 (1932), 202−3; *Science* 75, no. 1949 (1932), 481. Societies and agencies represented at the New Orleans meeting included ESA, United

States Forest Service, Izaak Walton League, National Park Service, United States Biological Survey, American Ornithological Union, National Parks Association, Game Survey of the Sporting Arms & Ammunition Manufacturers Institute, and the National Research Council.

17. Shelford, *Ecology* 16, no. 2 (1935), 274; Park, *Ecology* 18, no. 2 (1937), 307; Shelford, *Ecology* 14, no. 2 (1933), 240–45; Shelford, *Science* 77, no. 1994 (1933), 281–82.

18. V. E. S to C. C. Adams and enclosures 3/7/1933, WMUA-CCA, 1933 folder; Thompson, "Joseph Scattergood Dixon" in Clepper (ed.), *Leaders of American Conservation* (1971), 95; Kienholz, *Ecology* 15, no. 2 (1934), 208; Harold Ickes to V. E. S 5/12/1933, UIA-VES, box 1. Formal designation of natural areas by the Forest Service, under regulation of the Secretary of Agriculture began in 1931. By 1940, forty-one natural areas were set aside. These areas were intended for scientific and educational use exclusively. The areas were not large enough for best maintenance of large mammal species, but were large enough to be representative of other characteristic plants and animals in the different forest regions (Kendeigh, *Ecology* 22, no. 3 [1941], 339–42).

19. V. E. S to C. C. Adams and enclosures 3/7/1933, WMUA-CCA, 1933 folder; Ise, *Our National Park Policy* (1961), 349; C. C. Adams to V. E. S 3/21/1933, WMUA-CCA, 1933 folder; C. C. Adams to V. E. S 4/10/1933, WMUA-CAA, Shelford-Parks folder; RCC/Drew Sparkman Wetzel 6/1985.

20. Owens, *Conservation Under F. D. R.* (1983), 13–14, 83, 86; McElvaine, *The Great Depression* (1984), 154; RC/Charles Kendeigh 7/16/1985; Kendeigh, "The Fight to Preserve Natural Areas," unpublished memoirs, 7–8. During the period 1933–35, Shelford corresponded with a number of senior individuals in the National Park Service, the Department of Agriculture, the United States Senate and House of Representatives, and the Office of the President concerning his ESA committees' work in natural area preservation, overgrazing, national park standards, buffer areas, and the reintroduction of wolves into Yellowstone National Park (UIA-VES, box 1, appropriate year folders).

21. Wright *et al.*, Faunal Series, no. 1 (1933), 147–48; Shelford, *Science* 77, no. 2005 (1933), 535; Ise, *Our National Park Policy* (1961), 594; Wright and Thompson, Faunal Series, no. 2 (1935), 19–20, 25, 120–30.

22. Ise, *Our National Park Policy* (1961), 594; *Science* 83, no. 2151 (1936), 276. As of February 1934, research reserves had been designated in five national parks—Grand Canyon, Lassen Volcanic, Sequoia, Yellowstone, and Yosemite. An additional research reserve was recommended in Rocky Mountain National Park (Wright and Thompson, Faunal Series, no. 2 [1935], 123). By 1940 the number of research areas had increased to twenty-eight in ten national parks (Kendeigh, ESA study committee, "Progress Report for 1941," mimeo., WMUA-CCA, 1941 folder).

In 1936, the objectives of ESA's preservation plan for natural areas were to "provide and maintain representative natural areas from each extensive biotic community, to be used for preservation of the primitive in plant and animal life, as check areas in scientific study of modified biotic communities, and for continuous observation of cycle phenomena" (ESA, "The Nature Sanctuary Program" [1936], mimeo., 2 pp; UIA-VES, box 1).

The formation of and positive support given to the wildlife division, headed by George Wright, under National Park Service director Horace Albright accompanied Albright's recognition of the Park Service's need for more ecological information and a coherent policy toward wildlife in the early 1930s. Consequently, the Park Service's behavior concerning the increased use of ecological principles for park policy and management goes back more than half a century, is not "new," and is not only the result of "increasing influence of the environmental movement and its world view" on the Park Service since the mid-1960s as argued by Foresta (*America's National Parks* [1984], 96–99, 109). See also Swain, *University of California Publications in History* 76 (1963), 142, 166–69.

In 1985 the new director of the National Park Service, William P. Mott, said in a statement on Yellowstone National Park, "We're beginning to realize that we have to protect the very values we're trying to preserve by creating a buffer zone around the park that represents the entire ecosystem" (*Boston Sunday Globe,* 6/9/1985, Northern New England Edition, 16).

23. Keinholz, *Ecology* 15, no. 2 (1934), 209; V. E. S to R. E. Coker, 10/5/1937, UIA-VES, box 1; Swain, *Pacific Historical Review* 41 (1972), 327; Owens, *Conservation Under F. D. R* (1983), *passim;* Cart, *Pacific Northwest Quarterly* 63 (1972), 115–17; Shelford, *Ecology* 18, no. 2 (1937), 307; Jay "Ding" Darling quoted in Matthiessen, *Wildlife in America* (1959), 228; McElvaine, *The Great Depression* (1984), 167–68; Kendeigh, "The Fight to Preserve Natural Areas," unpublished memoirs, 37.

24. Shelford's statistical time report of his university duties, 1934–38, courtesy of Charles Kendeigh; RCC/James Carson, 12/1981 and 7/12/1984; V. E. S to W. C. Cooper 6/12/1945, UIA-VES, box 1.

25. V. E. S to ESA preservation and study committees 12/3/1936, WMUA-CCA, 1936 folder; V. E. S to ESA preservation committee 3/7/1936, UIA-VES, box 1; Ise, *Our National Park Policy* (1961), 434.

26. Shelford, "Conservation of Wildlife" in Parkins and Whitaker (eds.) *Our National Resources and Their Conservation* (1936), 489; Vestal, *Ecology* 17, no. 2 (1936), 312, 313, 316–18; E. Rachford to V. E. S 2/3/1936, UIA-VES, box 1; Harold Ickes to V. E. S 2/6/1936, UIA-VES, box 1. Ira Gabrielson to V. E. S 2/25/1936, UIA-VES, box 1; F. Silcox to V. E. S 3/4/1936, UIA-VES, box 1; Arno Cammerer to V. E. S 3/19/1936, UIA-VES, box 1.

27. Vestal, *Ecology* 16, no. 2 (1935), 275; V. E. S to ESA preservation and study committees 12/3/1936, WMUA-CCA, 1936 folder.

28. Shelford, *Bull. Ecol. Soc. Amer.* 19, no. 3 (1938), 23; Shelford, *Bull. Ecol. Soc. Amer.* 18, no. 1 (1937), 5; Kendeigh, "The Fight to Preserve Natural Areas," unpublished memoirs, 12; Park, *Ecology* 19, no. 2 (1938), 339; V. E. S to Robert E. Coker 10/15/1937, UIA-VES, box 1; V. E. S to W. C. Allee 11/30/1939, UIA-VES, box 1. The first complete summary of preservation activities and a listing of publications and personnel of the preservation and study committees appeared in the *Bulletin of the Ecological Society of America* for 1936 and 1937 (vol. 17, no. 1 [1936], and vol. 18, no. 4 [1937], 60–68). In 1937, Shelford told ESA president R. E. Coker that if the ESA constitution was not amended in certain ways regarding preservation activities, he

"would leave the Society and . . . take the majority of the ecologists with him." (R. E. Coker to R. F. Griggs 8/12/1944, WMUA-CCA, 1944 folder). Late that same year, Coker made an eloquent plea for an adequate endowment to support ESA activities, saying that ESA "has also undertaken to be a real force in the life of the country in respect to national problems, the proper solution of which can be derived only from the application of ecological knowledge and principles. It is said that other biological societies are developing the habit of looking to the Ecological Society of America for leadership and action in such matters. The service of the Society in this field is rendered chiefly through committees, and these committees have made a good deal of progress with very slight financial support from the Society." (*Bull. Ecol. Soc. Amer.* 18, no. 1 [1937], 3).

29. Shelford, ESA preservation and study committees, "Special Report of the Chairman," 1/16/1937, mimeo., UIA-VES, box 1; VES-PP.

30. Shelford and Hanson, "The Problem of Our Grasslands" in Parkins and Whitaker (eds.) *Our Natural Resources and Their Conservation* (1936), *passim.*

31. Shelford and Hanson, "The Problem of Our Grasslands" in Parkins and Whitaker (eds.), *Our Natural Resources and Their Conservation* (1936), 156–59; Shelford, *Science* 90, no. 2346 (1939), 564–65; Shelford *Science* 100, nos. 2590 and 2591 (1944), 135–40, 160–62.

32. Shelford, *Science* 100, nos. 2590 and 2591 (1944), 135–40, 160–62; Shelford, *Sci. Monthly* 55 (1942), 331–41. Shelford saw for himself, in the spring of 1904, the enormous number of rabbits and prairie dogs "reduced almost to extinction" in areas where poison was applied to kill both types of animals (Shelford, *Sci. Monthly* 55 [1942], 336).

33. V. E. S to Grassland Research Foundation 1/31/1948, UIA-VES, box 1; V. E. S to F. R. Lillie 4/24/1931, UCA-FRL, box VI, folder 6. Members of the NRC Committee on the Ecology of Grasslands in 1933 were H. C. Hanson, North Dakota State Agricultural College; K. M. King, University of Saskatchewan; W. P. Taylor, United States Biological Survey; B. C. Tharp, University of Texas; J. E. Weaver, University of Nebraska; and Shelford (chair).

34. NRC Committee on the Ecology of Grasslands, "Provisional Report" (1933), APS-CBD.

35. Shelford, "Memorandum to the Several Committees" (1931), UCA-FRL, box 6, folder 6; Shelford, *Science* 100, no. 2591 (1944), 162; V. E. S to Grassland Research Foundation 1/31/1948, UIA-VES, box 1; Shelford, *Audubon Mag.* 43, no. 6 (1941), 508–9; Shelford, Grassland Research Foundation "The problems of establishing," (1958), mimeo., courtesy of Charles Kendeigh.

The 8,616-acre tallgrass Konza Prairie in Kansas is being studied intensively by ecologists from Kansas State University. The principal project concerns the role of fire in maintaining the prairie in presettlement times. Plans are also underway to reintroduce bison, elk, and pronghorn (Kolata, *Science* 224, no. 4650 [1984], 703–4).

36. V. E. S to Grassland Research Foundation 1/31/1948, UIA-VES, box 1; J. M. Aikman to C. C. Adams 11/23/1939, WMUA-CCA. As of 1985, it was estimated that less than 1 percent of original American grassland remained from the 250 million acres

that existed before settlement by Europeans. The largest remaining trace of tallgrass prairie is in the Flint Hills of Kansas and the Osage Hills of Oklahoma, where the owners of two ranches (74,000 acres) are willing to see their land come under government protection. The Grassland Heritage Foundation succeeded in getting a bill introduced into Congress in 1979 for a Tallgrass Prairie National Reserve. This has not yet come to fruition (Begley and King, *Newsweek* 105, issue 22 [1985], 76–76B; Kendeigh, "The Fight to Preserve Natural Areas," unpublished memoirs, 14).

37. Shelford, *Ecology* 22, no. 1 (1941), 100–110; Kendeigh, "The Fight to Preserve Natural Areas," unpublished memoirs, 20–22; Shelford, *Science* 98, no. 2543 (1943), 280–81, with attachments, UIA-VES, box 1. During 1940–41, Shelford helped to prepare suggested changes in the Illinois fish and game code. Most zoological collecting gear used by faculty and students was illegal, and collecting for most fish, birds, and mammals could not be confined to the narrow periods specified by law. Eventually an arrangement for special permits was worked out through the State Natural History Survey and the State Department of Conservation (V. E. S to Judge S. Johnson 11/14/1940, V. E. S to A. C. Willard 12/16/1940, T. H. Frison to V. E. S 1/13/1941, and others, courtesy of Charles Kendeigh).

38. V. E. S to C. C. Adams 12/31/1943, WMUA-CCA, 1943 folder; Kendeigh, "The Fight to Preserve Natural Areas," unpublished memoirs, 16–18; Dexter, *Bull. Ecol. Soc. Amer.* 59, no. 3 (1978), 146–47; R. F. Griggs to C. C. Adams 7/25/1944, WMUA-CAA, 1944 folder; C. C. Adams to R. F. Griggs 8/4/1944, WMUA-CCA, 1944 folder.

39. V. E. S to C. C. Adams 11/4/1944, WMUA-CCA, 1944 folder; Shelford, *Bull. Ecol. Soc. Amer.* 25, no. 2 (1944), 12–13.

40. Kendeigh, "The Fight to Preserve Natural Areas," unpublished memoirs, 22–23; R. F. Griggs to ESA members 9/1944, WMUA-CCA, 1944 folder; R. F. Griggs to C. C. Adams 7/25/1944, WMUA-CCA, 1944 folder; C. C. Adams to R. F. Griggs 8/4/1944, WMUA-CCA, 1944 folder; V. E. S to R. F. Griggs 8/1944 quoted in Griggs to ESA members 9/1944, mimeo., WMUA-CCA, 1944 folder.

41. Kendeigh, "The Fight to Preserve Natural Areas," unpublished memoirs, 23; V. E. S to W. A. Dreyer 11/16/1944, WMUA-CCA, 1944 folder; S. C. Kendeigh to W. A. Dreyer 11/7/1944, WMUA-CCA, 1944 folder. The executive committee of ESA for 1944 consisted of R. F. Griggs, George Washington University and NRC; A. C. Redfield, Woods Hole Oceanographic Institution; W. A. Dreyer, University of Cincinnati; H. J. Oosting, Duke University; J. M. Aikman, Iowa State College; C. F. Korstian, Duke University; and O. Park, Northwestern University. The committee for 1945 was the same, except for the absence of Korstian.

42. Kendeigh, "The Fight to Preserve Natural Areas," unpublished memoirs, 23–24; taped interview with V. E. S. by M. Brichford 3/24/1965, UIA-VES, box 2; R. F. Griggs to ESA members 9/1944, WMUA-CCA, 1944 folder.

43. *Bull. Ecol. Soc. Amer.* 26, nos. 1 and 2 (1945), 4, 5; Kendeigh, "The Fight to Preserve Natural Areas," unpublished memoirs, 15–19, 23; V. E. S to C. C. Adams 10/1/1944, WMUA-CCA, 1944 folder; R. F. Griggs to C. C. Adams 10/6/1944; R. F. Griggs to C. C. Adams 11/27/1944, WMUA-CCA, 1944 folder.

44. Taped interview with V. E. S. by M. Brichford 4/1/1965, UIA-VES, box 2; Shelford, *Science* 100, no. 2603 (1944), 450–51.

45. V. E. S to C. C. Adams 11/4/1944, WMUA-CCA, 1944 folder.

46. A. H. Wright to V. E. S 1/9/1945, UIA-VES, box 1. Members of the NRC Committee for the Preservation of Natural Conditions in 1938 were H. E. Anthony (chair), American Museum; C. C. Adams, New York State Museum; H. I. Baldwin, New Hampshire Forestry and Recreation Department; R. E. Coker, University of North Carolina; W. S. Cooper, University of Minnesota; H. C. Hanson, North Dakota Agricultural College; E. Huntington, Yale; G. E. Nichols, Yale; E. A. Preble, Washington, D.C.; A. H. Wright, Cornell (*Bull. Ecol. Soc. Amer.* 19, no. 2 [1938], 16).

47. Kendeigh, "The Fight to Preserve Natural Areas," unpublished memoirs, 24; A. C. Redfield to C. Newcombe, S. C. Kendeigh, A. O. Weese, and V. E. S 4/25/1945, UIA-VES, box 1; VES-PP; A. C. Redfield to V. E. S 5/21/1945, UIA-VES, box 1.

48. V. E. S to ESA members 6/6/1945, UIA-VES, box 1. Shelford said he had "several letters" from prominent persons in the NRC concerning their dissatisfaction with the overlapping officers of the NRC and ESA (V. E. S to W. S. Cooper 6/12/1945, UIA-VES, box 1).

49. Shelford, "Excerpts from letters," no date, mimeo. UIA-VES, box 1.

50. Kendeigh, "The Fight to Preserve Natural Areas," unpublished memoirs, 24; *Bull. Ecol. Soc. Amer.* 26, nos. 1 and 2 (1945), 12; A. C. Redfield to C. Newcombe, S. C. Kendeigh, A. O. Weese, and V. E. S 4/25/1945, UIA-VES, box 1.

51. Kendeigh, "The Fight to Preserve Natural Areas," unpublished memoirs, 24–25; *Bull. Ecol. Soc. Amer.* 26, nos. 1 and 2 (1945), 12.

52. V. E. S to H. M. Hefley 12/20/1945, UIA-VES, box 1; Kendeigh, "The Fight to Preserve Natural Areas," unpublished memoirs, 26, 27, 29; A. O. Weese to V. E. S 1/16/1946, UIA-VES, box 1; H. M. Hefley to V. E. S 3/6/1946, UIA-VES, box 1. The original sponsors of the Ecologists' Union were L. R. Dice, University of Michigan; F. W. Emerson, New Mexico Highlands University; T. C. Nelson, Rutgers University; A. S. Pearse (past president of ESA), Duke University; G. H. Shull, Princeton University ; W. G. Van Name, American Museum of Natural History; A. O. Weese (past president of ESA), University of Oklahoma; C. T. Vorhies (past president of ESA), University of Arizona; P. S. Welch, University of Michigan; E. H. Wenrich, University of Pennsylvania; T. C. Frye, University of Washington; F. C. Gates, Kansas State College; Hefley; and Shelford (Kendeigh, "The Fight to Preserve Natural Areas," unpublished memoirs, 26–27).

53. Kendeigh, "The Fight to Preserve Natural Areas," unpublished memoirs, 26, 28; *Bull. Ecol. Soc. Amer.* 27, no. 1 (1946), 35–37, 43.

54. Kendeigh, "The Fight to Preserve Natural Areas," unpublished memoirs, 28–31; Behlen, *The Nature Conservancy News* 31, no. 4 (1981), 8, 9; *Science* 107, no. 2773 (1948), 189.

55. G. Fell quoted in Behlen, *The Nature Conservancy News* 31, no. 4 (1981), 8. In the spring of 1950, Representative Charles E. Bennett proposed legislation to create a "Nature Conservancy." This federally supported organization would aid the National

Park Service and the states in the preservation of natural areas. Congress never acted on this bill (Behlen, *The Nature Conservancy News* 31, no. 4 [1981], 8–9).

56. Dexter, *Bull. Ecol. Soc. Amer.* 59, no. 3 (1978), 147; *Science* 112, no. 2911 (1950), 446; VES-PP; VES-UI Acad. Appt. F.; RCC/Cinthya Whittaker 10/20/1989. The entire winter 1950–51 issue of *The Living Wilderness*, a publication of the Wilderness Society, was devoted to an inventory of 691 nature sanctuaries covering 1,088,046 square miles in the United States and Canada. The inventory was completed by the Committee for the Study of Plant and Animal Communities, of the ESA from 1938 to 1946 and of the Ecologists' Union from 1946 to 1950, Charles Kendeigh, chair. The inventory brought up-to-date Shelford's (1926) *Naturalist's Guide to the Americas*.

Curtis Newcombe suggested the name *Nature Conservancy* for the Ecologists' Union at the Columbus meetings on September 11, 1950. The formal motion to rename the society was made by Hurst Shoemaker of the Illinois zoology faculty (RCC/C. L. Newcombe 11/13/1981; RC/H. Shoemaker 8/22/1981). Newcombe said he suggested the designation "after the British organization of the same name, with which [he] had corresponded on numerous occasions" (RCC/C. L. Newcombe 2/7/1987).

CHAPTER 7. ENDINGS

1. Manchester, *The Glory and the Dream* (1973), 430; O'Neill, *American Society Since 1945* (1969), 4–5; author's observations. President Truman's statement was quoted in Manchester, *The Glory and the Dream* (1973), 488.

2. UIA-VES, box 1, folder 1946–47; RC/Charles Kendeigh 8/18/1981; RCC/Donald Hoffmeister 2/2/1984; Charles Child to V. E. S 3/23/1948, VES-PP.

3. Shelford, *J. Econ. Entomol.* 42, no. 3 (1949), 541; Shelford, *J. Econ. Entomol.* 43, no. 1 (1950), 107; Shelford, *J. Econ. Entomol.* 45, no. 1 (1952), 127, and no. 3 (1952), 544; Shelford, *J. Econ. Entomol.* 46, no. 3 (1953), 527–28.

4. Kendeigh, "The Fight to Preserve Natural Areas," unpublished memoirs, 49, 52–54, 56, 87, 88; Shelford, "History of the Committee of Natural Areas" (1947), mimeo., UIA-VES, box 1; Charles Brooks to V. E. S 5/5/1947, UIA-VES, box 1. Shelford became interested in ultraviolet light as a possible factor in influencing animal populations as early as 1918 (V. E. S to W. W. Coblenz 1/3/1955, UIA-VES, box 2).

5. RC/Dorothy Parmelee 7/13/1981; UIA-VES, box 1; RC/Clarence Berdahl 7/16/1985; George Stoddard to P. L. Windsor 6/12/1951, UIA-VES, box 1; E. S. Gibrala to V. E. S 6/27/1955, UIA-VES, box 1; V. E. S to Marine Biological Laboratory Corporation, Woods Hole 10/25/1946, UIA-VES, box 1; V. E. S to American Association of Economic Entomologists 11/6/1946, UIA-VES, box 1; RCC/Richard Brewer 6/16/1983.

6. Shelford, *Ecol. Monogr.* 21, no. 2 (1951), 149–81; Shelford, *Int. J. Biometer.* 5, no. 2 (1962), 44–58; Errington, *Ecol. Monogr.* 15, no. 1 (1945), 1–34; Kendeigh, *Ecol. Monogr.* 14, no. 1 (1944), 67–106; Shelford, *J. Mammal.* 35, no. 4 (1954), 533–38; Shelford, *Journal of Wildlife Management* 19, no. 2 (1955), 233–42.

7. Shelford, *Trans. Illinois State Acad. Sci.* 45 (1952), 158; Shelford, *Ecology* 34, no. 2 (1953), 422–25; Shelford, *Ecology* 32, no. 4 (1951), 760; V. E. S to Ira N. Grabrielson 4/10/1952, UIA-VES, box 1.

8. UIA-VES, box 1; V. E. S to H. H. Michaud 3/1/1954, UIA-VES, box 1.

9. Shelford, *Ecology* 32, no. 4 (1951), 760, 761; Shelford, *Ecology* 34, no. 2 (1953), 422–25. Shelford received financial support from the Wildlife Management Institute for his 1953 paper in *Ecology* detailing his life science complex (V. E. S to C. R. Gutermuth 12/15/1952, UIA-VES, box 2).

Over the past twenty to twenty-five years, evidence has accumulated for the effect of ultraviolet solar radiation on the reproduction, growth, behavior, and mortality of plants and animals. Photobiology is a relatively new scientific discipline, and from an environmental viewpoint, it provides challenges for the multidisciplinary scientist (Seliger "Environmental Photobiology" in Smith (ed.), *The Science of Photobiology* [1977], 169; Jagger, *Solar-UV Actions on Living Cells* [1985], xvi).

10. Shelford to Whom It May Concern 3/30/1955, courtesy of Charles Kendeigh. This letter was written about the time planning sessions were held concerning a new biology building at Illinois (Kendeigh, "The Fight to Preserve Natural Areas," unpublished memoirs, 93).

11. RCC/Stanley Auerbach 1/24/1984; *Bull. Ecol. Soc. Amer.* 36, no. 4 (1955), 116–18.

12. V. E. S to R. Pillsbury 12/19/1955, courtesy of Charles Kendeigh; RC/Lois Bennett 10/29/1986; Shelford and Winterringer, *American Field Naturalist* 61, no. 1 (1959), 89–95; RC/Richard Brewer 6/16/1983. The Nature Conservancy made its first land acquisition on June 2, 1955, with the receipt of the deed for New York's Mianus River Gorge Reserve (Behlen, *The Nature Conservancy News* 31, no. 4 [1981], 14).

13. RC/Betty Bennett 8/22/1981; RC/Lois Bennett 10/28/1986. Betty Bennett continued competitive swimming into adulthood and holds thirteen national records for backstroke, won from 1978 to 1983 in the thirty-to-forty-five-year age group for 50-, 100-, and 200-yard (and meter) distances. She also set world records for the 100- and 200-meter backstroke in 1978 and the 200-meter backstroke in 1983. In 1968, Mary Bennett (now Sheppard) swam in the AAU National Finals and in the Olympic trials. That year she ranked in the top twenty women swimmers in the world for the 200- and 400-meter freestyle. She later swam and dove for the University of Michigan (RC/Lois Bennett 1/14/1987).

14. *Bull. Ecol. Soc. Amer.* 36, no. 4 (1955), 114; Behlen, *The Nature Conservancy News* 31, no. 4 (1981), 16–17; RCC/Nathan Riser 9/15/1983; RCC/Stanley Auerbach 1/24/1984.

15. RC/Hilda Tillman 8/12/1984; RCC/Hilda Tillman 2/3/1982 and 8/29/1984.

16. J. G. Sutton to V. E. S 11/12/1956, UIA-VES, box 2; J. A. Behnke to V. E. S 6/24/1958, UIA-VES, box 2. On the evening of October 6, 1958, Shelford presented a lecture on the history of ecology to the History of Science Society on the Illinois campus (mimeo., UIA-VES, box 2).

17. RC/Charles Kendeigh 8/20/1981; V. E. S to Clarence Goodnight 7/16/1959, courtesy of Charles Kendeigh; RCC/Charles Kendeigh 5/15/1984.

18. V. E. S to G. H. Lowery, Jr., 6/4/1959, courtesy of Charles Kendeigh; taped interview with V. E. S. by M. Brichford 4/1/1965, UIA-VES, box 2.

19. RCC/Charles Kendeigh 5/15/1984; V. E. S to Doris and Leslie Shelford 9/24/1959, courtesy of Charles Kendeigh; RCC/Jane Dirks-Edmunds 3/8/1982.

20. T. Sperry to interested parties 1957, courtesy of Charles Kendeigh; Martha Shackleford to V. E. S 4/7/1958, UIA-VES, box 1; V. E. S to Grassland Research Foundation 4/18/1958, courtesy of Charles Kendeigh; Grassland Research Foundation officers' and directors' statement, 2/7/1959 to 4/13/1959, courtesy of Charles Kendeigh.

21. Harold Hefley to Grassland Research Foundation members 3/10/1959, courtesy of Charles Kendeigh; V. E. S to Martha Shackleford 3/16/1961, courtesy of Elizabeth Shackleford; V. E. S to J. J. Crockett 7/18/1963, courtesy of Elizabeth Shackleford; Paul Buck to Grassland Research Foundation members 10/24/1966, courtesy of Charles Kendeigh.

22. RC/Lois Bennett 10/29/1986; VES-PP; RC/Lois Bennett 7/18/1985; RCC/Lois Bennett 1/14/1987; Lois Bennett to Joy Elliott 9/28/1971.

23. RCC/Lois Bennett 1/14/1987; RC/Lois Bennett 7/18/1985 and 10/29/1986; taped interview with V. E. S. by M. Brichford 4/1/1965, UIA-VES, box 2; Knight, *At. Nat.* 19, no. 2 (1964), 146–48; Waloff, *J. Anim. Ecol.* 33 (1964), 532–33; Niering, *Am. Sci.* 52, no. 4 (1964), 433A–434A; Taylor, *The Living Wilderness* 28, no. 87 (1964), 27. Shelford's daughter, Lois Bennet, said, "When he was having so much trouble finding a publisher, I asked him if someone had already published something similar. He said that 'no one would be such a fool as to attempt it.' "

24. RC/Lois Bennett 1/14/1987; RC/Lois Bennett 10/29/1986; RCC/Lois Bennett 2/19/1984; RC/Lois Bennett 8/21/1981, and 7/18/1985; V. E. S to David Henry 9/29/1967, VES–UI Acad. Appt. F. On March 24, 1965, Shelford's remarks on his life were taped by Maynard Brichford, archivist at the University of Illinois. A second taping session was required on April 1, 1965, because of a mechanical malfunction. Shelford was upset over the need for retaping and was not feeling well; consequently, his speech is difficult to understand.

25. RC/Lois Bennett 10/29/1986; RC/Hurst Shoemaker 8/24/1981; RCC/Charles Kendeigh 2/22/1985; RC/Harry Shelford 7/15/1981.

26. Kendeigh, *Bull. Ecol. Soc. Amer.* 49, no. 3 (1968), 97–100; RCC/Stanley Auerbach 1/24/1984; RCC/Lois Bennett 7/18/1987; RC/Lois Bennett 8/21/1981 and 7/18/1985; *New York Times* 12/27/1968, 1 and 20, and 12/28/1968, 1 and 12.

Bibliography

Adams, C. C. 1913. *Guide to the study of animal ecology.* New York: Macmillan Co.
————. 1917. The new natural history—ecology. *Amer. Mus. J.* 7:491–94.
Adams, H. 1918. *The education of Henry Adams.* Boston: Houghton Mifflin.
Allee, W. C. 1939. An ecological audit. *Ecology* 20(3):418–21.
————. 1958. *The social life of animals.* Boston: Beacon Press.
Allee, W. C., A. E. Emerson, O. Park, T. Park, and K. P. Schmidt. 1950. *Principles of animal ecology.* Philadelphia: W. B. Saunders.
Allee, W. C., and S. Tashiro. 1914. Some relations between rheotaxis and the rate of carbon dioxide production of isopods. *J. Anim. Behav.* 4:202–14.
Allen, G. E. 1975. *Life science in the twentieth century.* New York: John Wiley and Sons.
Babbitt, H. E. 1932. *Sewage and sewage treatment.* New York: John Wiley and Sons.
Barila, T. Y., R. D. Williams, and J. R. Stauffer, Jr. 1981. The influence of stream order and selected stream bed parameters on fish diversity in Raystown Branch, Susquehanna River drainage, Pennsylvania. *J. Appl. Ecol.* 18(1):125–31.
Bates, J. L. 1957. Fulfilling American democracy: The conservation movement, 1907–1921. *The Mississippi Valley Historical Review* 44 (1): 29–57.
Batzli, G. O. 1975. The role of small mammals in arctic ecosystems. In *Small mammals: Their productivity and population dynamics,* ed. F. B. Golley, K. Petrusewicz, and L. Ryszkowski, 243–68. Cambridge: Cambridge University Press.
————. 1981. Populations and energetics of small mammals in the tundra ecosystem. In *Tundra ecosystems: A comparative analysis,* ed. L. C. Bliss, O. W. Heal, and J. J. Moore, 377–96. Cambridge: Cambridge University Press.
Begley, S., and P. King. 1985. The prairie's last stand. *Newsweek* 105, no. 2 (June 3), 76–76B.
Behlen, D. 1981. Thirtieth anniversary issue: A history. Pt. 2, Taking root. *The Nature Conservancy News* 31(4):7–11.
Bird, R. D. 1930. Biotic communities of the aspen parkland of central Canada. *Ecology* 11 (2): 356–442.
Boller, P. F., Jr. 1970. The new science and American thought. In *The gilded age,* ed. H. W. Morgan, 239–57. Syracuse: Syracuse University Press.
Brehm, A. E. 1895. *From the North Pole to the Equator: Studies of wildlife and scenes in many lands.* London: Blackie and Sons, Ltd.
Brewer, R. 1960. A brief history of ecology. Pt. 1, Pre–nineteenth century to 1919. *Occasional Papers of the C. C. Adams Center for Ecological Studies,* no. 1, 1–18.

Burgess, R. L. 1977. The Ecological Society of America: Historical data and some preliminary analysis. In *History of American ecology*, ed. F. N. Egerton, 1–24. New York: Arno Press.

Burnham, J. C., ed. 1971. *Science in America: Historical selections*. New York: Holt, Rinehart, and Winston.

Carpenter, J. R. 1939. The biome. In Plant and animal communities, ed. T. Just, 75–91. *Am. Midl. Nat.* 21 (1).

Cart, T. W. 1972. "New Deal" for wildlife. *Pacific Northwest Quarterly* 63:113–20.

Cherry, D. S., and J. Cairns, Jr. 1982. Biological monitoring. Pt. 5, Preference and avoidance studies. *Water Res.* 16(3):263–301.

Cittadino, E. 1980. Ecology and the professionalization of botany in America, 1890–1905. *Studies in the History of Biology* 4:171–98.

Clayton, J. 1970. *The Illinois fact book and historical almanac 1673–1968*. Carbondale, Illinois: Southern Illinois University Press.

Clements, E. S. 1948. Frederic Edward Clements. *National Cyclopedia of American Biography*, vol. 34, 266–67.

———. 1960. *Adventures in ecology: Half a million miles . . . from mud to macadam*. New York: Pageant Press.

Clements, F. E. 1904. *The development and structure of vegetation*. Botanical Survey of Nebraska 7, Studies in Vegetation of the State. Lincoln, Nebraska.

———. 1905. *Research methods in ecology*. Lincoln, Nebraska: The University Publishing Co.

———. 1916. *Plant succession: An analysis of the development of vegetation*. Publication no. 242. Washington, D.C.: Carnegie Institution of Washington.

———. 1917. The development and structure of biotic communities. Abstract of a talk given at Ecological Society of America meetings in New York City, Dec. 27–29, 1916. *J. Ecol.* 5:120–21.

———. 1936. Nature and structure of the climax. *J. Ecol* 24(1):252–84.

Clements, F. E., and V. E. Shelford. 1939. *Bio-Ecology*. New York: John Wiley and Sons.

Commager, H. S. 1950. *The American mind: An interpretation of American thoughts and character since the 1880's*. New Haven: Yale University Press.

Cook, R. E. 1977. Raymond Linderman and the trophic-dynamic concept in ecology. *Science* 198 (4312): 22–26.

Cook, S. G. 1980. *Cowles Bog, Indiana. Henry Chandler Cowles, 1869–1939: A study in historical geography and the history of ecology*. Unpublished, written for the Indiana Dunes National Lakeshore.

Cook, W. C. 1930. Review of V. E. Shelford's *Laboratory and field ecology*. *Ecology* 11(3): 611–14.

Cooper, W. S. 1913. The climax forest of Isle Royale, Lake Superior, and its development. *Bot. Gaz.* 55 (1): 1–44, 115–40, 189–235.

Cowles, H. C. 1901. The physiographic ecology of Chicago and vicinity: A study of the origin, development, and classification of plant societies. *Bot. Gaz.* 31(2 and 3):73–108, 145–82.

———. 1904. The work of the year 1903 in ecology. *Science* 19(493):879–85.

Bibliography

Cowles, H. C. 1908. An ecological aspect of the conception of species. *Amer. Nat.* 42(496):265–81.

―――. 1909. Present problems in plant ecology: The trend of ecological philosophy. *Amer. Nat.* 43:356–68.

Cox, D. L. 1979. Charles Elton and the emergence of modern ecology. Ph.D. dissertation, Washington University, St. Louis, 232 pp.

Cravens, H. 1978. *The triumph of evolution: American scientists and the heredity-environment controversy, 1900–1941.* Philadelphia: University of Pennsylvania Press.

Curtis, J. T., and R. P. McIntosh. 1951. An upland forest continuum in the prairie forest border region of Wisconsin. *Ecology* 32:476–96.

Davenport, C. B. 1898. The fauna and flora of Cold Spring Harbor, L.I. *Science* 8(203):685–89.

―――. 1901. Zoology of the twentieth century. *Science* 14(348):315–24.

―――. 1903. The animal ecology of the Cold Spring sand spit, with remarks on the theory of adaptation. *Decennial Publications of the University of Chicago, The Biological Sciences,* 10:155–76.

Dexter, R. W. 1978. History of the Ecologists Union, spinoff from the E.S.A. and prototype of The Nature Conservancy. *Bull. Ecol. Soc. Amer.* 59(3):146–47.

Drude, O. 1906. The position of ecology in modern science. In *Congress of arts & sciences, universal exposition, St. Louis, 1904,* vol. 5, *Biology, Anthropology, Psychology, Sociology,* ed. H. J. Rogers, 179–90. Boston: Houghton Mifflin.

Dulles, F. R. 1972. *Twentieth century America.* Reprint of 1945 book. Freeport: Books for Libraries Press.

Ecological Society of America. 1921. Preservation of natural conditions. Committee on the Preservation of Natural Conditions, ESA. Springfield, Illinois: Barnes.

Egerton, F. N. 1976. Ecological studies and observations before 1900. In *Issues and ideas in America,* ed. B. J. Taylor and T. J. White, 311–51. Norman: University of Oklahoma Press.

Egler, F. E. 1951. A commentary on American plant ecology, based on the textbooks of 1947–1949. *Ecology* 32(4): 673–94.

Ellis, E. R. 1970. *A nation in torment: The Great American Depression, 1929–1939.* New York: Coward-McCann.

Elton, C. S. 1927. *Animal ecology.* New York: Macmillan Co.

―――. 1931. Review of V. E. Shelford's *Laboratory and field ecology. J. Ecol.* 19(1):216–17.

―――. 1940. Scholasticism in ecology. *J. Anim. Ecol.* 9(1):151–52.

―――. 1960. *The ecology of animals.* New York: John Wiley and Sons.

―――. 1962. *Animal ecology.* London: Sedgwick and Jackson, Ltd.

―――. 1966. *The pattern of animal communities.* London: Methuen and Co., Ltd.

Engel, R. 1983. *Sacred sands: The struggle for community in the Indiana dunes.* Middletown, Conn.: Wesleyan University Press.

Errington, P. L. 1945. Some contributions of a fifteen-year local study of the northern bobwhite to a knowledge of population phenomena. *Ecol. Monogr.* 15(1):1–34.

Evans, M. A. E., and H. E. Evans. 1970. *William Morton Wheeler, biologist.* Cambridge: Harvard University Press.

Evers, R. A. 1965. Arthur Gibson Vestal, 1888–1964. *Trans. Illinois State Acad. Sci.* 57(2):77–81.

Ewan, J. 1971. Frederick E. Clements. In *Dictionary of scientific biography.* Vol. 3, ed. C. C. Gillespie, 317–18. New York: Scribners.

Farber, P. L. 1982. The transformation of natural history in the nineteenth century. *Journal of the History of Biology* 15(1):145–52.

Faulkner, H. U. 1957. *American political and social history.* 7th ed. New York: Appleton-Century-Crofts.

————. 1959. *Politics, reform, and expansion, 1890–1900.* New York: Harper.

Foresta, R. A. 1984. *America's national parks and their keepers.* Washington, D.C.: Resources for the Future.

Ganong, W. F. 1904. The cardinal principles of ecology. *Science* 19(482):493–98.

Gleason, H. A. 1917. The structure and development of the plant association. *Bull. Torrey Bot. Club* 44:463–81.

————. 1926. The individualistic concept of the plant association. *Bull. Torrey Bot. Club* 53:7–26.

Golley, F. B., ed. *Ecological succession.* Benchmark Papers in Ecology 15. Stroudsburg, Pennsylvania: Dowden, Hutchinson, and Ross.

Guthrie, R. L., ed. 1961. The Rumsey Trail is formally dedicated. *Arboretum Newsletter* 11(1):1–4.

Haeckel, E. 1904. *The wonders of life: A popular study of biological philosophy.* New York: Harper and Bros.

Hagley, E. A. C. 1973. Timing sprays for codling moth (Lepidoptera:Olethreutidae) control on apple. *Can. Entomol.* 105:1085–89.

————. 1976. Effect of rainfall and temperature on codling moth oviposition. *Environ. Entomol.* 5(5):967–69.

Hayes, S. P. 1959. *Conservation and the gospel of efficiency: The progressive conservation movement, 1890–1920.* Cambridge: Harvard University Press.

Heidgerd, R. P., and W. M. Shoemaker II. 1974. *The Schoonmaker family, descendents of Hendrick Jochemez Schoonmaker, 1624–1683.* Pt. 1. New Paltz, New York: Schoonmaker Family Assoc., Huguenot Historical Society.

Hellebust, J. A. 1970. Light: Plants. In *Marine ecology,* vol. 1, pt. 1, ed. O. Kinne, 125–58. New York: Wiley-Interscience.

Holmes, R. W. 1957. Solar radiation, submarine daylight, and photosynthesis. In *Treatise on marine ecology and paleoecology,* vol. 1, ed. J. W. Hedgpeth, 109–28. The Geological Society of America Memoir 67. Baltimore: Waverly Press.

Horn, W. 1905. Systematischen Index der Cicindeliden. *Deutsche Entomologische Zeitschrift,* Suppl. 2, 56 pp.

Hornaday, W. T. 1914. *Wildlife conservation in theory and practice.* New Haven: Yale University Press.

Howard, L. O. 1932/34. Biographical memoir of Stephen Alfred Forbes, 1844–1930. *Biogr. Mem. Nat. Acad. Sci.* 15:3–25.

Hutchinson, G. E. 1940. Review of F. E. Clements and V. E. Shelford's *Bio-Ecology. Ecology* 21(2):267–68.

Bibliography

Hyman, L. H. 1957. Charles Manning Child 1869–1954. *Biogr. Mem. Nat. Acad. Sci.* 30:72–103.

Ise, J. 1961. *Our national park policy: A critical history.* Baltimore: Johns Hopkins University Press.

Jagger, J. 1985. *Solar-UV actions on living cells.* New York: Praeger.

Jones, J. R. E. 1948. A further study of the reactions of fish to toxic solutions. *J. Exp. Biol.* 25(1):22–34.

———. 1964. *Fish and river pollution.* London: Butterworths.

Kendeigh, S. C. 1941. Natural and wilderness areas within the national forests. *Ecology* 22(3):339–43.

———. 1944. Measurement of bird populations. *Ecol. Monogr.* 14(1):67–106.

———. 1954. History and evaluation of various concepts of plant and animal communities in North America. *Ecology* 35(2):152–71.

———. 1968. Victor Ernest Shelford, Eminent Ecologist—1968. *Bull. Ecol. Soc. Amer.* 49(3):97–100.

———. 1979. Invertebrate populations of the deciduous forest: Fluctuations and relations to weather. *Ill. Biol. Monogr.* 50.

Kleinschmidt, A. 1955. Brehm, Alfred Edmund. In *Neue Deutsche Biographie,* vol. 2, 569–70. Berlin: Behaim-Bürkel, Duncker, und Humblot.

Knight, P. 1964. Review of Victor E. Shelford, *The ecology of North America. At. Nat.* 19(2):146–48.

Knisley, C. B. 1979. Distribution, abundance, and seasonality of tiger beetles (Cicindelidae) in the Indiana Dunes region. *Proc. Indiana Acad. Sci.* 88:209–17.

Knudsen, M. 1922. On measurement of the penetration of light into the sea. Conseil Internat. pour l'Exploration de la Mer, Pub. de Circ. 76, 1–16.

Kofoid, C. A. 1930. Review of V. E. Shelford's *Laboratory and field ecology. Ecology* 11(3):609–14.

Kolata, G. 1984. Managing the inland sea. *Science* 224(4650):703–4.

Krogh, A. 1914. On the influence of the temperature on the rate of embryonic development. *Zeitschr. für Allgem. Physiol.* 16:163–77.

Kwiat, A. 1905. Doings of societies. *Entomol. News* 16(4):121–28.

Langdon, J. 1979. Mark Twain in Elmira. *The Chemung Historical Journal,* 6 pp.

Lindeman, R. L. 1942. The trophic-dynamic aspect of ecology. *Ecology* 23(4):399–418.

Link, A. S., and W. B. Catton. 1967. *American epoch: A history of the United States since the 1890s.* Vol. 1, *1897–1920.* 3d ed. New York: Alfred A. Knopf.

———. 1967. *American epoch: A history of the United States since the 1890's.* Vol. 2, *1921–1941.* 3d ed. New York: Alfred A. Knopf.

———. 1967. *American epoch: A history of the United States Since the 1890's.* Vol. 3, *1939–1966.* 3d ed. New York: Alfred A. Knopf.

MacMahon, J. A. 1981. Successional processes: Comparisons among biomes with special reference to probable roles of and influences on animals. In *Forest succession: Concepts and application,* ed. D. C. West, H. H. Shugart, and D. B. Botkin, 277–304. New York: Springer Verlag.

Manchester, W. 1974. *The glory and the dream: A narrative history of America, 1932–1972.* Boston: Little, Brown, and Co.

Matthiessen, P. 1959. *Wildlife in America.* New York: Viking Press.

Mayer, H. M., and R. C. Wade. 1969. *Chicago: Growth of a metropolis.* Chicago: University of Chicago Press.

McElvaine, R. S. 1984. *The Great Depression: America, 1929–1941.* New York: Times Books.

McIntosh, R. P. 1980. The relationship between succession and the recovery process in ecosystems. In *The recovery process in damaged ecosystems,* ed. J. Cairns, Jr., 11–62. Ann Arbor: Ann Arbor Science Publishers.

————. 1981. Successional and ecological theory. Chapter 3 in *Forest succession: Concepts and applications,* ed. D. C. West, H. H. Shugart, and D. B. Botkin, 10–23. New York: Springer Verlag.

————. 1985. *The background of ecology: Concept and theory.* Cambridge: Cambridge University Press.

Merriam, C. H. 1890. *Results of a biological survey of the San Francisco Mountain region and desert of Little Colorado, Arizona.* U. S. Department of Agriculture, Division of Ornithology and Mammalogy, North American Fauna, no. 3. Washington, D.C.: United States Government Printing Office.

Miller, G. F. 1969. *The academy system of New York.* New York: Arno Press and *The New York Times.*

Minter, J. E. 1948. *The Chagres: River of westward passage.* New York: Rhinehart and Co., Inc.

Möbius, K. 1877. *Die Auster und die Austernwirtschaft.* Berlin: Verlag von Wiegandt, Hempel und Parey. Transl. By H. J. Rice in *Report of the U.S. Commissioner of Fish and Fisheries for 1880,* 683–751.

Muller, C. H., J. T. Tanner, and A. A. Lindsey. 1978. Awards, Eminent Ecologist Award for 1978, S. Charles Kendeigh. *Bull. Ecol. Soc. Amer.* 59(4):168–69.

Nash, A. 1967. *Wilderness and the American mind.* New Haven: Yale University Press.

Newman, H. H. 1948. History of the department of zoology in the University of Chicago. *Bios* 19(4):215–39.

Niering, W. A. 1964. Review of Victor E. Shelford, *The ecology of North America. Am. Sci.* 52(4):433A–34A.

Olson, J. S. 1958. Rates of succession and soil changes on southern Lake Michigan sand dunes. *Bot. Gaz.* 119(3):125–70.

O'Neill, W. L. (ed.) 1969. *American society since 1945.* Chicago: Quandrangle Books.

Oppenheimer, J. M. 1967. *Essays in the history of embryology and biology.* Cambridge, Massachusetts: M.I.T. Press.

O'Riordan, T. 1971. The third American conservation movement: New implications for public policy. *Journal for American Studies* 5(2):155–71.

Osborn, H. 1937. *Fragments of entomological history: Including some personal recollections of men and events.* Pt. 1. Columbus: H. Osborn.

Owens, A. L. 1983. *Conservation under F.D.R.* New York: Praeger Publishing Co.

Park, B. L. 1960. *Cortland—our alma mater: A history of Cortland Normal School and State*

Bibliography

University of New York Teachers College at Cortland, 1896–1959. Ithaca: Cayuga Press.

Perrett, G. 1982. *America in the twenties: A history.* New York: Simon and Schuster.

Philips, R., and B. Fleenor. 1970. Investigation of benthic marine flora of Hood Canal, Washington. *Pac. Sci.* 24:275–81.

Phillips, J. V. F. 1931. The biotic community. *J. Ecol.* 19(1):1–24.

———. 1934. Succession, development, the climax, and the complex organism: An analysis of concepts. Pt. 1. *J. Ecol.* 22(2):554–71.

———. 1935. Succession, development, the climax, and the complex organism: An analysis of concepts. Pt. 2, Development and the climax. *J. Ecol.* 23(1):210–46.

———. 1935. Succession, development, the climax and the complex organism: An analysis of concepts. Pt. 3, The complex organism: Conclusions. *J. Ecol.* 23(2): 488–508.

Pianka, E. R. 1978. *Evolutionary ecology.* New York: Harper and Row.

Pool, R. J. 1954. Frederick Edward Clements. *Ecology* 35(2):109–12.

Powers, E. B. 1914. The reactions of crayfishes to gradients of dissolved carbon dioxide and acetic and hydrochloric acids. *Biol. Bull.* 27(4):177–200.

———. 1917. The gold fish (*Carassius carassius*) as a test animal in the study of toxicity. *Ill. Biol. Monogr.* 4:121–94.

Pruitt, W. O., Jr. 1978. *Boreal ecology.* The Institute of Biology, Studies in Biology No. 91. London: Edward Arnold.

Riddle, O. 1949. Charles Benedict Davenport, 1866–1944. *Biogr. Mem. Nat. Acad. Sci.* 25:75–110.

Riedl, H., B. A. Croft, and A. J. Howitt. 1976. Forecasting codling moth phenology based on pheromone trap catches and physiological-time models. *Can. Entomol.* 108(5):449–60.

Robinson, G. O. 1975. *The Forest Service: A study in public land management.* Baltimore: Johns Hopkins University Press.

Rock, G. C. and P. L. Shaffer. 1983. Developmental rates of codling moth (Lepidoptera: Olethreutidae) reared on apple at four constant temperatures. *Environ. Entomol.* 12(3):831–34.

Roethele, J. W. 1980. Shifting sands. *The Nature Conservancy News* 30(6):12–15.

Rogers, D. 1961. *Oswego: Fountainhead of education.* New York: Appleton-Century-Crofts.

Saffo, M. B. 1987. New light on seaweeds. *Bio Science* 37(9):654–64.

Schantz, H. L. 1945. Frederick Edward Clements (1874–1945), an obituary. *Ecology* 26(4):317–19.

Schmidt, K. P. 1957. Warder Clyde Allee, 1885–1955. *Biogr. Mem. Nat. Acad. Sci.* 30:3–40.

Sears, P. B. 1966. *The living landscape.* New York: Basic Books.

Seastedt, T. R. 1984. The role of microarthropods in decomposition and mineralization processes. *Annu. Rev. Entomol.* 29:25–46.

Seliger, H. 1977. Environmental photobiology. In *The science of photobiology,* ed. K. C. Smith, 143–73. New York: Plenum Press.

Semper, K. G. 1881. *Animal life as affected by the natural conditions of existence.* New York: D. Appleton and Co. Reprint. New York: Arno Press.

Shankland, R. 1951. *Steve Mather of the national parks.* New York: Alfred A. Knopf.

Shannon, D. A. 1955. *The Socialist Party in America: A history.* New York: Macmillan Co.

Sheldon, A. L. 1968. Species diversity and longitudinal succession in stream fishes. *Ecology* 49(2):194–98.

Shelford, V. E. 1906. Horn's Systematischen Index der Cicindeliden. *J.N.Y. Entomol. Soc.* 14:5–8.

———. 1907. Preliminary note on the distribution of the tiger beetles (Cicindela) and its relation to plant succession. *Biol. Bull.* 14(1):9–14.

———. 1908. Life histories and larval habits of the tiger beetles (Cicindelidae). *J. Linn. Soc. Lond. Zool.* 30:157–84.

———. 1911. Ecological succession. Pt. 1, Stream fishes and the method of physiographic analysis. *Biol. Bull.* 21(1):9–34.

———. 1911. Ecological succession. Pt. 2, Pond fishes. *Biol. Bull.* 21(3):127–51.

———. 1911. Ecological succession. Pt 3, A reconnaissance of its causes in ponds with particular reference to fish. *Biol. Bull.* 22(1):1–38.

———. 1911. Physiological animal geography. *J. Morphol.* 22(3):551–618.

———. 1912. Ecological succession. Pt. 4, Vegetation and the control of land animal communities. *Biol. Bull.* 23(2):59–99.

———. 1912. Ecological succession. Pt. 5, Aspects of physiological classification. *Biol. Bull.* 23(6):331–70.

———. 1913. *Animal communities in temperate America as illustrated in the Chicago region: A study in animal ecology.* The Geographic Society of Chicago, Bulletin no. 5. Chicago: University of Chicago Press.

———. 1913. The reactions of certain animals to gradients of evaporating power of air: A study in experimental ecology. *Biol. Bull.* 25(2):79–120.

———. 1914. A comparison of the responses of sessile and motile plants and animals. *Amer. Nat.* 48(575):641–74.

———. 1914. An experimental study of the behavior agreement among the animals of an animal community. *Biol. Bull.* 26(5):294–315.

———. 1914. Modification of the behavior of land animals by contact with air of high evaporating power. *J. Anim. Behav.* 4:31–49.

———. 1914. Review of *Adams's guide to the study of animal ecology. Science* 39(1007): 580–81.

———. 1915. Principles and problems of ecology as illustrated by animals. *J. Ecol.* 3(1):1–23.

———. 1917. Color and color-pattern mechanism of the tiger beetles. *Ill. Biol. Monogr.* 3(4):399–32. Reprint. 1957, Johnson Reprint Corp., 5–134.

———. 1917. An experimental study of the effects of gas waste upon fishes with especial reference to stream pollution. *Bull. Illinois State Lab. Nat. Hist.*, vol. 11, art. 6, 380–424.

Bibliography

Shelford, V. E. 1918. A comparison of the responses of animals in gradients of environmental factors with particular reference to the method of reaction of representatives of the various groups from protozoa to mammals. *Science* 48(1235):225–30.

————. 1918. The relation of marine fishes to acids with particular reference to the Miles acid process of sewage treatment. *Publ. Puget Sound Biol. Sta.* 2(39):97–111.

————. 1919. Fortunes in wastes and fortunes in fish. *Sci. Monthly* 9:97–124.

————. 1920. Our aquatic biological resources. *Geogr. Rev.* 9:250–63.

————. 1920. Physiological life histories of terrestrial animals and modern methods of representing climate. *Trans. Ill. State Acad. of Sci.* 13:257–71.

————. 1920. The preservation of natural conditions. *Science* 51(1317):316–17.

————. 1921. National parks. *Science* 53(1375):431.

————. 1926. Methods for the experimental study of the relations of insects to weather. *J. Econ. Entomol.* 19(2):251–61.

————. 1926. *A naturalist's guide to the Americas.* Baltimore: Williams and Wilkins Co.

————. 1926. Terms and concepts in animal ecology. *Ecology* 7(3):389.

————. 1927. An experimental investigation of the relation of the codling moth to weather and climate. *Bull. Illinois Nat. Hist. Survey* 16(5):311–440.

————. 1929. *Laboratory and field ecology: The responses of animals as indicators of correct working methods.* Baltimore: Williams and Wilkins Co.

————. 1929. The penetration of light into Puget Sound waters as measured with gas filled photoelectric cells and ray filters. *Publ. Puget Sound Biol. Sta.* 7:151–68.

————. 1930. Ways and means of improving the quality of investigation and publication in animal ecology. *Ecology* 11(1):235–37.

————. 1931. Some concepts of bioecology. *Ecology* 12(3):455–67.

————. 1932. Basic principles of classification of communities and habitats and the use of terms. *Ecology* 13(2):105–20.

————. 1932. An experimental and observational study of the chinch bug in relation to climate and weather. *Bull. Illinois Nat. Hist. Survey* 19, art. 6, 487–547.

————. 1932. Life zones, modern ecology, and the failure of temperature summing. *The Wilson Bulletin* 44:144–157.

————. 1933. Conservation versus preservation. *Science* 77(2005):535.

————. 1933. Nature sanctuaries—a means of saving natural biotic communities. *Science* 77(1994):281–82.

————. 1933. The preservation of natural biotic communities. *Ecology* 14(2):240–45.

————. 1934. Faith in the results of controlled laboratory experiments as applied in nature. *Ecol. Monogr.* 4:491–98.

————. 1934. Life zones and modern ecology. *Problems of Ecology and Biocenology* 1:3–11.

————. 1935. The physical environment. Chapter 14 in *A handbook of social psychology,* ed. C. A. Murchison, 567–95. Worcester: Clark University Press.

————. 1936. Conservation of wildlife. In *Our natural resources and their conservation,* ed. A. E. Parkins and J. R. Whitaker, 485–526. New York: John Wiley and Sons.

Shelford, V. E. 1938. An open letter to ecologists. *Bull. Ecol. Soc. Amer.* 19(3):23–24.

——. 1938. The organization of the Ecological Society of America 1914–19. *Ecology* 19(1):164–66.

——. 1939. Grassland as a site for basic research on terrestrial animals. *Science* 90(2346):564–65.

——. 1941. List of reserves that may serve as nature sanctuaries of national and international importance in Canada, the United States, and Mexico. *Ecology* 22(1):100–110.

——. 1941. The nature sanctuary idea. *Audubon Mag.* 43(6):503–10.

——. 1942. Biological control of rodents and predators. *Sci. Monthly* 55:331–41.

——. 1943. The abundance of the collared lemming (*Dicrostonyx groenlandicus* (T.R.) var. Richardsoni Mer.) in the Churchill area, 1929–1940. *Ecology* 24(4):472–84.

——. 1943. Twenty-five-year effort at saving nature for scientific purposes. *Science* 98(2543):280–81.

——. 1944. The conflict between science and biological industry. *Science* 100(2603): 450–51.

——. 1944. Deciduous forest man and the grassland fauna. *Science* 100(2590 and 2591):135–40, 160–62.

——. 1944. Memorandum to the descendents of John Shelford, born 1769, died 1840, Keysoe, England. Marking the 100th anniversary of the landing of Eli & Phoebe Shelford, in New York, Christmas 1844 by his great-great grandson, V. E. Shelford. Mimeo., 10 pp.

——. 1944. Two open letters. *Bull. Ecol. Soc. Amer.* 25(2):12–15.

——. 1945. The relation of snowy owl migration to the abundance of the collared lemming. *Auk* 62:592–96.

——. 1949. Notes on the Rumsey family of Orange County, New York. Reprinted from *The Independent Republican,* Goshen, New York, 7 pp.

——. 1949. Termite treatment with aqueous solution of chlordan. *J. Econ. Entomol.* 42(3):541.

——. 1950. Termite treatment with aqueous solution of chlordan. *J. Econ. Entomol.* 43(1):107.

——. 1951. A ground plan for a biological research plant. *Ecology* 32(4):760–63.

——. 1951. Fluctuations of forest animal populations in east central Illinois. *Ecol. Monogr.* 21(1):183–214.

——. 1951. Fluctuations of non-forest animal populations in the upper Mississippi Basin. *Ecol. Monogr.* 21(2):149–81.

——. 1952. Paired factors and master factors in environmental relations. *Trans. Illinois State Acad. Sci.* 45:155–60.

——. 1952. Termite treatment with aqueous solution of chlordan. *J. Econ. Entomol.* 45(1):127.

——. 1952. Termite treatment with aqueous solution of chlordan. *J. Econ. Entomol.* 45(3):544.

——. 1953. An experimental approach to the study of plant and animal reproductivity and population with a life science building plan. *Ecology* 34(2):422–26.

Shelford, V. E. 1953. Termite treatment with one percent solution of chlordan. *J. Econ. Entomol.* 46(3):527.

──. 1954. The antelope population and solar radiation. *J. Mammal.* 35(4):533–38.

──. 1954. Some lower Mississippi Valley flood plain biotic communities: Their age and elevation. *Ecology* 35(2):126–42.

──. 1956. Charles Manning Child. *Bull. Ecol. Soc. Amer.* 37(1):32–34.

──. 1962. Paired factors of the physical environment operating on the sensitive periods in the life history of organisms. *Int. J. Biometeor.* 5(2):44–58.

──. 1963. *The ecology of North America.* Urbana: University of Illinois Press.

Shelford, V. E., and W. C. Allee. 1912. An index of fish environments. *Science* 36(916):76–77.

──. 1913. The reactions of fishes to gradients of dissolved atmospheric gases. *J. Exp. Zool.* 14(2):207–66.

Shelford, V. E., and M. W. Boesel. 1942. Bottom animal communities of the island area of western Lake Erie in the summer of 1937. *Ohio J. of Sci.* 42(5):179–90.

Shelford, V. E., and S. Eddy. 1929. Methods for studying stream communities. *Ecology* 10(4):382–91.

Shelford, V. E., and F. W. Gail. 1922. A study of light penetration into sea water made with the Kunz photo-electric cell with particular reference to the distribution of plants. *Publ. Puget Sound Biol. Sta.* 3(65):141–76.

Shelford, V. E., and H. C. Hanson. 1936. The problem of our grasslands. In *Our natural resources and their conservation,* ed. A. E. Parkins and J. R. Whitaker 147–59. New York: John Wiley and Sons.

Shelford, V. E., and J. Kunz. 1926. The use of photo-electric cells of different alkali metals and color screens in the measurement of light penetration into water. *Transactions Wisconsin Academy of Sciences, Arts and Letters* 22:283–98.

──. 1929. Use of photo-electric cells for measurement in ecological work. *Ecology* 10(3):298–311.

Shelford, V. E., and S. Olson. 1935. Sere, climax and influent animals with special reference to the transcontinental coniferous forest of North America. *Ecology* 16(3):375–402.

Shelford, V. E., and E. C. Powers. 1915. An experimental study of the movements of herring and other marine fishes. *Biol. Bull.* 28:315–34.

Shelford, V. E., and E. D. Towler. 1925. Animal communities of the San Juan Channel and adjacent areas. *Publ. Puget Sound Biol. Sta.* 5:33–73.

Shelford, V. E., and A. C. Twomey. 1941. Tundra animal communities in the vicinity of Churchill, Manitoba. *Ecology* 22(1):47–69.

Shelford, V. E., A. O. Weese, D. I. Rasmussen, A. MacLean, N. M. Wismer, and J. H. Swanson. 1935. Some marine biotic communities of the Pacific coast of North America. Pts. 1 and 2. *Ecol. Monogr.* 5:249–354.

Shelford, V. E., and G. S. Winterringer. 1959. The disappearance of an area of prairie in the Cook County, Illinois, Great Forest Preserve District. *Am. Midl. Nat.* 61(1):89–95.

Shelford, V. E., and R. E. Yeatter. 1955. Some suggested relations of prairie chicken abundance to physical factors, especially rainfall and solar radiation. *J. Wildl. Manag.* 19(2):233–42.

Shreve, F. 1915. *The vegetation of a desert mountain range as conditioned by climatic factors.* Publication no. 217. Washington, D.C.: Carnegie Institution of Washington.

Sprugel, D. C. 1980. A "pedagogical genealogy" of American plant ecologists. *Bull. Ecol. Soc. Amer.* 61(4):198–99.

Stenseth, N. C. 1977. Demographic strategies in fluctuating populations of small rodents. *Oecologia* 33(2):149–72.

Sterling, K. B. 1977. *The last of the naturalists: The career of C. Hart Merriam.* New York: Arno Press.

Stevenson, E. 1967. *Babbitts and bohemians—the American 1920's.* New York: Macmillan Co.

Storr, R. J. 1966. *Harper's university: The beginnings. A history of the University of Chicago.* Chicago: University of Chicago Press.

Strausbaugh, P. D. 1938. William Earl Rumsey. Notes and News, *Castanea* 3:53–55.

Summerhayes, V. S., and C. S. Elton. 1923. Contributions to the ecology of Spitsbergen and Bear Island. *J. Ecol.* 11(1):214–68.

Sumner, F. B. 1921. The responsibility of the biologist in the matter of preserving natural conditions. *Science* 54(1385):39–43.

Swain, D. C. 1963. Federal conservation policy, 1921–1933. *University of California Publications in History* 76:160–70.

———. 1972. The National Park Service and the New Deal, 1933–1940. *Pacific Historical Review* 41:312–32.

Tansley, A. G. 1935. The use and abuse of vegetational concepts and terms. *Ecology* 16(3):284–307.

———. 1940. Henry Chandler Cowles, 1869–1939. *J. Ecol.* 28:450–452.

———. 1953. *The British Islands and their vegetation.* Vol. 1. Cambridge: Cambridge University Press.

Taylor, W. P. 1964. Review of Victor E. Shelford, *The ecology of North America. The Living Wilderness* 28(87):27.

Thompson, B. H. 1971. Joseph Scattergood Dixon. In *Leaders of American conservation,* ed. H. Clepper, 96. New York: Ronald Press.

Thomson, J. A. 1895. Introductory essay. In *From North Pole to Equator: Studies of wildlife and scenes in many lands,* by A. E. Brehm, xv–xxxi. London: Blackie and Sons, Ltd.

Thoreau, H. D. 1893. *Excursions: The Writings of Henry David Thoreau.* Vol. 9. Riverside Edition. Boston and New York: Houghton Mifflin.

Thorson, G. 1957. Bottom communities (sublittoral or shallow shelf). In *Treatise on marine ecology and paleoecology,* vol. 1, ed. J. W. Hedgpeth, 461–534. The Geological Society of America Memoir 67. Baltimore: Waverly Press.

Tingley, D. F. 1980. *The Structuring of a state: The history of Illinois, 1899–1928.* Urbana: University of Illinois Press.

Tobey, R. C. 1981. *Saving the prairies: The life cycle of the founding school of American plant ecology, 1895–1955.* Berkeley: University of California Press.

Bibliography

Torrey, B., and F. H. Allen, eds. 1906. *The journal of Henry David Thoreau*. Vol. 12. New York: Houghton Mifflin.

Towner, A. 1892. *Our county and its people: A history of the valley and county of Chemung from the closing years of the eighteenth century.* Syracuse: D. Mason and Co.

Trefethen, J. B. 1961. *Crusade for wildlife: Highlights in conservation progress.* Harrisburg: Stackpole Co..

Udall, S. L. 1963. *The quiet crisis.* New York: Holt, Rhinehart, and Winston.

University of Chicago. 1927. *Register of doctors of philosophy of the University of Chicago. June 1893–June 1927.* Chicago: The University of Chicago Press.

Usher, M. B., R. G. Booth, and K. E. Sparkes. 1982. A review of progress in understanding the organization of communities of soil arthropods. *Pedobiologia* 23(2):126–44.

Van Cleave, H. J. 1947. A history of the department of zoology in the University of Illinois. *Bios* 18(2):75–97.

Vestal, A. G. 1913. An associational study of Illinois sand prairie. *Bull. Illinois State Lab. Nat. Hist.* 10:1–96.

———. 1914. Internal relations of terrestrial associations. *Amer. Nat.* 48:413–45.

Wallwork, J. A. 1983. Oribatids in forest ecosystems. *Annu. Rev. Entomol.* 28:109–30.

Waloff, N. 1964. Review of Victor E. Shelford, *The ecology of North America. J. Anim. Ecol.* 33:532–33.

Ward, H. B. 1930. Stephen Alfred Forbes. *Science* 71(1841):378–81.

———. 1934. Robert H. Wolcott. *Science* 79(2054):422–23.

Warren, C. E. 1971. *Biology and water pollution control.* Philadelphia: W. B. Saunders.

Watters, M. 1951. *Illinois in the Second World War.* Vol. 1, *Operation home front.* Springfield: Illinois State Library.

Weaver, J. E., and F. E. Clements. 1929. *Plant ecology.* New York: McGraw-Hill.

Weiner, D. R. 1984. Community ecology in Stalin's Russia: "Socialist and bourgeois" science. *Isis* 75(279): 684–96.

Wells, M. M. 1913. The resistance of fishes to different concentrations and combinations of oxygen and carbon dioxide. *Biol. Bull.* 25(6):323–47.

Wennekens, M. P. 1959. Marine environment and macrobenthos of the waters of Puget Sound, San Juan Archipelago, Southern Georgia Strait and Strait of Juan de Fuca. Ph.D. dissertation, University of Washington, Seattle, 298 pp.

Whittaker, R. H. 1951. A criticism of the plant association and climatic climax concepts. *Northwest Sci.* 25:17–31.

———. 1953. A consideration of climax theory: The climax as a population and pattern. *Ecol. Monogr.* 23(1):41–78.

———. 1972. An hypothesis rejected: The natural distribution of vegetation. In *Botany: An ecological approach,* W. A. Jensen and F. B. Salisbury, 689–91. Belmont, California: Wadsworth.

Willis, H. L. 1967. Biomass and zoogeography of tiger beetles of saline habitats in the central United States (Coleoptera: Cicindelidae). *The University of Kansas Science Bull.* 47(5):145–313.

Worster, D., ed. 1973. *American environmentalism.* New York: John Wiley and Sons.

Worster, D., ed. 1977. *Nature's economy: The roots of ecology.* San Francisco: Sierra Club
Books.

Wright, G. M., J. S. Dixon, and B. H. Thompson. 1933. *Fauna of the national parks of
the United States: A preliminary survey of faunal relations in national parks.* Faunal
Series, no. 1. Washington, D.C.: United States Government Printing Office.

Wright, G. M., and B. H. Thompson. 1935. *Fauna of the national parks of the United
States: Wildlife management in the national parks.* Faunal Series, no. 2. Washington,
D.C.: United States Government Printing Office.

Index

217

Index